Raising and Educating a Deaf Child

Raising and Educating a Deaf Child

Marc Marschark

OXFORD UNIVERSITY PRESS
New York   Oxford

Oxford University Press

Oxford   New York

Athens   Auckland   Bangkok   Bogotá   Buenos Aires   Calcutta
Cape Town   Chennai   Dar es Salaam   Delhi   Florence   Hong Kong   Istanbul
Karachi   Kuala Lumpur   Madrid   Melbourne   Mexico City   Mumbai
Nairobi   Paris   São Paulo   Singapore   Taipei   Tokyo   Toronto   Warsaw

and associated companies in

Berlin   Ibadan

First published by Oxford University Press, Inc., 1997

First issued as an Oxford University Press paperback, 1998

Oxford is a registered trademark of Oxford University Press

Library of Congress Cataloging-in-Publication Data
Marschark, Marc.
Raising and Educating a Deaf Child/
Marc Marschark.
p. cm. Includes bibliographical references and index.
ISBN 0-19-509467-0
ISBN 0-19-512658-0 (pbk.)
1. Children, Deaf.   2. Children, Deaf—Language.
3. Parents of handicapped children.   I. Title
HV2391.M26   1996   362.4'2' 083—dc20   96-5504

1 3 5 7 9 10 8 6 4 2

Printed in the United States of America

To my father (and role model),
Herbert L. Marschark

Preface

A preface is something that comes at the beginning of a book, but it is invariably something that the author writes last. I suppose that's a good thing, because it allows one to look back and reflect on all of the work that has gone into the book and to look ahead, with hope, to how it will be received. For me, this feels a little like being a parent: I can see how this book has developed during the time I have been working on it and now, with some trepidation, I have to give up control and send it out into the world. It is thus time to get some perspective.

Looking back, my motivation for writing the book was the feeling that despite all of the excellent research relevant to children who are deaf, very little of the resulting information trickles down to the people who need it most: parents, teachers, and other professionals involved with deaf children on a day-to-day basis. My goal, therefore, has been to take what we know from a wide variety of investigations and explain it in everyday language. Because of my own perspective on the field and the needs and sensitivities of many people who hopefully will read this book, the endeavor turned out to be rather more time-consuming and difficult than I originally expected. I wanted to be sure that readers got "the whole truth and nothing but the truth," but that sometimes required decisions about whether it was worth even starting on some important points that I knew would seem trivial unless they were put in what would be a rather complex context. Compromises were therefore necessary, and in the acknowledgments, I credit a variety of people who helped me to work through these issues. I was also helped by something Albert Einstein wrote almost fifty years ago that remains just as true today:

> Anyone who has ever tried to present a rather abstract scientific subject in a popular manner knows the great difficulties of such an attempt. Either he succeeds in being intelligible by concealing the core of the problem and by offering to the reader only superficial aspects or vague allusions, thus deceiving the reader by arousing in him the deceptive illusion of comprehension; or else he gives an expert account of the problem, but in such a fashion that the untrained reader is unable to follow the exposition and becomes discouraged from reading any further.
>
> If these two categories are omitted from today's popular scientific literature, surprisingly little remains. . . . It is of great importance that the general public be given an opportunity to experience—consciously and intelligently—the efforts and results of scientific research. It is not sufficient that each result be taken up, elaborated, and applied by a few specialists in the field.[1]

Taking heed of Einstein's cautions, I have tried to summarize what we know from research concerning deaf children and deaf education while remaining true to the original significance and generality of the findings (if perhaps not always to what the original author had in mind). I fully admit that in the process, I raise almost as many of these questions as I answer. As I emphasize repeatedly, however, there are few "right" answers in this field, and what is right for one child will be wrong for another. So, my goal has been to show what kinds of questions we should be asking and where to look for the answers. Perhaps most important, I argue for the need to accept the many differences among deaf children and between deaf and hearing children without viewing these differences as deficiencies or disabilities that need to be corrected.

This book is in no way intended to be a how-to manual. Instead, I have focused on broad issues like alternatives for effective communication, the importance of diverse social experiences, and the need for consistency in parenting. In a variety of situations I have been quite specific, but only going so far as I could with confidence. For example, it should not seem odd to parents and teachers when I suggest that they need to read to their children and students. Nor should it surprise anyone when I suggest that this activity is all the more important for deaf children, who may lack other opportunities for exposure to English. I hope I have explained fully the bases for these recommendations.

I have learned a lot from writing this book. Some things I learned from doing background research in areas with which I was less familiar. Other things I learned by discussing issues with friends and colleagues who grew up deaf, with parents of deaf children, and with people who have been involved with deaf children in a variety of ways. In particular, I have learned a lot from challenging my own assumptions about deaf children. It turns out that some of the "facts" I had previously held as true are not really facts at all, but assumptions that I either made myself or accepted from others. Which of these misapprehensions were my own fault and which were someone else's is not really important. What *is* important is that until I was actually immersed in a community of people who are Deaf, until I taught deaf students, and until I knew deaf people who I could really call friends, I did not know as much as I thought I did. I do not feel embarrassed about that, and neither should parents or teachers of deaf children ever look back and feel ashamed of what they did not know. We all learn. Those of us willing to accept a role in the lives of deaf children constantly have to challenge assumptions about what deaf children can and cannot do and explore new avenues to allow them to reach their potentials. Therein lies the pursuit of excellence both for deaf children and for those who love them.

Rochester, N.Y.   M. M.
February 1996

Note

1. Albert Einstein, foreword to *The Universe and Dr. Einstein*, by Lincoln Barnett (New York: William Morrow and Company, 1948).

Acknowledgments

First, I want to express my great thanks to Professors Harry Lang and John Albertini who read several previous drafts of this book, worked through many issues with me, and provided valuable content information as well as editorial help. Always insightful and with good humor, they were never reluctant to tell me the truth. I fear I never would have actually finished this project without the support and encouragement of our "Book Club" meetings; I owe them a great debt. Thanks are due to Sandy Harvey and Claudine Storbeck who each read an earlier draft of the book and provided me with important feedback. I also owe a lot to the many colleagues at the National Technical Institute for the Deaf who have been supportive of this work—and of me—in a variety of ways. In particular, I want to express my appreciation to my many deaf colleagues for their acceptance, patience, and advice.

A variety of people have shared with me their specific expertise and experiences (whether they knew it or not) and deserve special mention: Steve Baldwin, John Bonvillian, Gerry Buckley, Ruth Campbell, Cathy Chovaz, Cesare Cornoldi, Mary Elsie Daisey, Vince Daniele, Tony DeCasper, Jim DeCaro, Robert Davila, Mary Elsie Daisy, Vicki Everhart, Susan Fischer, Susan Foster, Larry Goldberg, Gail Kovalik, Lynn Koester, Lorrie Marantz, Matthew Moore, Heather Mohay, Anna Pani McLin, Kay Meadow-Orlans, Bob Pollard, Cathy Quenin, Janie Runion, Pat Spencer, Michael Stinson, Ted Supalla, Ginny Swisher, Cristina Vaccari, Virginia Volterra, Gerry Walter, and Dean Woolever.

Ed Shroyer was kind enough to allow me to use artwork from his book

Signing English, and Sarah Perkins was the wizard who put it all into useable form. The following allowed the reprinting of various materials as noted throughout the book: *Deaf Life* magazine, Sugar Sign Press, National Information Center on Deafness, National Captioning Institute, National Cued Speech Association. Warm thanks are due to Joan Bossert and Oxford University Press for their continuing support in our many collaborations and their patience when this book was delayed by my move to NTID.

Finally, I want to thank my wife, Janie Runion, for her willingness to move from Greensboro, North Carolina, to Rochester, New York, and her neverending encouragement as I pursue goals that will always be just out of my reach.

Contents

Foreword

It was a pleasure for me some months ago to review an "almost-final" draft of *Raising and Educating a Deaf Child* written by Marc Marschark. At first glance, I saw the book as a comprehensive guide to understanding the implications of being deaf. More important, this book concentrates on the implications of raising or teaching a child who is deaf or hard of hearing. In each of its chapters, I found information that parents will find valuable in making knowledgeable decisions about their children's lives.

The complexity of raising children who *can* hear, in meeting their social, psychological, and educational needs is a tough enough job for parents. When children are identified as deaf or hard of hearing, that job is made even more complex and, at times, overwhelming. Parents often experience a sense of loss, anger, guilt, and confusion. As parents, we have an unquenchable thirst for knowledge and understanding about our children. Often, we are unprepared for raising a deaf or hard-of-hearing child. Our child is often times the first person we have ever met who is deaf or hard of hearing.

We turn to the "professional" in search of answers, cures, and assurances of a bright future. All too often, these well-meaning and sometimes biased professionals leave parents feeling at arms' length with their own deaf children. Our children are seen as "broken" and in need of repair or therapy instead of having a different way of communicating and learning. They are seen as cases to be handled instead of individuals who are as unique and special as any other child, hearing or deaf. Many families have depended on trusted and well-respected family doctors, only to find that their only knowledge of deaf children was gained from medical textbooks that talked about the "pathology of hearing impairments." We have also depended on family members or friends who, as this book points out, "may not be right but are never uncertain."

As a young mother I remember sitting with my morning coffee wondering about this question or that, mulling over whether it would be better to adopt Plan A or Plan B for our deaf son. In the evenings my husband and I would go over the limited reading materials we could find that seemed related in any way to our son's needs. In looking back, and watching other families go through the same experiences as ours, I know that getting information about your child's needs is probably the most challenging and most critical aspect of being a hearing parent of a child who is deaf or hard of hearing. That's why I am so excited about this book. I believe that *Raising and Educating a Deaf Child* is the kind of book that should sit on your kitchen table; the book that should be there with that morning cup of coffee and for discussion after the children are tucked into bed for the evening.

I said that at first glance, I saw *Raising and Educating a Deaf Child* as an important information resource guide. As I looked closer, I saw more. This book is like a fine tapestry, the chapters woven together to reveal the shapes of future challenges and potential for future successes. In the foreground of its pages are the answers to the fundamental questions parents most often ask. Also woven into the tapestry are the questions many families are afraid to let surface when beginning their quest for knowledge and understanding of the unique child they will nurture. You will taste and savor the rich cultural heritage of deaf people—their successes, heartaches, and victories. You will grow to appreciate the culture and will relish in sharing that culture with your child. You will find the vocabulary and terminology specific to deafness explicitly defined. The many signing systems that have evolved over the years, educational philosophies, and models are explained within these chapters. This information will shape your understanding of the intricacies involved and challenges faced with respect to educating children who are deaf or hard of hearing.

Also included are the subtle but clear details that help parents decide exactly which answers are best for their unique child. All too often, parents are preached to, lobbied, and pushed into decisions based on the philosophies of others, rather than being allowed to arrive at their own conclusions. Not this time! *Raising and Educating a Deaf Child* leaves you with a sense of confidence and assurance that, despite the many challenges you will face raising your deaf or hard-of-hearing child, they will have futures just as bright and just as successful as anyone.

The thread that ties the pieces of *Raising and Educating a Deaf Child* together is unlike any I have encountered before. Although written by a researcher, the language and explanation of complex issues are clear and easy to understand. It addresses not only the questions we so obviously need to ask, but also the concerns, misconceptions, and fears that parents of deaf children often find hard to articulate and perhaps harder to confront. This book will weave you through the complex patterns of what it means to be deaf versus what it means to be Deaf, of the similarities and differences between Deaf and Hearing culture, of the causes of hearing loss, and the all-important questions of communication choices. Perhaps more important, it shows clearly the twisting design of language acquisition and the implications for other aspects of language development. Throughout this book, like a woven shawl over your shoulders, you will find a warm recognition of the kinds of emotional issues that parents deal with in order to reach complete acceptance of their children and acknowledgment of their special needs.

The best decisions that parents make for their children are the ones that are the most informed. We must not deny the inherent ability in ourselves to know our children even in the midst of confronting and learning about something we've never had to face before—deafness. I know that to be the kind of parent you want to be, you must become knowledgeable about deafness. *Raising and Educating a Deaf Child* will equip families raising children who are deaf or hard of hearing with the knowledge, understanding, and armor to face the many responsibilities that await them. Never before has there been such a comprehensive guide to raising a deaf or hard-of-hearing child. It touches on every aspect and topic that you will face sooner or later. In all likelihood, you will face these challenges sooner than you may think.

Timing is critical and not to be treated lightly. Your child should not be on the path of low expectations simply because you do not feel capable of making decisions regarding his or her communication needs and school program choices. Hearing parents of deaf children often delay making these important decisions because the topic seems so intimidating and the possible consequences of a "wrong" decision so great. How much better it would be if we could resolve those issues early and allow childhood to be natural and enjoyable. What a different picture you will get from talking with other parents who have been through what you are going through now. What an impact meeting and befriending Deaf adults will have on your family. Deaf adults provide our children with strong self-identities and help parents to see that a bright future is a reality.

I know you will enjoy this book and I hope that you will use it daily. May you know the same kind of joy that raising a son who is Deaf has given to my family. The days have not all been easy. The nights have not always been

serene. Our decisions have not always been correct. The things we would
have changed might have been avoided if we had had a resource guide such
as *Raising and Educating a Deaf Child*. You can learn the right questions to
ask, determine with wisdom the answers, and make informed decisions that
best accommodate your child's attributes, capabilities, and aptitudes. With
Raising and Educating a Deaf Child at your side, you can become a successful
parent raising a child who is growing up Deaf.

SANDY HARVEY
Executive Director
American Society for Deaf Children

Raising and Educating
a Deaf Child

1

A Deaf Child in the Family

You can do anything except hear.

I. King Jordan,
President of Gallaudet University,
addressing Gallaudet students

Parents of a deaf child, like the parents of any child who has special needs, want answers to what seem to be some simple and straightforward questions—questions like: What kind of language experience is best for my child, speech or sign language? Will my child ever learn to speak normally? Does being deaf affect how smart a child is? What kind of school is best? Will my child be able to get a good job? Regrettably, these questions are not as simple as they might appear, and parents may sometimes get contradictory information from professionals who are supposed to have the answers. Great strides have been made over the last twenty years in psychological and educational investigations relating to children who are deaf, but sincere differences of opinion still exist, just as they do in education generally and in various guides to "good parenting." Physicians, school officials, and counselors thus may have different responses to the same questions—differences that also will be affected by whether they, themselves, are deaf or hearing. In other cases, there simply will be no right answers.

These cautions notwithstanding, deaf children will be as happy, smart, and successful as hearing children, as long as they are given equal opportunities. It is true that every child is different, every family is different, and every school is different. Nevertheless, there is enough good information available about the growth and education of deaf children to allow parents to make enlightened decisions. Not all of those decisions will be easy, and some of them may turn out to have been wrong. Hearing parents unfamiliar with deafness will have some particular challenges with regard to raising

3

their deaf children, especially if a child has multiple handicaps, and they will vary widely in how they respond to the situation. Some will take the initiative and become active in fostering their children's development, spending extra time with them on school work, language skills, and in play. Those parents also will probably learn sign language if their children's hearing losses prevent early learning of spoken language. Eventually, their deaf children will be involved in all of the normal activities of young kids, from dinner-table conversation to Girl Scouts. As a result, those children will have essentially all of the learning opportunities of their hearing peers in both social and academic areas.

Other parents will leave the initiative up to schools and to others "who should know." They will follow available advice for the most part, but they will be hesitant or unable to seek out new information and new strategies. Either they will fear that they might make matters worse, or they will not be able to imagine that they could do much to make matters better. Those parents typically will find it much harder to make the time to learn *and use* sign language, even when it is clearly appropriate, or to make other modifications to day-to-day family life such as installing visual doorbells or television caption decoders (see Chapter 2). They simply will not realize how much more they could do to help their children succeed!

Being the parent of a deaf child is even more challenging when the child has multiple handicaps. Recent estimates suggest that over 20 percent of all deaf children have one or more handicaps beyond their hearing losses. Those handicaps include both physical challenges and impediments to normal **cognitive development**.[1] In decreasing order of their frequency, the most common physical challenges accompanying severe hearing loss in children are vision problems (including blindness), cerebral palsy, orthopedic problems, epilepsy, and heart disorders. The most common intellectual challenges are learning disabilities, mental retardation, and emotional or behavioral problems This is not to say that those conditions are particularly frequent; they occur in only about 1 to 10 percent of children who are deaf. Because they are receiving medical care for those conditions, children with multiple handicaps tend to have their hearing losses diagnosed earlier than children without other challenges. Often, however, hearing loss is considered secondary while parents and doctors deal with more immediate medical problems. It is only after doctors turn out to be unhelpful in dealing with their child's behavior that many parents seek help from organizations that understand and specialize in the problems of deaf children. Everyone involved may overlook the fact that without access to language, multiply-handicapped deaf children cannot understand what is happening to them and what others want from them. Establishing an effective means of communication should be a first priority with such children, not something to take care of later. Otherwise, medical issues may be resolved, but behavioral difficulties will remain and perhaps increase.

Part of the difficulty is that what most hearing people know about being deaf and about deaf people is limited to what they have seen in movies like *The Miracle Worker* and *Children of a Lesser God* or what they have gleaned from popular television shows. Other people have had personal contact with someone who is deaf—either a member of their extended family or, more likely, a child in the neighborhood. When I meet hearing people who say they "know" a deaf person, however, I am struck by the fact that regardless of the closeness of the relationship, the hearing person rarely seems to know any sign language. Often, they say that they can **fingerspell** a little—a form of communication that plays a relatively small role in communication among deaf people but adds to the erroneous assumption that **American Sign Language (ASL)** is somehow related to English (see Chapter 3). Some of those well-meaning individuals do know a few basic signs, typically less than a dozen, but they readily admit that they never have actually carried on any kind of a normal dialogue with their deaf "friend." What kind of friend can that be? What kind of relationship can you have with someone when you do not share a common language? What must it be like to grow up unable to have regular conversations with your parents—not to be able to talk to them about school, about love, or about God?

Certainly there are language and cultural differences to be surmounted by anyone who really wants to understand what it means to be deaf, but if we are willing to expend the time and energy, most deaf people are willing to aid in our education. There is also a wealth of literature about deaf children and about the Deaf community, much of it published very recently (see the suggested readings at the end of the book). For parents in need of "hard data," the task is somewhat more difficult. Some of the information they need is published in places and in jargon not easily accessible to the public and, to be honest, some of it is biased and poorly researched. The goal of this book, therefore, is to provide a description of recent advances in research and practice that is both objective and understandable. In so doing, its aim is to help readers gain a better understanding of the context, abilities, and needs of deaf children, with an eye toward improving their opportunities and the likelihood of their success.

The chapters to follow will provide several different perspectives on the development of deaf children, no one of which will give a complete view of the whole story. Taken together, however, they will provide a broad view of what we know about the growth and education of deaf children and what parents and teachers can do to optimize them.

A View from Within

Before I talk about what it is like to grow up deaf, it is important to clarify some basic terminology and issues as they are perceived from both Deaf and hearing communities (see also Moore and Levitan's *For Hearing People Only*, in the suggested readings). Only then can we avoid the kinds of overgeneralization and faulty assumptions that have plagued the field in the past.

BIG D AND LITTLE d

Let's start with the fact that the word *deaf* appeared in both capitalized and uncapitalized form in the preceding paragraph. Most commonly, *Deaf* is used as an adjective, referring to deaf people who see themselves as part of a community bound together by a common culture and, most often, a common language—ASL. That community has a rich history of art, humor, literature, and customs in addition to sharing most of those enjoyed by hearing people. In this sense, it offers the same kind of cultural enhancement available to African-American, Hispanic, or Jewish families who can appreciate both mainstream American culture and a link to a special heritage. Although *deaf* is sometimes used as a generic adjective, many people now use it to refer only to lack of hearing, preferring to use *Deaf* as a more restricted sociocultural term.

Part of the reason for this attention to the word *deaf* comes from the fact that people who are deaf have long been described in medical terms rather than as a people with a rich tradition and cultural pride. For similar reasons, the term *deafness* is frowned upon by some Deaf people who argue that it carries a connotation of pathology (meaning "with disease or illness"), although the National Association of the Deaf uses the term quite freely in its publications.[2] It is difficult to talk about the field without a noun, however, as can be seen by the fact that the word has slipped into this book occasionally despite my efforts to use alternatives.

What exactly is meant by *deaf*? Hearing losses are not all-or-none, but there is a continuum of hearing loss from those so subtle that they might not be noticed to losses so severe that hearing aids and other amplification devices are essentially worthless. In this book, I will not use the word *deaf* to refer either to people who have lost some of their hearing as a normal part of growing older or to people who have slight hearing losses, perhaps from ear infections as toddlers. Consistent with my primary focus, I will apply it only to those children and adults with hearing losses that are classified as severe to profound—hearing losses that eliminate the use of speech and hearing for all of the practical purposes of day-to-day life (see Chapter 2).

HEARING LOSSES VERSUS HEARING IMPAIRMENTS

For most hearing parents of deaf children, their child's hearing loss is at first seen as a major problem that will interfere with family life, education, and potential success. While family life certainly is different when hearing parents have a deaf child, there is no reason why hearing loss should create any insurmountable obstacles to either education or career success. Some parents of deaf children will be told about all the things their child supposedly cannot do, but as the quote at the start of this chapter indicates, most educators of deaf children and deaf people themselves do not see hearing loss in the same light. To people who understand Deaf culture, hearing loss is a sign of community membership rather than a limiting characteristic. Admittedly, this perspective has created some discussion within the Deaf community concerning its apparent conflict with the demands of deaf people for special consideration under the **Americans with Disabilities Act (ADA)** and other legal safeguards. This issue will be addressed later in several contexts (see especially Chapter 6). For now, we will focus on the practical issue: Most parents of deaf children will need to seek advice and assistance from government and educational agencies charged with supporting children with special needs. Therefore, parents and practitioners need to be aware of the several terminological categories that might be used to describe a child in any particular situation.

The term *hearing impaired* is one that is used frequently. According to the World Health Organization, an impairment is any loss of physiological or psychological structure or function considered normal for human beings, a disability is any restriction or lack of ability to perform "normally" due to an impairment, and a handicap is a disadvantage for a particular individual, resulting from an impairment or disability, that limits or prevents that person's full functioning in appropriate social and career roles. By these medical definitions, all deaf children have impairments, those with hearing parents have disabilities, and in the reality of today's world, most will be handicapped. An alternative and more accurate description, however, is that because of their hearing losses, deaf children lack full access to information and opportunities normally available to hearing children. Some of those experiences can be made available through sign language, but not all. To the extent that the absence of particular kinds of experience affects deaf children's learning or behavior, there may be consequences for other aspects of development. Nevertheless, whether or not such differences make any difference in the grand scheme of growing up is separate from the terms we use to describe them. In other words, differences between deaf and hearing children need not imply deficiencies.

Although the above definitions are intended as medical descriptions, they have become generic labels that are applied widely to deaf children and deaf people. With their own language, culture, and traditions, members of the Deaf community resent those labels, and the community prides itself as unique among groups who would normally be considered handicapped. Consistent with this community self-image, studies involving deaf children have indicated that the best way to optimize their academic, career, and social success is to consider them a linguistic and cultural minority that deserves appropriate educational considerations. Deaf children can be members of multiple cultures, but their development and education clearly depend on experiences that may not be available to them from hearing environments. The reasons for this situation and its implications will require several more chapters. Meanwhile, my goal is to emphasize the potential of deaf children, not traditional labels.

SIGN LANGUAGE

One final terminological distinction we have to make is that between sign language and American Sign Language or ASL (once called Ameslan). The issue will be discussed in depth in Chapter 3, but for the moment we can use the term *sign language* to refer to any language that makes primary use of the hands and face to communicate **grammatically** through visual-spatial means. *American Sign Language*, in contrast, refers to a specific sign language used in the United States and in English-speaking parts of Canada. There is no universal sign language any more than there is a universal spoken language, and attempts in this regard (for example, **Gestuno**) have little more use than Esperanto. Knowing ASL myself, and having experienced both British Sign Language (BSL) and Italian Sign Language (LIS), I can confirm that there is no more carry-over from ASL to BSL or LIS than there is from English to French or Italian.

In the following sections, I will remain true to the above terminology in the hope of keeping some difficult issues from becoming confused. Rest assured that the distinctions are important and will surface again later. Meanwhile, I will choose my words carefully.

A Deaf Child in the Family

Imagine for the moment a hearing American couple adopting an eighteen-month-old hearing toddler from a non-English-speaking country. Bridging the language gap seems like it would be relatively easy: The child will have some words and a few simple sentences in her native language, but not too many. The new family and the community then flood the child with language, both intentionally and unintentionally, and eventually she becomes fluent in English rather than the language of her native country.[3] At the same time, of course, she learns more than just a particular language. Through the speech that she hears, the child also learns who people are, about social rules and customs, about objects and events in the world, and about the uses of communication. This same process occurs quite naturally for the vast majority of young children in essentially all cultures. Language learning in more "natural" situations may be a bit less contrived and explicit than in the case of an international adoption—after all, most parent-child interactions involve language, regardless of which one it is—but the process is fundamentally the same.

Now consider the situation of a child who cannot hear. In the United States alone, there are close to a million children who have some degree of hearing loss, and one in a thousand babies is born with a hearing loss sufficient to prevent the hearing and understanding normal speech. Some people are surprised to learn that over 90 percent of those children are born into hearing families. Hearing parents who discover that they have a deaf child are probably the most surprised of all! The diagnosis of a hearing loss is so unexpected for children who are not multihandicapped that it typically is not made until a deaf child is between two and three years of age, when his language has fallen noticeably behind his playmates or when the preschool teacher suggests that something might be wrong. Boys are only slightly more likely to have serious hearing losses than girls, but the warning signs of hearing loss are often recognized later for them, because boys are notorious as slower language learners.[4]

The relatively late diagnoses of hearing loss, on average, might be viewed two ways. From one perspective, if it takes two to three years to discover that a child is deaf, perhaps hearing loss does not have much of an impact during the first months of life. After all, how much hearing does a child need at that age? From another perspective, and the one that turns out to be correct, the late discovery of a hearing loss can have significant and far-reaching consequences. Late diagnoses mean that for the first months of life, when most infants are hearing and beginning to learn the sounds of their native language, deaf children are not. Deaf infants do not hear their mothers coming down the hall nor do they turn to look when she enters the room. They are not soothed by their parents' voices and do not respond their to parents' attempts to have "baby talk" conversations. While these might seem like relatively minor problems to some people, they will have a lasting impact on the children, their parents, and on the relationships between them.

There are, of course, ways other than speech in which parents can communicate with their deaf children, just as they do with their hearing children: by touching, holding, and even through smell. Within the first twenty-four hours after birth, for example, babies can distinguish their mothers from other women by how they smell, and by three days after birth, they can recognize their mothers by sight.[5] On the mother's side, several investigations have found that hearing mothers with deaf babies touch them more than do mothers with hearing infants. They also use more frequent and more exaggerated facial expressions with their deaf infants, and they bring more things into their babies' lines-of-sight so that they can share experiences and play together. But our knowledge about this apparent compensation for the lack of hearing in mother-child interactions comes from observing mothers who already know that their infants are deaf and therefore recognize the need to do something more than talk to their babies.

Our naive assumption might be that hearing parents who unexpectedly have a deaf baby go through a fairly long period of unintentionally treating him as though he could hear. They would talk to him and expect him to respond with attention, smiling, and his own share of gurgling and cooing. Hearing parents might also touch and cuddle their deaf babies more than they would hearing babies, even before they suspect that their babies could be deaf. It likely would not take most of these parents very long to discover that talking to their babies was not as soothing as holding and stroking them, and those parents might be quickly "trained" by their babies to use more physical contact and face-to-face communication, even if they are unaware of it. Unfortunately, there is no way to evaluate this possibility, because as soon as a baby is identified as deaf, parents are likely to change their behavior.

During the first year or so of life, babies normally experience a variety of things that will have important consequences for language, social, and cognitive development. In the case of deaf babies of hearing parents, their early understanding of the world will be somewhat different from hearing babies and different from other deaf babies who have deaf parents. Later chapters will consider some specific consequences of a deaf child being born into a hearing family. Chapter 4, for example, will look at the effects of hearing losses on early social relationships, and Chapter 5 will examine language learning in young deaf children. First, however, it will be worthwhile to consider several different perspectives on deaf children and to get some background on issues relevant to deaf people. Throughout this discussion and the coming chapters, it is important to keep in mind that perspective is everything for the deaf child and for his parents, just as it is for educators and others who are interested in the welfare of deaf children. One memorable reminder of this came in a March 11, 1990, *60 Minutes* television interview with Dr. I. King Jordan, president of Gallaudet University, who became deaf as a young adult. During the discussion, the woman interviewing Jordan asked him if he would want to take a "miracle pill" that would allow him to hear. Jordan countered by asking the interviewer whether she would want to take a pill that would make her into a man. His point was clear: Being Deaf is his identity, and he is quite comfortable with who he is.

The Importance of Language

For those children whose hearing losses are sufficient to prevent their efficiently learning an oral (speaking) and aural (hearing) language, sign language can provide a viable alternative method for communication—the advice of out-of-date grandmothers and pediatricians notwithstanding. The dilemma for many parents is deciding when hearing losses are sufficiently severe (see Chapter 2). For many, learning sign language seems a drastic step. Perhaps it is not quite as drastic as it would be if they were told they had to learn Chinese and use it all of the time, because you cannot speak Chinese and English at the same time. However, learning to sign and using it *all the time* is not an easy feat, and even those parents who sign and speak simultaneously have no guarantees that their children will be either fluent signers or fluent users of English (see Chapter 3).

The question To sign or not to sign? is just one of many issues facing the family of a deaf child, but it is perhaps the most central one. From soon after birth, and maybe even before (see Chapter 4), language plays an essential role in parent-child relationships. Contrary to some popular beliefs, sign language works every bit as well as spoken language in educational settings and social relationships. Parents need to recognize that the majority of children who have greater hearing losses are unlikely ever to learn language through oral-aural means alone. It is true that about 25 percent of deaf children have some understandable speech, and **speechreading** or lipreading is certainly helpful to those children who have partial hearing losses. Nevertheless, many people are surprised to learn that the average deaf adult with years of speechreading practice does not read lips any better than the average hearing adult.

I know that this is counterintuitive. I once described this finding to a class of Italian special education students who would eventually have deaf children in their classes. (It is important to note that almost all deaf children in Italian schools are taught using spoken language only, and some Italian teachers do not even know that Italian Sign Language exists.) My interpreter, an Italian educator familiar with deaf children in that country, was so convinced of the effectiveness of speechreading that she refused to translate my assertion to the contrary. She could not bring herself to tell those future teachers of deaf children something she "knew" was false. After finishing the lecture on my own in my poor Italian, I suggested that anyone who wanted to see how difficult it is to read lips should try a very simple experiment (one that readers can also try at home): Down the hall, we found a television set. We watched it first with normal volume, then with very low volume, and then with the volume off. While comprehension was still perfect at low volume, everyone was startled when it suddenly became impossible when the volume was turned off. My colleague never brought up the topic again.

The presence or absence of communication in early and later childhood has broad consequences for development. For deaf children with greater hearing losses, this most often translates into a signing (communication) versus speaking (no communication) dichotomy. As we will see later, those deaf children who learn to sign at a young age also tend to be better adjusted emotionally, tend to do better in school, and tend to have better social relationships with their signing parents and peers relative to children raised in speech-only environments. The situation is more cloudy for children with mild to moderate hearing losses, who may learn spoken language more easily. In any case, the most important thing is full access to *some* language—and the earlier the better.

Regrettably, many parents still complain that they have trouble getting information and advice about the pros and cons of sign language, and Chapter 3 therefore is intended to give them all of the information they need. Some of this difficulty might result from their being understandably sensitive and confused when they first learn that their child is deaf. Still, I have heard too many stories of audiologists leaving parents standing in clinic hallways with mouths open and heads buzzing, and too many accounts of misdiagnoses or denials of early hearing losses by trusted pediatricians to consider professionals guiltless in this failure to convey the necessary information about dealing with childhood hearing loss. An excellent (if sad) example of this was recounted recently by two of my colleagues. When they noticed that their three year old son was not playing with other children, and his teacher reported that he was not talking to anyone in school, they had his hearing tested by an audiologist in an otolaryngology practice. They described what happened:

> During the visit, the audiologist took Bernard to his office, while we waited in the waiting room. Approximately 15 minutes later, the audiologist came back dragging Bernard, who was crying. He told us that he

could do nothing for Bernard, as he was not cooperative during the test. He told us to bring him back when he was good and ready. We were furious at the way he had handled our son and demanded that he do the test again in our presence and with our assistance. At first he was hesitant to comply, but we were persistent in our demand.

In the testing room, the audiologist handed Bernard an abacus with colored beads for him to move from one side to the other each time he heard a sound. There was no communication or explanation on the part of the audiologist to Bernard, and it was clear that Bernard was tentative and frightened with not knowing what was expected of him.

At this point, Bernard's father intervened, and turned the testing session into a game which his son clearly enjoyed. To the surprise of the audiologist, the test was now completed smoothly. It showed that Bernard had a significant hearing loss. Then, the doctor appeared on the scene.

The otolaryngologist told us that Bernard had "inner ear deafness." We asked for further explanation about the nature of the deafness and what recourse, if any, we had. He told us that he couldn't explain any more about it, and at that point a hearing aid dealer came into the office to talk with the otolaryngologist. After the hearing aid dealer left, the otolaryngologist told us he had to leave for lunch. We were dumbfounded at his rudeness in leaving us hanging and demanded time to speak to him. We proceeded to ask him what we should do to help Bernard and he simply told us to go to a hearing and speech clinic. Then he left the office. We left as well, dumbfounded!

This kind of experience is not unusual, and you can imagine the hurt and anger experienced by parents in such situations. Actually, *these* parents are deaf! Imagine what the experience would have been like for hearing parents who would have had almost no idea what the audiologist and otolaryngologist were talking about!

Hearing Loss as Pathology?
Differences versus Deficiencies

Family doctors are most accustomed to dealing with hearing children. The frequency of severe to profound hearing loss in the general population is so low that most pediatricians encounter deaf children only rarely, if ever. Moreover, **congenital** and early onset hearing losses are not so easily noticed unless one is looking for them. When physicians do encounter young children with serious hearing losses, they tend to view them in terms of the pathology model acquired during their medical school training. From their perspective, being deaf is considered a serious handicap and an impediment to normal development. True, being deaf, like having any other impairment, deprives deaf children of some of the experiences available to normally hearing children (like the enjoyment of music or the sound of oncoming cars). Other experiences may simply be different than they would be if their hearing were intact (like the rules of children's games or the way they learn to read). Anyone who has ever watched a basketball game between two deaf schools or the enthusiasm fostered by their cheerleaders, however, knows that some things never change.

The different experiences of hearing and deaf children will affect how they view and interact with the world in a variety of subtle and not-so-subtle ways. In the case of deaf children of deaf parents, their full range of natural experiences will lead to their passing through the various developmental stages at the same rate as hearing children. For deaf children of hearing parents, early experiences may not blend so readily into the background of family and community life. For them, the potentially limited or atypical nature of their experiences are more likely to lead to differences in their social, language, and perhaps their intellectual functioning relative to hearing children. My primary reason for emphasizing differences between deaf and hearing children at this point is a practical one. There is an understandable impulse on the part of many of us to deny or minimize handicaps that are not visible. A Deaf man once told me that deaf people do not receive as much understanding or consideration as those with other handicaps because deaf people "look too normal." Indeed, it is easier for most people to accept the obstacles faced by someone in a wheelchair than those faced by someone with a learning disability, easier to recognize the challenges encountered by someone who is blind than those of someone who is deaf. But denying a child's hearing loss (or any other possible impediment to full access), no matter how stress-reducing to parents or grandparents in the short run, does no one any good in the long run. Eventually, overlooking children's difficulties catches up with them, with their parents, and with society. Sometimes the realization comes too late; it always comes at a higher price.

Let us return to the language-learning issue as an example. It is easy enough to understand the desire of most hearing parents to have a child who speaks and acts normally. The truth is, however, that most deaf children will never sound like their hearing brothers and sisters. Delaying the learning of sign language in the hope of developing better speaking skills in deaf children simply does not work in most cases. In fact, such delays can make matters more difficult for both children and their parents. The first years of life are when basic language skills develop, and the first two to three years are generally recognized as a critical period for language learning. There is no substitute for natural language learning, and language acquisition that begins at age three or four is not natural.

It should be apparent by this point that the necessity of early language—any language—is an assumption that guides most of our thinking about the normal development of both deaf and hearing children. For centuries, philosophers and scientists have sought to understand the relation between language and thinking (see Chapter 8). Although the language we use does not *determine* the way we think, as was once believed, the language that children learn and the context in which they learn it will affect the way that they view the world. It is not just the explicit teaching in the classroom that requires and contributes to fluency in language. In addition, the vast majority of most children's experience comes in the form of language or accompanied by language. Our perceptions and conceptions of the world will be colored as much by the way something is described as by its factual content. Most of young children's experiences in the world will be shaped by the language of parents who are communicating with a particular purpose in mind. It does not matter much if the parents are using English, Japanese, ASL, or BSL; the content and effects of that communication are always present. Therefore, if a child does not receive any language, an essential component of development will be missing. Parents of deaf children with greater hearing losses can compensate for their children's lack of hearing if they are aware of the loss and are willing and able to learn sign language, but early awareness by hearing parents that their child is deaf is the exception. The primary issues we need to consider thus will concern how parents normally interact with their deaf infants, both before and after the diagnoses of their hearing losses, and the consequences of those interactions for a happy and healthy childhood.

Family Adjustment to Early Childhood Hearing Loss

The diagnosis of a significant hearing loss in a young child and a hearing family's adjustment to its new situation have a variety of ramifications. The most important thing to keep in mind is that the entire family is affected by having a deaf child. Although mothers tend to take the greater share of responsibility for dealing with the added necessities of a deaf child (or any other child with special needs), the effects of such changes are felt by each member of the family. Frequently forgotten in the new and sometimes stressful situation are the older children, who now are likely to receive relatively less attention than they did prior to their sibling's diagnosis (see Chapter 9). One couple I know avoided this problem by putting a note on their door requesting visitors to remember to pay attention to the hearing four-year-old sister of a deaf toddler. Whatever the methods, the goal of parents and children alike in this situation is to maintain comfortable and "normal" interactions within the home. In this, the whole family is involved and has to work together with patience and understanding.

It is well worth emphasizing that no matter how upset a hearing couple may be when they discover that their child is deaf, those feelings do pass. Any stress between the parents because of their different ways of responding to the situation also will dissipate, and there is no evidence that having a deaf child influences marriages in any way that affects their success or failure. Once the initial surprise passes, parents start to collect useful information on what it means to be deaf and about accommodating their child's hearing loss. Things that initially may have seemed overwhelming are recognized as less burdensome than they originally appeared. Not surprisingly, research has shown that those mothers who receive emotional and practical support from their family and friends are best able to cope with the demands of having a deaf child. This finding reinforces the impression that support groups consisting of other parents and professionals involved with young deaf children can be invaluable resources.

Down the road, mothers' abilities to function and deal with their children's being deaf will affect the child in a variety of ways. Mothers who are more secure and confident about themselves tend to treat their deaf children in ways that lead to better social and emotional adjustment in childhood and eventually better performance in school. Findings of this sort clearly indicate the need for greater support and training for hearing parents throughout their deaf children's childhood. Parents need to be educated about childhood deafness and its consequences, about the possible special needs of deaf children that must be addressed to ensure normal development, and about the educational alternatives open to deaf children and their families.

Just as the causes and characteristics of childhood deafness vary widely, so do the early experiences of deaf children and the abilities of parents and families to adapt to the changes that accompany having a deaf child. These changes are not always dramatic and need not be negative. Nevertheless, parental acceptance of children's hearing losses and adjustment to their needs are essential for a normal childhood. Therefore, this book is not a how-to guide to raising a deaf child, but a guide to understanding the implications of being deaf and of having a deaf child in the family or in a classroom. This understanding has implications not only for parents and teachers of deaf children, but for anyone who has contact with deaf children or with children who are academically or emotionally challenged for any reason.

It is essential to remember that as with most generalities, those that are applied to deaf children in this book are rarely accurate in individual cases. The strengths and weaknesses of each child must be considered, and we must be aware that deaf children may be even more variable than hearing children (who clearly differ considerably from each other even within families). Perhaps most importantly, parents should be wary of taking advice about deaf children from people who are not knowledgeable about deafness or do not have first-hand experience. In this situation, *knowledgeable* does not necessarily refer to those of us who are trained in a relevant field and have diplomas or certificates hanging on the office wall. Professionals will be able to provide important information related to language, hearing aids, and so on. We often have our own biases, however, usually based on where and how we were trained. I therefore believe that because we are seen as authorities, parents and teachers sometimes may be too quick to accept our advice as necessarily the only true path. To really understand what it means to have a deaf child, there is no substitute for chatting with other parents who have been or are currently working their ways through similar issues. At this juncture, local groups or national organizations like the American Society for Deaf Children (listed at the end of the book) can be important sources of information and support.

In the spirit of avoiding some of the common overgeneralizations about early childhood hearing loss, let us look at some of them. Most of these are discussed at various places later in this book. Just to clear up some of the inaccurate claims at the outset, however, it is generally *not* true that:

Deaf children who learn to sign will not learn to speak.
Deaf children and adults are very quiet.
Hearing aids enable deaf children to understand speech (by amplifying sound, they do help to hear speech, but understanding it is a different matter, see Chapter 2).
Cochlear implants are a very effective kind of hearing aid (Chapter 2).
All deaf children can be taught to "read lips" (Chapter 3).
Deaf children are less intelligent than hearing children (Chapter 8).
Deaf children have more emotional difficulties than hearing children (Chapter 9).
Mainstreaming is the best way to educate all deaf children (Chapter 6).
Deaf children will not have many friends (Chapters 6 and 9).

American Sign Language is a form of English (Chapter 3).
All deaf people know sign language.
Deaf people all wish that they could hear and seek hearing friends .
Deaf people cannot drive cars because they cannot hear.

It *is* generally true that:

Deaf children cannot hear how much noise they are making.
Hearing aids may enable some deaf children with partial hearing losses to understand speech (Chapter 2).
Cochlear implants are not yet as helpful as many people claim (Chapter 2).
Speechreading is very difficult, especially in English (Chapter 3).
Deaf children tend to have more academic difficulty than hearing children, especially in learning to read and write (Chapter 7).
Deaf children may have behavioral problems in school that are traceable to home environments (Chapter 9).
Mainstreaming in public schools may work for some deaf children but has drawbacks for others (Chapter 6).
Many deaf adults are members of Deaf social groups (Chapter 2).
American Sign Language is a language in its own right and differs from English in grammar and vocabulary (Chapter 3).
Most deaf people hold regular jobs and are fully functioning members of society.
Most deaf people resent the patronizing attitudes of hearing people.

Summary

Most deaf children have hearing parents, and those parents often are unprepared to deal with the emotional and practical issues related to having a deaf child. Whether due to denial or misunderstanding, diagnoses of hearing losses in children who are not multihandicapped typically are not made until between two and three years of age. Many parents then strive to have their child learn spoken language. Later chapters will discuss the fact that educating deaf children in spoken language only works for a minority of children, particularly those with lesser hearing losses, while children with greater hearing losses typically do not benefit significantly from such experience. Delays in deaf children's access to language during the most critical stages of development (the first two to three years) have a variety of consequences in social, language, and academic areas.

Sign language can provide deaf children with access to the information flow of people around them, provided that their parents and teachers are competent and consistent signers. Learning to sign as an adult is as difficult as learning any foreign language, however, and many people have considerable difficulty in learning a second language, whether spoken or signed. This situation may be even more complex for hearing parents who have discovered that their child is deaf and may be receiving conflicting and incomplete advice. Although many hearing parents will view their deaf child as disabled, the vast majority of deaf people are fully normal contributing members of the community. Within the Deaf community, art, Deaf history, and Deaf culture provide deaf people with a unique identity and a large network of friends. Therefore, most deaf people resent patronizing attitudes that suggest that their lives are any less full or important than those of hearing people.

In most respects, then, deaf and hearing children are the same. Like hearing children, deaf children's success begins with acceptance and communication at home. Attention to their special needs acknowledges that deaf children may be different from hearing peers, but those differences should not be taken to mean that deaf children are in any way defective. Instead, it is essential that we recognize that deaf children vary greatly—just like hearing children—and we have to treat them as individuals. Optimizing their opportunities in school and the social world requires a more complete understanding of deaf people and deaf issues than most hearing people will ever obtain in their own communities. The remainder of this book therefore will provide a survey of what we currently know about the language, social, and intellectual development of deaf children and will extensively consider the educational and practical issues confronting them and their families. First, we will consider characteristics of deaf children—and of the deaf population in general—as well as the importance of communication and language, whether signed or spoken.

Notes

1. Words in bold are defined in the glossary at the end of the book.

2. Disagreement over issues like use of the term *deafness* reflects some of the political disagreement within the Deaf community itself. There are prominent Deaf people known for being particularly radical, and others are known for being not "Deaf enough." Such differences of opinion are present in any group (and especially in minority groups), and for the most part, I avoid dealing with them in this book. However, just as I fault some hearing professionals

for not always informing parents of deaf children about the full range of options available to them, I fault some deaf professionals for doing the same thing.

3. Throughout this book, *English* is used in a general sense to refer to the language spoken in a deaf child's social environment. Most of available evidence with regard to deaf children's development is based on children who use either ASL, English, or some combination of the two, but there is no reason to believe that these differ from other signed or spoken languages.

4. It is interesting to speculate on why boys tend to be later talkers than girls. There does not appear to be any clear biological or physical reason for this to occur. The answer might lie in the different ways in which adults treat boys and girls. Parents tend to talk to their baby girls more than their baby boys and tend to let the boys cry longer than the girls before trying to soothe them with soft words. Boys, in contrast, appear to have the advantage in early physical activity, and parents are more likely to move their sons' arms and legs around playfully than they do with their ("more delicate"?) daughters. Perhaps herein lie the beginnings of gender-related differences in talkativeness and rough-and-tumble play.

5. The preference for their mother's smell is an ability seen only in infants who are breast fed; bottle-fed babies do not seem to learn that distinction. Importantly, the evidence for babies being able to recognize their mothers by sight comes from hearing babies who might take advantage of the correspondence between their mother's familiar voice (see Chapter 4) and her appearance. It is unknown whether deaf babies show the same ability.

2

Practical Aspects of Being Deaf

I know one man who got a cochlear implant. He always goes on and on about how wonderful it is. One day, he discovered that it had been without a battery for several weeks. What does that tell you?

A mutual friend

If we really want to understand the development of deaf children, we need a feeling for the worlds they grow up in and the various factors that shape their futures. We already have touched on the kinds of adjustments that are necessary for parents with deaf children, and more detailed discussions about families, communities, and educational environments will follow in several different chapters. Before considering the details of deaf children's early development within either hearing or deaf families, it will be helpful to consider some of the practical aspects of being deaf.

In the Lands of the Deaf

During the 1960s, when I was growing up just outside Washington, D.C., I knew about Gallaudet University (then Gallaudet College), which is the only free-standing liberal arts college for deaf students in the United States. My only experience on the campus, attending basketball games, impressed me primarily because they were so noisy. I noticed a lot of hearing aids at the games, but I do not recall their making much of an impact on me at the time. My mother once explained that because most of the students could not hear, the vibrations of the big bass drum in the bleachers were just as important as its sound. I am sure that she meant it both as a science lesson and cultural lesson, but all it meant to me was that I could join in, stamping my feet and cheering as much as I wanted—no one seemed to notice.

Living now in Rochester, New York, where there are about 10,000 people who are deaf and another 60,000 who are hard of hearing,[1] it is easy for me to forget how difficult it must be for the only deaf child in a town or county that has scarce resources and little understanding of what it means to be deaf. A colleague who grew up deaf in Kansas recently captured this well when he told me: "There were only three interpreters in the whole state when I was growing up. When one of them was out on disability with CTD [**cumulative trauma disorder**[2]], it was a big deal. Medical, legal, and educational activities all were disrupted." In contrast, Rochester, New York, alone has over 175 interpreters!

Most deaf children and their parents will have experiences more like that of my Kansas friend than a child lucky enough to grow up deaf in Washington, D.C. or Rochester, New York.[3] Unless they happen to live in a metropolitan area or a city that has a residential school for the deaf, neither children nor their parents will interact with—much less really get to know—any other deaf children or deaf adults. This situation has implications not only for interpreting and other services, but also for the availability of deaf role models and sign language teachers for deaf children and their parents.

Although a variety of early intervention programs are available in this country (see Chapter 6), most hearing parents of deaf children initially have to rely on their own resources and those of a variety of public and private groups (see the list of organizations serving deaf children and their families at the end of the book). Local school boards also may be helpful, but parents first have to understand the issues and know the right questions to ask. The remainder of this chapter therefore provides preliminary information about the frequency and causes of various kinds of hearing loss and the kinds technology that help to support hearing for those with only partial losses and help to make life more natural and pleasant for those with greater or lesser hearing losses. It also provides a brief description of the Deaf community, which has long played an active role in American culture through art, science, and industry.

Describing the Deaf Population

I have already noted that any attempt to provide complete and precise descriptions of "deaf people" or "deaf children" is unlikely to succeed. Like the members of any other group, deaf individuals in the United States vary widely. In some ways, they vary even more widely than the population of normally hearing individuals. In the case of the deaf children, there is variation contributed by differences in whether their hearing losses are congenital or **adventitious,** stable or **progressive,** caused by medical factors related to their hearing losses, by whether they are born into deaf or hearing families, and by the quality and type of education they receive. Whether or not these variables are any more important than the many factors that affect hearing children, they add to the normal sources of variation that can influence development and as such seem destined to make for a more diverse population.

As will become clear through the rest of this book, it appears that several direct and indirect effects of hearing loss have a greater impact on deaf children's development than anything experienced by most hearing children. To the extent that deaf children begin their lives by heading down somewhat different roads than hearing children, simple comparisons between the two groups will yield only partial information—and can lead to misleading conclusions. Consideration of differences among deaf children will be more informative in many cases, especially insofar as they highlight aspects of children's situations that are particularly influential with regard to fostering subsequent development. Because of variability within this group, expressions like "the typical deaf child" will be seen to be of little use. While trying to avoid unfounded stereotypes, it must be acknowledged that they are the result of how individuals within a group are perceived. Stereotypes thus are often rooted in fact, even if they are not universally applicable.

In order to understand the influence of individual differences among children who are growing up deaf, it is important to understand the character of the community in which they are immersed. The definitions and the **demographics** of hearing loss have to be considered together in this context for the simple reason that the number of people counted as deaf will depend on how the term is defined. According to the National Institutes of Health, for example, there are more than 28 million people in this country, or over 12 percent of the population, who have some form of hearing loss—up from estimates of 13.4 million in 1971. If we accept these numbers as even approximately correct, hearing loss is easily the single most widespread disability in the United States, and probably in the world.

The problem with this broad definition is that it includes both people like my father, who have hearing losses mild enough to interfere with conversations in noisy rooms but not on the telephone, and people like my racquetball partner, who has no hearing at all.[4] Deciding exactly how we want to carve up the population pie, therefore, depends on our goal. We could, for example, divide people by whether or not they use sign language. In this country, there are approximately 200,000 people who were either born deaf or lost their hearing before they acquired spoken language, and who use sign language as their primary form of communication. These people and many others who lost their hearing as children or adolescents are clearly deaf—and likely Deaf—meaning that most of them feel that they are members of the Deaf community. Another 200,000 or so people have congenital or early onset hearing losses but use spoken language as their primary form of communication, most often because their hearing losses are less severe. These people, like Miss America 1994, Heather Whitestone, are clearly deaf even if they are not Deaf in the cultural sense.

In contrast to a definition based on language preferences, some investigators have defined a deaf person as someone who lacks the capacity to hear and understand speech by age nineteen, the average age at which Americans enter the work force. This category includes well over a million people, some of whom use sign language and some of whom do not. Alternatively, if we remove the age limit, we get the definition that I find most enlightening, one that defines a deaf person as one for whom "the sense of hearing is nonfunctional for the ordinary purposes of life." This group has over five million Americans in it.

Focusing on children, federal estimates of the **prevalence** of hearing loss during the school years (ages six to seventeen years) indicate that over 840,000 (almost 2 percent) of the more than 42 million children attending school in the United States have some degree of hearing loss sufficient to be detected. Over 135,000 of those children are likely to have hearing losses that may be a major obstacle to their academic success, although accurate data are difficult to obtain. A recent study by Gallaudet University, for example, reported only 46,099 children identified as deaf or hard of hearing within the United States educational system.

Hard of hearing is a term frequently encountered in reference to hearing loss. To most people, hard-of-hearing people represent a larger group than deaf people. Deaf people are those who fit into a definition like the one about not having sufficient hearing for it to play a role in day-to-day life. Hard-of-hearing people, in contrast, also include people like our parents or grandparents who simply do not hear quite as much as they used to. Some educators and public officials describe hard-of-hearing people not as those with a broader range of hearing losses, but as those who have been able to acquire a spoken language, regardless of the extent of their hearing losses. The most interesting aspect of this last distinction is that, rightly or wrongly, it highlights the frequent centrality of spoken language in deciding who is deaf and who is not. In most cases, of course, those children who show the greatest skill for acquisition of a spoken language will be those who have more **residual hearing.** It seems odd, however, that two children with identical hearing losses might be differentially identified as deaf and hard of hearing solely because of the emphasis their parents have placed on sign language or spoken language, respectively. In the present context therefore, the term *hard of hearing* will be avoided, and references to various degrees of hearing loss, where necessary, will be based on **audiological** definitions.

Causes and Consequences of Early Hearing Loss

Before discussing hearing loss, let's consider hearing. This section is somewhat technical, and some readers may wish to skip it and come back to it later, if necessary, as a reference. In either case, after treatments of hearing and hearing loss, we will be in a position to consider the early identification of hearing losses and various aids to support hearing after those losses are determined.

MECHANISMS OF HEARING

Sound

Remember the old question, "If a tree falls in the forest and there is no one to hear it, does it make a sound?" Technically, according to a (deaf) physicist I know, the fact that a falling tree sets up a compressional wave train that *could* be heard makes the answer yes. In order for sounds to be heard, however, there has to be (1) a force that sets up vibrations in (2) a medium (like air or water) that conducts the vibrations to (3) a receiver that can decode the **acoustic** vibrations into an **auditory** event. If we were actually standing in the forest when the tree fell, pressure waves, caused by the tree splitting or falling and hitting the ground, would create vibrations in the air molecules around it, and those vibrations—or sound waves—would wash over us and travel some distance until they faded out. Our perception of the sound would vary both in loudness (related to the amount of pressure) and in frequency (related to the wavelength, the distance between waves).

The decibel (dB) is the common unit of measurement for the loudness of sounds. For example, the loudness of normal speech in an otherwise quiet environment is about 60–65 dB. The music of rock bands begins at about 85–90 dB and goes up to 115 dB. This volume is 10 percent louder than a jackhammer, and many of our more senior rock musicians now have significant hearing losses. Travelling in a car at 55 miles per hour, with the windows rolled up, air conditioning and heat off, and no one talking produces background noise of about 80 dB. NASCAR drivers like the retired Richard Petty, in contrast, are constantly bombarded with noise of 100 dB and more, perhaps explaining why some of them have apparent hearing losses and affections for loud country music. Equally loud automobile noise can be caused by three children, a dog, and a radio in an air conditioned car on the way to the beach. Luckily, that noise does not last long, and its effects are only temporary.

Loudness is not the only factor affecting whether we can hear speech, because the particular frequency or pitch of a sound makes a big difference in what is heard. Normally, humans can hear sounds in the range of 20 to 20,000 hertz (Hz). Dogs, by contrast, can hear sounds over 30,000 Hz; hence the effectiveness of "silent" dog whistles too high-pitched for us to hear. When it comes to human speech, losses that affect hearing in the range of 500 Hz to 2000 Hz are those that are most troublesome, because those are the frequencies at which the important features of spoken language are expressed. Vowels tend to fall in the lower frequency range, while consonants fall in the higher frequency range. Vowels are also louder than consonants, but they are not as important for distinguishing one word from another; and hearing a sound is not the same as being able to understand it.

For children with hearing losses already present at birth or appearing soon thereafter, the particular frequencies affected can vary considerably, with a comparably broad range of implications. Thus, while statistics and descriptions of the severity of hearing loss usually cite decibel loss in the better ear across all frequencies (referred to as the PTA or **pure tone average**), consideration of any individual child must focus on qualitative as well as quantitative aspects of auditory loss and any remaining ability to discriminate sounds. This caution is especially important with milder hearing losses, in which the patterns of frequency loss tend to vary most widely. The sensorineural hearing losses (see next section) frequently seen in older adults, in contrast, tend to affect the ability to hear sounds at higher frequencies before the lower frequencies. This explains why my father can hear me better than he can hear my wife.

With this background, the physics of sound and hearing becomes easy: To say that a sound has a higher frequency means that more waves occur per unit of time. If you imagine blowing into a two-liter soda bottle filled halfway with water, it will make a higher-pitched sound than blowing into an empty container. When there is water in the bottle, the vibrations created in the bottle's neck do not have as much room to expand in the smaller areas, resulting in smaller wavelengths and the higher frequency sounds. Similarly, the shorter vocal cords and smaller chest volumes of most females compared to males usually makes their voices higher in frequency. Different production devices thus have different characteristic frequencies of sound, and the same device often can be made to make higher or lower frequency sounds by changing its shape, as one does with a slide whistle or a trombone. To perceive the full range of sound, reception devices (like ears) have to be able to be sensitive to and respond appropriately to that variability.

Ears

As most of us learned in middle school, the outer ear (auricle) funnels vibrations in the air through the ear canal (external auditory meatus) to the eardrum (tympanic membrane), which vibrates in response to the changing pressure. That vibration causes small movements in the three-bone chain of the hammer (malleus), anvil (incus) and stirrup (stapes) of the middle ear, the smallest bones in the human body. The linked movement of the hammer, anvil, and stirrup (collectively known as the ossicles) transmits the vibrations through its connection to the oval window (actually another membrane, like the eardrum), which causes vibrations in the inner ear fluids that lie on its other side. Higher frequencies have shorter distances between waves and therefore make for faster vibrations that are passed along this chain.

The inner ear houses the organs of balance, most notably the semicircular canals, and the cochlea. The snail-like spiral of the cochlea contains, among other things, a soft tube that holds the sensory cells that actually "receive" sound. The sensory cells themselves are actually four parallel rows of hair cells. There are about 3,500 of these hair cells in an inner row along the basilar membrane and another 20,000 smaller cells in the three outer rows. When the oval window creates movement in the fluids of the inner ear, the basilar membrane rubs against the adjacent tectorial membrane, creating a shearing force on the hair cells similar to the feeling of rubbing your hand back and forth on velvet. This stimulation of the cells, in turn, creates nerve impulses that are carried to the auditory centers of the brain by the auditory nerve—at least in most people.[5]

MECHANISMS OF HEARING LOSS

When illness, accident, or hereditary factors reduce the amount of hearing someone has, the resulting losses generally are categorized as either conductive, sensorineural (or sensory-neural), or central. The first two categories are the ones of primary interest here.

Conductive Hearing Loss

Conductive hearing losses are those that hinder the transmission of vibrations through the mechanism of the middle ear. Usually, the damage is to either the eardrum or the ossicles, which restricts the vibration of the bones against the oval window, although conductive losses also can include blockage of the ear canal. Some children are born with or develop severe problems with their ear drums or ossicles, and in some cases one or more ossicles may be missing or malformed.[6] Most frequently, conductive losses are the result of severe or repeated middle ear infections, collectively referred to as **otitis media,** that inflame and damage the eardrum or the ossicles, thus reducing the perceived intensity of sound. Otitis media accounts for over ten million visits to the family doctor each year in this country. Many children have repeated bouts of ear infections that can temporarily impair their eardrums and their hearing. Repeated cases can sometimes lead to speech impediments which usually disappear with speech therapy. More severe cases lead to varying degrees of permanent hearing loss, making otitis media one of the most common nongenetic causes of hearing loss seen in infants and children.

Sensorineural and Central Hearing Loss

Sensorineural hearing losses typically involve the cochlea or its connections to the auditory nerve (from "sensory" to "neural"). Central hearing losses involve auditory centers of the brain or the "brain end" (rather than the "ear end") of the auditory nerve. Both kinds of losses usually affect particular frequencies of sound—unfortunately, precisely those frequencies needed to hear speech. Because sensorineural and central hearing losses actually reduce or eliminate the transmission or reception of nerve impulses representing sound, people with such hearing losses cannot benefit from bone conduction, and they cannot hear their own voices. **Tinnitus,** a condition most common in older adults (see Note 6), also may occur in sensorineural hearing losses with such intensity that the ringing that sufferers hear can be confused with telephones or doorbells. On reading an earlier draft of this chapter, one deaf friend wrote in the margin, "I've had it consistently for 30 years. It screams at me like a music that haunts."

Sensorineural hearing losses can be either congenital or acquired. Those that are congenital can result from illnesses of either mother or fetus prior to birth, from illnesses during childhood, or from hereditary (genetic) factors that are not yet fully understood. At one time, maternal rubella (German measles) was the single greatest cause of hearing loss in children, culminating in the rubella epidemic of 1963–65, which led to 30,000–40,000 babies being born deaf. With the development of a rubella vaccine in 1969, rubella has receded as a major cause of congenital and early onset deafness. According to recent statistics for children enrolled in special education programs, the three most frequent medical causes of childhood hearing loss among those with those that are diagnosed are meningitis (24 percent), premature birth (14 percent), and otitis media (12 percent); with rubella causing about 6 percent of all cases. In addition, other medical causes such as measles, mumps, and incompatibility in the Rh factor of maternal and fetal blood add to accidents as the most frequent causes of hearing loss in children. Some **etiologies** are never discovered.

At least twenty-eight sex-linked genetic variations have been shown to involve hearing loss and, overall, hereditary factors have been assumed to account for the hearing losses in about 20 percent of deaf children. However, genetic causes account for a full 50 percent or more of the cases with known origins, and the global estimate of 20 percent of all cases is probably too low. The important point here is that the diversity in the causes of hearing loss will lead to diversity in their impact on deaf children as they grow up. With the exception of many hereditary etiologies, many causes of childhood hearing loss also affect other sensory systems or various parts of the brain. This relationship means that the identification of any particular factor as responsible for differences between deaf and hearing children needs to be approached with considerable caution. Characteristics or behaviors typically attributed to some generic condition called *deafness* may well be the result of related factors rather than, or in addition to hearing loss per se.

DEGREES OF HEARING LOSS

If a hearing loss affects only the intensity of sound perception, amplification can improve reception if the loss is not too great. Loss of intensity frequently is not uniform across all frequencies, however, and as I have already noted, higher frequencies usually are affected more than lower frequencies.

Regardless of the kind or cause of childhood hearing loss, the measurement of most practical interest is what is called the "loss of pure tone receptivity in the better ear." This is essentially the limit of potential hearing in any particular frequency range. Hearing is considered normal with losses up to 25 decibels (dB) in the better ear. Losses from 26 to 40 dB are mild, those from 41 to 55 dB are moderate, and those from 56 to 70 dB are moderately severe. Hearing losses from 71 to 90 dB are severe and those over 91 dB in the better ear are considered profound. Most frequently, conductive hearing losses are less severe, ranging up to about 60 dB. Hearing losses above that level typically are of the sensorineural variety and are the ones that cause difficulty for children growing up in hearing environments.

Early Identification of Hearing Losses

As noted in Chapter 1, congenital or early onset hearing losses in children usually are not recognized immediately, but are suspected only when the children fail to meet certain milestones for language and social development. In these cases, representing about 70 percent of all children with hearing losses, it is the parents who recognize that something is wrong and eventually seek out an audiologist to check their child's hearing or an oto-laryngologist, an ear, nose, and throat doctor, to determine the reasons for the problem. Other parents may first look to psychologists to explain their children's behavior problems. Sometimes, however, hearing losses are not detected until children are screened as part of kindergarten placement, and I have been told that in Vermont the average age at diagnosis is six and one-half years. Overall, the average age for detection of childhood hearing losses in the United States is between two and three years, although it is somewhat earlier for profoundly deaf children. The sad part is that hearing loss could be detected even before a newborn leaves the hospital.

Currently, the only babies screened for hearing loss at the time of birth are those who are considered to be at high risk due to premature birth, maternal illness, multiple handicaps, or other factors. Fifty to 70 per cent of the congenital hearing losses are thus missed. In fact, within hours after birth, babies could be tested using a technology that measures the auditory brain stem response (ABR). This inexpensive test (less than $50) uses a device like an earphone to send a clicking sound into a newborn's ears. Electrodes attached to the scalp detect electrical responses from the inner ear, and a computer determines if those responses show the inner ear to be functioning normally. ABR has replaced a variety of earlier early-detection methods because of its high accuracy and low cost, and has now been the detection method of choice for almost twenty years. Just becoming popular in the United States is a test of evoked otoacoustic emissions, which shows promise as another effective, quick, and inexpensive method of testing cochlear functioning. Invented in England in mid-1970s, the test involves fitting a newborn with a soft-tipped earphone/microphone that sends soft clicks. The clicks make the eardrum vibrate, activating the inner ear; the pattern and intensity of the echo provides indicate the likelihood of hearing loss. The test requires less than 1 minute per ear, and a full assessment and documentation can be done in only three minutes. The problem is that without proper training, false positives (incorrect diagnosis of hearing loss in a healthy ear) can be as high as 25 percent.

Because of the importance of the first three years of life for language development, an Early Identification of Hearing Impairment (EIHI) panel convened by the National Institutes of Health (NIH) recently urged that a greater proportion of newborns be tested for hearing loss before they leave the hospital. Screening all newborns seems prohibitively expensive, but there are ways to identify a greater proportion of children who may have hearing losses. One way suggested by NIH would be to test babies in neonatal (newborn) intensive care units, 1 to 3 percent of whom have been found to have an increased risk of moderate to profound sensorineural hearing loss, and all children who have bacterial meningitis, which is associated with a 5 to 30 percent incidence of profound hearing losses. The EIHI panel went further, suggesting that all children be tested during the first three months of life. Screening outside of the hospital would reduce costs, and the possibility of false positives would be lower because of the later testing.

Lest it sound as if we have the right tools but are just not using them, it must be emphasized that neither ABR nor evoked otoacoustic emissions are perfect. According to a colleague of mine who served on the EIHI panel, the primary impediment to wider testing is the false positive issue mentioned above. The problem is that approximately one in ten babies who tests positive—that is, has test results that indicate a hearing loss—actually will have normal hearing. According to my friend, there was concern on the panel that telling parents that they have a deaf baby when they really do not would cause too much mental anguish for parents. Depending on one's perspective, such occasional anguish may be well worth the price. Certainly there is nothing that a parent would do for a deaf baby that would in any way be disadvantageous for a hearing baby. In my view, any parents who even begin to suspect a hearing loss should make their way to the nearest ABR machine.

Technological Tools for Deaf People

Once a hearing loss is identified, a variety of technological and educational tools are available to children and to their parents and teachers. When people think of the ways in which technology might affect the lives of children and adults who are deaf, they naturally think first of hearing aids and, more recently, of cochlear implants. Technology in this area has seen important advances over the last twenty years, but hearing aids are just one of several areas that have made great strides. In addition to aids that assist with hearing, there are also a variety of devices that deaf people use to replace hearing or reduce the reliance on it. These technological aids are particularly important for people who have little or no residual hearing, providing a personal and emotional independence that eliminates the need to rely on hearing relatives and friends. In addition, they make life more pleasant and more "normal."

Aside from hearing-assistive devices, most technological aids used by people who are deaf rely on visual information or signals.[7] For deaf parents, there are baby monitors that pick up babies' crying or other noises and flash signal lights to get the parents' attention. Home devices include vibrating alarm clocks and safety alarms, lights that flash in place of the doorbell, and lights that indicate when the telephone is ringing. Perhaps the two most important devices for most deaf people are the **TTY** and the **caption decoder.**

TTYs

A TTY is essentially a visual telephone (with letters, not pictures) for people who are deaf. A caller types in one part of a telephone conversation, a receiver reads it and types a reply, and so on. The early models of the TTY used in the Deaf community, like my first one in 1982, were refurbished Western Union teletypewriters. They were about the size of a three-drawer file cabinet and as heavy as a full one. Actually, that's where the TTY got its name: TTY is the telegraphy name for Teletype, the brand name for the machines made by a Bell Telephone subsidiary to translate code into printed words for Western Union. In the 1980s, there was a movement to change the name to TDD, for "Telecommunications Device for the Deaf," but TTY still seems to be the favorite term. Basic TTY models now consist of a standard (QWERTY) keyboard, a horizontal window with LED display, and an acoustic coupler. The model now on my desk (a big one by current standards at 9 in. x 9 in.) also includes a printer to keep track of conversations, a direct-connect plug so that it does not actually require a telephone, and a TTY answering machine. In addition, it has an "announcer" that would allow deaf users to tell the receiver that they are deaf. When the announcer button is pressed, a digitized voice says, "Hearing-impaired caller, use TDD"—clearly it is an older model!

A TTY produces a series of tones when the character keys are pressed. Those tones are picked up via the telephone handset through the acoustic

Table 2-1 Commonly Used Abbreviations that Speed Up TTY Communication

CUZ -	"Because"
GA -	"Go Ahead," it's your turn
HD -	"Please hold," for a short time (like pulling up a chair)
	PLS HD - "Please hold," for a longer time (like going to look for a person)
MIN -	"Minute"
MSG -	"Message"
PLS -	"Please"
Q -	"?"
R -	"Are"
SK -	"Stop Keying," signing off or hanging up
	GA to SK - "if you don't have anything else, I'm hanging up now"
TK -	"Thank"
TKS -	"Thanks"
TMW -	"Tomorrow"
U -	"You"
UR -	"Your"

Months and days of the week are abbreviated: JAN, DEC, MON, WED, etc.

coupler or via the direct connect cord and sent through standard phone lines. At the other end, a phone is placed on a similar coupler, and the tones are decoded into characters and shown on the display. Because typing speeds are slower than speech, TTY calls take longer than speech calls, and long-distance carriers now give TTY customers lower long-distance telephone rates in recognition of this fact. In addition, there are a variety of abbreviations and conventions that make for faster or more polite conversations. Some of these are shown in Table 2-1. (For a complete list of TTY conventions and etiquette, see Cagle and Cagle's *GA and SK Etiquette* in the suggested readings.) Many companies and essentially all public offices, including 911 in most areas, now have TTY capability. This availability usually is indicated by either separate TTY telephone numbers or the designation *V/TTY*, which means the number handles both voice and TTY calls.

TTYs are relatively inexpensive, and they are available in models ranging from pay TTY telephones in many airports and public buildings to portable versions that are barely bigger than a hand calculator. This was not always the case. It was not until the early 1960s that three deaf men, Robert Weitbrecht, Andrew Saks, and Jim Marsters, invented the acoustic coupler when AT&T and other large companies failed to do so because they felt there was not enough financial incentive. The three men then started hooking couplers up to discarded and refurbished teletypewriter machines. This breakthrough allowed deaf people to communicate over long distances in real time rather than through letters or telegrams for the first time, and it radically changed their lives, culture, and community. The complete story of the TTY, from Alexander Graham Bell to the present is delightfully captured in Harry Lang's book *A Phone of Our Own* (see suggested readings).

RELAY SERVICE

Another telecommunications advance that is important for people who are deaf was made possible by the TTY and the cooperation of telephone companies in the United States. For a deaf person who wants to call a hearing person or business that does not have a TTY, or for a hearing person who does not have TTY but wants to call a deaf person, there is now a nationwide "Relay" system. The Relay system involves calling a hearing operator using a toll-free 800 number (different in each state). The operator reads TTY messages from deaf callers and types spoken messages from hearing callers, and the entire conversation is guaranteed to be confidential. This network has freed deaf people from having to depend on hearing friends to make calls for them or to have to make personal visits when they want to make doctor appointments or reservations, consult lawyers, or inquire about goods or services from companies that do not have TTYs. A good Relay operator, like a good sign language interpreter, will tell the deaf person everything that the hearing person says and often will include information about the emotional state of the person if it is important to the conversation (e.g., "she's crying" or "he's yelling"). Some hearing people apparently are not aware of this fact, however. A deaf friend thus recently saw on his display "I hate getting these calls!" as an operator faithfully typed exactly what his veterinarian's receptionist said when the Relay operator informed her that it was a Relay call.

It was an important day in the American Deaf community when President Bill Clinton inaugurated the Relay system in 1993 by telephoning Frank Harkin, the deaf brother of U.S. Senator Tom Harkin of Iowa. A large group of hearing and deaf dignitaries, including Senator Harkin, were gathered around the president in the White House when he made the call. Unfortunately, Frank was on the phone at the time, telling a deaf friend that the president was going to be calling him. After the president got a busy signal, Senator Harkin called his brother's neighbor, who went next door and told Frank to get off the phone!

Figure 2-1 Symbols indicating that a film or video includes closed captions. The television-balloon is a registered trademark of the National Captioning Institute, reprinted by permission.

CAPTIONING AND DECODERS

Most people know that the symbols shown in Figure 2-1 mean that a television program is closed captioned. What does that mean? In its simplest form, it means that with the correct kind of decoding equipment, you can see printed text corresponding to what is being said. Decoders do not do the captioning. Rather, someone has to actually type in captions for each program, preferably at the time of the original production.

Captioned programs are not new. Open captions, meaning ones that are always visible, have been used in foreign films for many years, and they are used by local television stations to warn of serious weather or other emergencies without interrupting a broadcast. In 1971, WGBH, the public broadcasting station in Boston, used open captions on an episode of Julia Child's *The French Chef*, and in 1973 it started open captioning ABC-TV news and rebroadcasting it for deaf viewers a few hours later. As captioning started to expand, hearing viewers complained that open captions were distracting, and closed captions were developed. With the help of the National Captioning Institute and the Federal Communications Commission, broadcasters started to include captions on Line 21, a special signal band of commercial television broadcasts. Those signals can be decoded by a **caption decoder,** a device about the size of a TV cable box, or by decoder circuitry built into all thirteen-inch or larger televisions sold in the U.S. since 1990 (at a cost of about twenty-five cents per television set).

All kinds of programming are now captioned, either through pre- or postprogramming additions of captions or through real-time captioning, in which the captions are typed in by a captioner as a program is proceeding (for example, during special live news and sporting events). This does not mean that all programming is captioned. A recent report from the National Center for Accessible Media reported that although 100 percent of prime-time programming on public broadcasting stations is captioned, captioning is available on only about 36 percent of the programming on pay channels like HBO and The Disney Channel, 25 percent of local newscasts, and only 5 percent of all of the educational and children's videos now being released. That means that deaf children will often encounter uncaptioned videos in school and will have no access to the content of most instructional programming.

In 1981, video movies with captions began to be produced for home rental, and most deaf movie fans now eventually get to see their favorite actors and the season's hot movies. Unfortunately, it can take as long as six months for a popular movie to be released on tape, and only about 20 percent of all entertainment videos currently being released are captioned. Most third-rate, "B" movies are never be captioned, and all too frequently, a deaf person will rent a videotape with one of the labels shown in Figure 2-1 only to find that there are no captions after all![8]

Captions, when done properly, are an integral part of a program and do not detract from the original audio or video content. This requires that captions be paced as closely as possible to the audio track and to each utterance by the actors. Captions change with changes in video images and generally use the original wording, unless changes are necessary to avoid overwhelming the viewer with captions that are too fast to be able to read them all. Similarly, technical, scientific, and other difficult vocabulary may be presented at a slower rate to accommodate viewers' possible unfamiliarity with the material. As you can imagine, such modifications make it particularly difficult to caption educational materials for deaf college students, as professors who talk too fast for hearing students often cannot slow themselves down for a to-be-captioned lecture intended for other classrooms.

In addition to providing deaf people with access to television broadcasts, captioning is valuable in many other ways. Captioning has been shown to improve the reading skills and social communication skills of deaf children and of hearing children learning English as a second language. It is particularly helpful to older adults who have partial hearing losses as a normal part of the aging process. Captions also are useful in noisy environments or where the sound of a television would be distracting (for example, health clubs and airports), and it has now been accepted by most people. While the value of captioning is just starting to be realized, the battle to have all television and video material captioned continues to be an uphill one. The battle must be won in the end, however, and meanwhile captioners and caption researchers are pushing captioning technology and potential to its limits.

Hearing Aids and Related Technology

As I described in the previous section, some kinds of hearing loss involve the reduced intensity of sound, a situation that often can be improved through the use of some amplification device—that is, by making everything louder. Other hearing losses are more complex, involving losses of particular frequencies or damage to the nerves that carry sound-related impulses to the brain. Amplification devices do relatively little for people with hearing losses of these kinds, except in serving a signaling function. In some cases, such devices let the user know when some sound-related event is happening, when someone is approaching, or when someone is speaking to them, even if they cannot understand what is being said.

HEARING AIDS

Hearing aids come in a variety of styles, models, and even colors, but they are all relatively simple devices. Regardless of whether they fit behind the ear, fit in the ear, or are strapped to a child's chest, hearing aids consist of a microphone, a receiver/amplifier with volume control, a miniature speaker, a battery, and an acoustically designed earmold (see Figure 2-2). Amplified sound picked up by the microphone passes from the receiver to the speaker, through a tube, and into the plastic earmold, which is custom-molded for each user to ensure a snug fit.

Even in the simplest cases, the use of technology for improving hearing is not as straightforward as it might seem. Comprehension is a process that happens in the brain, not in the ear. The listener has to have sufficient information from the ear to analyze several different kinds of information in order to understand what is spoken. If a particular deaf child does not understand English speech, hearing aids will help him to the same extent as speaking louder to someone who does not speak English—not at all. Further, most hearing aids are not specifically tuned to speech sounds the way that (functioning) human ears are. That means that all sounds are amplified, and background noise often is so loud and disturbing that it eliminates any chance of improving speech reception. On the cutting-edge in hearing aid technology are digital hearing aids that can be programmed to particular frequency patterns of hearing loss and adjusted to block out background

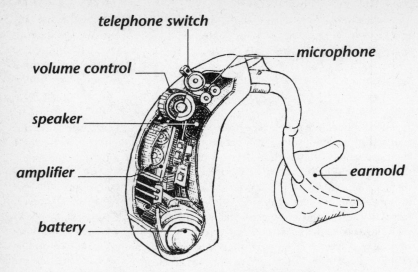

Figure 2-2   Schematic diagram of a hearing aid

noise. Unfortunately, such devices are not yet available to most deaf children at a price their parents can afford.

Because of the limitations of most hearing aids, some people with greater hearing losses do not find the trouble and discomfort they cause to be worth the small amount of information they provide. For people with profound hearing losses, aids are of no use anyway. One recent study found that deaf children of deaf parents were only half as likely as deaf children of hearing parents to wear hearing aids, even when their hearing losses were the same, so necessity is clearly not the only factor involved. For some people hearing aids may be a matter of habit (like professional tennis players wearing their watches during important matches). For others, there are personal or cultural reasons for wearing or not wearing them. A few deaf people prefer not to use hearing aids on principle, feeling that it would compromise their Deaf identities, but these are exceptions, and most Deaf people who can benefit from them do wear hearing aids. Yet others prefer not to wear hearing aids for cosmetic reasons. A teacher at a school for the deaf once told me that her students did not like wearing their hearing aids because they "weren't sexy." A boy in the class quickly corrected her, however, saying he did not mind wearing them at school, but he would never wear them if he was "trying to pick up hearing girls."

For children with some residual hearing, the use of hearing aids can be very important. Not only do they provide children with access to the language of hearing parents and siblings, but in cases of progressive hearing loss, they can provide a temporary bridge that will allow those children to more easily acquire sign language and reading skills in addition to some speech skills. Hearing aids must be approached cautiously with very young children, because too much amplification can damage the young ear, perhaps speeding up or causing more hearing loss.

LOOP SYSTEMS

Most newer hearing aids include special circuitry and a T (telephone) switch that improves their operation with telephones and in large meeting rooms, theaters, and religious buildings equipped with loop systems. The essence of loop circuitry is an electronic telecoil in the hearing aid that picks up magnetic signals generated by a telephone handset or closed-circuit loop system and feeds them directly to the hearing aid receiver, something like using a direct-connect computer modem. This system improves sound quality in situations where it normally would suffer, thus providing access to more information. Since 1988, federal law has required that all new telephones include circuitry that is consistent with hearing aid telecoils, making them more useful for many people with partial hearing losses.

COCHLEAR IMPLANTS

The term *cochlear implant* refers to the surgical implantation of a set of electrodes directly into the cochlea. As with a hearing aid, the user has one of several models of external device that includes a microphone and a receiver that converts sound to electrical energy. Unlike a hearing aid, the cochlear implant system includes a micro–speech processor, which generates electrical signals corresponding to sounds varying in pitch and loudness and sends them directly to nerve fibers in the cochlea (for those who have them). The U.S. Food and Drug Administration has approved the use of cochlear implants for **prelingually** deaf children beyond age two, as well as adults, while some other countries have approved them only for adults.

Cochlear implant technology is improving rapidly, but there are several factors that make the issue of their use rather complex. On the practical side, cochlear implants are extremely expensive, and the surgery is uncomfortable as well as potentially dangerous (for example, because the auditory nerve is close to the facial nerves, facial paralysis can occur). The people who so far have benefited most from implants are adults who had already learned spoken language and then lost their hearing. For them, the information transmitted by implants often provides access to speech again, even allowing them to use the telephone in some cases. Many of those people report feeling less isolated and more confident in social situations after their implant surgery. One author, in fact, recently suggested that the psychological benefits of a cochlear implant seem greater than the audiological benefits. (See also the quote at the beginning of this chapter.) The difficult issues arise when implants are considered for children or for severely to profoundly deaf adults who have never learned spoken language. For these groups, the results thus far have been mixed. Some prelingually deaf adults have gained rudimentary hearing, and those who are most motivated have improved their speech skills with extensive therapy. Nevertheless, the benefits have not been large.

From the perhaps understandable viewpoint of hearing parents who can afford them, cochlear implants appear to be the answer to their dreams—a way to make their child "hear" and perhaps learn to speak. But, is that really what happens? Do the results really justify the expensive surgery and risks involved? Most people have heard or read about successful cases of implants in children, and some parents' testimonials about their child's sudden abilities to hear and speak are both moving and convincing. Interestingly, the public does not hear about unsuccessful cases, and little objective data is available from people who do not have vested interests in the success of implants, as do doctors, families, and implant manufacturers. One recent study, however, found that although cochlear implants improved hearing in a group of profoundly deaf children, they did not do so any better than hearing aids. Further, the increase in hearing observed was still insufficient for the processing of speech.

Many members of the Deaf community and some others involved in deaf education and research argue that the decision by parents to implant their deaf children violates the children's rights by performing unnecessary surgery on them. Given the less-than-spectacular success with prelingually deaf adults, they argue that the risks of the nonreversible implant surgery are too great (you cannot take out an implant the way you can a hearing aid), and it destroys any natural residual hearing. Moreover, deaf people who are comfortable with their identities as Deaf believe that "forcing" cochlear implants on children does not allow them the opportunity to develop normal identities and freedom of choice. Having a cochlear implant, in their view, communicates to the child that being deaf is bad. They believe that this message may leave children forever caught between Deaf and hearing cultures, belonging to neither.

Some other Deaf people, admittedly, are threatened by the message of wanting to convert deaf children to "hearing" children. Recall that over 90 percent of deaf children have hearing parents. That means that the Deaf community is composed largely of people who themselves had hearing parents. They know what it is like growing up deaf, and also recognize the quality of their lives as Deaf people. These are things that hearing parents can never know. Hearing parents know what it is like growing up hearing, and know only the quality of their lives as hearing people. Is it wrong for them to want the same experience for their children?

It is still too soon to know the long-term consequences of cochlear implants for language and intellectual development in deaf children. The long-term social and cultural issues also are unclear—both for the children and for the Deaf community. At present, therefore, it is difficult to decide what is right and what is wrong, and probably there is no one answer.

The Cultural Context of Being Deaf

The Deaf community may only have come into the public limelight recently, but it has existed for a long time. That community, with its rich culture of theater, art, and writing, has contributed many famous scholars, artists, and public figures to this country and others. It is rarely seen by most hearing people, however, and many do not even know it exists.[9] In part, this situation follows from the nature of our society and the practicalities of being deaf in a hearing society. Most deaf adults and their children are part of a social group that is relatively more restricted or at least more clearly bounded than other groups defined by, say, religious affiliation, political interests, or race. Such separateness should not be too surprising. As one author asked, "Why would anyone choose to be with people with whom they could communicate only with great difficulty?"

Like any other subculture, the Deaf community has its own social structures, organizations, attitudes, values, and cultural history. The National Association of the Deaf (NAD) has been existence since 1880, but recent years have seen the mobilization of a variety of other Deaf groups and greater political activity by them and the NAD. Among the results of such activities are the **Americans with Disabilities Act** and the creation of the National Institute on Deafness and Other Communication Disorders, a division of the National Institutes of Health, which will have a long-range impact on the quality and extent of research relating to hearing loss and deaf children. These changes are primarily reforms to the hearing culture in which the Deaf community is immersed, but they are providing new opportunities for people who are deaf and a new understanding of deaf people by hearing people.

Several authors have referred to Deaf people as an ethnic group. In reality, members of the Deaf community are defined primarily by their fluent use of American Sign Language, but knowledge of the cultural tradition of the community is also essential. This situation is consistent with the *Oxford English Dictionary* definition of an ethnic group as one delineated by a cultural background and claiming official recognition of its group identity. From this perspective, some hearing children of deaf parents also are part of the Deaf ethnic group, even though they are not deaf.

For deaf children of deaf parents, growing up in the context of this social group likely has some rather specific consequences. Most deaf adults are not fully assimilated into the larger, ethnically mixed society, and their deaf children will not be either. There is a considerable amount of support from the Deaf community itself, and various chapters in this book will describe evidence suggesting that deaf children of deaf parents may have a variety of advantages over deaf children of hearing parents in both social and academic domains. At the same time, this cultural and language-based separation creates some natural differences between deaf and hearing individuals, similar to, but perhaps more pronounced than those that characterize other ethnic groups. Before considering the details of growing up deaf within hearing and Deaf cultures, however, we need to understand the centrality of communication for deaf as well as hearing children. We also have to consider the special situation encountered by deaf children in hearing families, where most parents are unable to communicate effectively with them. These topics, together with descriptions of sign language and several alternative communication systems, are the subjects of Chapter 3.

Summary

There are about 25 million people in the United States who have some degree of hearing loss, most of them older people who have begun to lose what once was normal hearing. Over a million adults and children never did have normal hearing and consider themselves deaf or hard of hearing. Hearing losses in these people can be from a variety of causes, including infant, childhood, or maternal illness; accidents; or hereditary factors. Genetic hearing losses appear to account for close to half of the cases, and deaf children of deaf families represent an important core in the Deaf community.

Being deaf and being Deaf are not the same thing. Capital-d Deaf is applied to people who are part of the historical and cultural community of deaf people and who use American Sign Language as their primary means of communication. Over 90 percent of deaf children have hearing parents; for them, access to the Deaf community is something that usually will not start until they are well into their school years. This affiliation is a natural one, and there is nothing that parents either should or can do to stop it. For emotional, social, and academic purposes, parents are much better supporting and perhaps even seeking it out rather than fighting it (see Chapter 6).

Deaf people are not evenly distributed around the country, and tend to be more concentrated around residential schools for the deaf, where there are historical and social ties, and in cities like Washington, D.C., Rochester, New York, and Northridge, California, where there are college programs specifically designed for students who are deaf. Within those population centers, parents and teachers are likely to have a variety of sources of information available to them about educational and other options for deaf children, but in outlying areas, information and access may be more limited. I thus have met several families that have moved to a city with a residential school for the deaf, allowing their child to live at home while having the most available options and support.

The causes and extent of hearing losses vary greatly, as do deaf people's use of spoken or signed communication and their involvement in the Deaf community. Deaf children will vary in whether their hearing losses occurred prior to or after they learned spoken language and whether their hearing losses are stable or progressive. These factors, as well as the degree and frequencies of their hearing losses, will play a major role in social, language, and academic development, issues to be considered through the remainder of this book. Most central for development is the fact that the first three years of life are the most critical for language acquisition, whether spoken or signed. Because most hearing losses are not identified until children are in their second year, many deaf children lose out on educational opportunities that could have been available if they had had earlier screening of their hearing and early interventions to support parent-child communication.

There are a variety of strategies and technologies to help deaf people to offset their lack of hearing. Some technologies support hearing (hearing aids, loop systems, cochlear implants), while others rely on vision to make life more comfortable and convenient as well as safer (TTYs, captioning, doorbell lights). Hearing aids can be effective with hearing losses that involve only the *amount* that can be heard, because hearing aids amplify sound. Newer technologies have led to programmable hearing aids, although these still do not help children with profound hearing losses. Cochlear implants, which send intensity and frequency information directly to the cochlea, are seen as the next technological step by many people. Their reviews to date are mixed, however, and they raise a host of ethical and medical questions when they are surgically placed in children.

Deaf culture and a variety of technologies make being deaf rather different from having some other disability, and the Deaf community has a long tradition of being a social and artistic subgroup within the larger society. Membership within that group has privileges and advantages that some of us can only admire from the outside.

Notes

1. Rochester's large deaf population (almost 10 percent of the total) stems largely from the presence of the National Technical Institute for the Deaf, one of eight colleges of the Rochester Institute of Technology, and the historic Rochester School for the Deaf. With such a large presence, the area is particularly "user-friendly" to people who are deaf, who also are attracted by the active Deaf community.

2. Interpreters, like assembly line workers and high-volume computer users, are particularly prone to what is called Cumulative Trauma Disorder (CTD) or Repetitive Motion Injury (RMI). CTD is a musculoskeletal injury (different from Carpel-Tunnel Syndrome, which is a nerve injury) resulting from overuse of particular muscles in repetitive, high-acceleration activities. Although other signers, deaf and hearing, may also suffer from CTD, interpreters are particularly prone to it because they often need to sign faster to keep up with teachers and other speakers, sign larger for bigger audiences, and sign for longer periods of time than the rest of us. As many as 45 percent of interpreters suffer from the problem and they can be out of work on disability for as long as a year. Symptoms include pain, stiffness, tingling, and loss of feeling in the fingers and hands.

3. There are a few other cities in the United States with proportionally large deaf populations, such as Riverside, California, and Hartford, Connecticut. The examples I use are those with which I am personally familiar.

4. Clearly, hearing loss is a frequent problem for older people. Thirty to 35 percent of Americans between sixty-five and seventy-five years of age and over 40 percent of those over seventy-five have some degree of hearing loss, but this book is not about them.

5. Sound also can be carried through the bones of the body via bone conduction just as it can through solid materials outside of the body (remember the hero in old western movies putting his ear to the railroad tracks to listen for the train?). Most fetuses thus are able to hear their mothers' but not fathers' voices during the last part of pregnancy, when their heads are resting on their mothers' pelvises (see Chapter 4). To demonstrate bone conduction of sound for

yourself (unless you are deaf), try tapping on your teeth with the soft end of a finger.

6. In older adults, the bones of the middle ear may lose some or all of their flexibility, a condition called otosclerosis. The result is frequently a humming or ringing in the ears, known as **tinnitus.** One way to overcome the annoyance of tinnitus is with an auditory masker, a device that looks like a hearing aid but produces white noise that "masks" the ringing. Maskers also are sometimes used to demonstrate to hearing people what it is like to be deaf, because they block most incoming sound.

7. In the 1950s through the 1970s, there were a variety of attempts to use tactile information instead of visual information (for example, a device that produced patterns on the skin corresponding to sounds), but none of these proved effective enough to justify their costs. The Picturephone, a telephone that has a videoscreen to allow face-to-face communication, is another "advance" that has gone by the wayside as a consequence of high cost, poor quality, and technological complications. Similar devices put in a new appearance every few years, and AT&T is currently testing a new one that makes use of personal computers as the sending-receiving device.

8. Unfortunately, deaf people cannot get the full effect of large-screen films in theaters. For many years, deaf moviegoers in many cities were able to pay half price for admission, on the assumption that they missed half of the film's content by not hearing the dialogue and music. Theater owners in many cities have now abandoned the practice, arguing that deaf patrons take up a full seat just like hearing patrons. Researchers are now working on several ways to allow deaf people to see closed-captioned films in movie theaters, but they are not yet cost-effective enough to be coming anytime soon to a theater near you.

9. In recent years, several books have been published about the Deaf community, some written by deaf individuals and others by hearing people within the community or close to it. These works provide new and valuable insights into a diverse subculture that otherwise might be inaccessible to hearing people. In their book *Deaf in America,* for example, Carol Padden and Tom Humphries provide exciting insights into the vibrant Deaf culture. Bonnie Poitras Tucker provides a very different perspective in *The Feel of Silence,* that of a deaf person who grows up entirely within hearing culture.

3

Communicating with Deaf Children

I use speech in situations where it is helpful, but this is entirely a matter of free choice. My entire education was taken in a residential environment, from elementary school through college, where sign language was the dominant language used in and out of the classroom. In fact, I learned ASL before I learned English. . . . What is important to success is not how people communicate but the extent to which they are willing to apply themselves in pursuit of their life's goals.

Robert R. Davila,
former Deputy Secretary, U.S. Department of Education,
Deaf Life (July 1995)

To this point, I have described several similarities and differences between deaf children and hearing children. Throughout, I have been careful to emphasize that differences observed between deaf and hearing children are natural and normal consequences of differences in their early environments and should not be seen as problems to be corrected. Deaf children are not "broken" hearing children, and trying to make them more like hearing children is unlikely to be the best way to support their development. Instead, we have to accommodate to their needs and perhaps alter our approaches to education and child rearing. In this regard, it would not be an exaggeration to suggest that most of the ways in which deaf and hearing children are different and the factors on which their success depend revolve around the availability and effectiveness of early communication.

Language is an essential component of normal development for all humans. Unfortunately, exposure exclusively to spoken language usually is not very successful for deaf children who have more severe prelingual hearing losses. While it is important for parents to strongly support deaf children's spoken language, it should not be to the exclusion of sign language. Similarly, while it is important for parents to strongly support deaf children's sign language, I do not believe that this should be done to the exclusion of spoken language. The important thing is to establish an effective mode of parent-child communication as early as possible. Postponing the beginning of sign language learning until they have given up on speech training is a common pitfall for parents of deaf children (see Chapter 5). It is also one to avoid unless you want to put all of your eggs into one very precarious basket. After exploring all of the available evidence, we will see that it clearly points to three conclusions: (1) There is no single, correct answer to the language question that applies to all or even most deaf children, (2) there are places for both signed and spoken language in the lives of many deaf children, and (3) sign language will play a vital role in the lives of most deaf children and its value should not be underestimated.

Availability of Language for Deaf Children

In the 1960s, about 90 percent of hearing parents used only spoken language with their deaf children, while the remainder used one or more of the forms of manual communication described below. Since that time, American Sign Language (ASL) has been on the rise, and recent surveys indicate that most deaf students sign at least some of the time. Still, fewer than half of the children who use sign language in school also sign when they are with their families, and only a small fraction of those are able to carry on normal, everyday conversations with their parents. This situation does not mean that signing is really unnecessary; in most cases, it means that children and parents are being short-changed in their interactions.

Despite occasional claims to the contrary, there is no evidence at all to suggest that the early use of manual communication (signs or gestures) by deaf children hampers their development of skills in spoken language or in any other area. Gestures, in fact, appear to be an essential prelude to language development, establishing the rules and contexts of interpersonal communication for both deaf and hearing children. Denying the use of gestures to deaf children, as is done in many programs emphasizing spoken language, thus seems more likely to hurt them than to help them. Moreover, the available evidence clearly indicates that, on average, deaf children who learn sign language as preschoolers show better academic achievement and social adjustment during the school years, and they also show superior gains in learning to read and write in English (see Chapter 7). Children of hearing parents who become deaf after learning language also tend to exhibit better academic and social abilities than children who became deaf prior to learning language. Thus, the important factor is not necessarily the ability to speak, but the ability to communicate through language, whatever its form, from an early age.

Also contrary to popular claims, spoken language skills in deaf children usually do not result in their full assimilation into hearing society. In this case, it is important to distinguish between those deaf children who have greater hearing losses and those children with enough residual hearing to benefit from speech training. This latter group is not *deaf* in the sense of being unable to use and understand speech for the purposes of day-to-day living, even though their hearing losses may have some effect on their development and academic achievement. Many children who are truly deaf eventually will find themselves with friends, dates, and spouses who are deaf. As described in Chapter 2, they eventually will become involved in Deaf social clubs and other Deaf organizations that play an important role in the Deaf community and Deaf culture. They do not give up roles in the hearing community and hearing culture, but rather they are able to draw from both groups.

Over 80 percent of American schoolchildren with severe to profound hearing losses now receive some kind of sign language education in school. Because most hearing parents cannot communicate effectively with their deaf children, residential schools and other special programs are important environments where they learn a large part of their social skills and social roles as well as academic subjects (see Chapters 6 and 9). Deaf children born to deaf parents who use sign language, in contrast, will be exposed to language from the beginning of their lives—a language that serves both social and educational functions. Most deaf children of deaf parents thus learn more about life and about who they are at home, in the context of the supportive Deaf community.[1]

Before describing sign language as it is taught and used by deaf children, two important distinctions should be noted. The first concerns what we mean by manual communication and sign language, and how they relate to the language actually experienced by deaf children. *Manual communication* is now recognized as somewhat of a misnomer, even though it is often used in contrast to *spoken communication*. The error here is that although many people who learn to sign use only their hands (and most hearing people notice only the hands), true sign languages like ASL include a variety of other features as well. Facial expression is particularly important, for example, in the way it carries grammatical information. Emotion is communicated by signing rate and size as well as by facial expression and sign selection.[2] Even talking about deaf children learning sign language rather than manual communication is somewhat misleading, because it is extremely rare that deaf children are exposed *exclusively* to sign language. Many deaf adults rely solely on ASL in communication among themselves, but their communication with deaf children and hearing individuals frequently includes mouth movements and sign modifications which increase the number of "comprehension cues" available to the receiver. Some of these are actually part of ASL (e.g., sign modification to signify extent or duration), but others are included to ensure communication with less-than-fluent language users.

In educational settings, a multiplicity of language cues for deaf children is made quite explicit through artificial means, and most sign-language-oriented schools for deaf children actually employ either **Simultaneous Communication** (SC) or **Total Communication** (TC). Simultaneous Communication refers to the concurrent production of both sign and speech and is the most common means of educational communication between deaf children and hearing individuals who can sign. Within the classroom, many schools make use of Total Communication, a method which utilizes all potentially available sources of linguistic communication, including sign, speech, and amplification through the use of hearing aids. While such methods are designed to give deaf children access to as much information as possible, it should not be assumed that they result in deaf children who are fluent in both ASL and English. SC and TC are not the same as ASL, any more than they are the same as English. Fluency in each of those "real" languages will require exposure to them and considerable instruction if they are not learned naturally.

A second important distinction to keep in mind is that between real languages, such as English or ASL, and the gestures and pantomime that accompany them both. Gestures and body language are normally used to facilitate both signed and spoken communication. Complex gesture and pantomime also have been shown to develop out of necessity when deaf children grow up in hearing families without the benefit of exposure to sign language, although they are insufficient to communicate more than the most basic information between child and parent.

The relation between gestures and signs as they are used and understood by young deaf children will be considered in Chapter 5. Looking ahead, deaf and hearing children tend to use many of the same gestures, both before they actually learn a signed or spoken language and in their day-to-day use of language as they get older. If these gestures are common to speakers of both sign language and English, clearly they cannot be said to be part of ASL any more than they are part of English. It just happens that hearing people tend not to notice how frequently they use gestures—an oversight that can be remedied by careful observation during any five-minute conversation.

Everything You Always Wanted to Know about Sign Language

Like a spoken language, a signed language consists of a large vocabulary of arbitrary signs, together with a set of rules, or a **grammar**, that governs both the formation of individual signs and combinations of signs into phrases and sentences.[3] In addition to the repertoire of formalized signs, a variety of which are found at the end of the book, signed languages contain a set of number signs (Figure 3-1) and a manual alphabet (Figure 3-2).

Number signs are used just as they are in spoken language: The signs represent number concepts just as the words *ten* and *ten million* do. Spelling also fills the same function in sign language as it does in spoken language, at least in part. We can spell words in English when they are new or when we do not know how to pronounce them, but we normally do not use spelling in our everyday conversations. Fingerspelling is used primarily in cases where there are no conventional signs for particular ideas or where a sign is obscure or unknown, but for a variety of reasons it also occurs in conversational signing even when there is an available sign. Fingerspelling thus does not replace signing, but supplements it.[4] In fact, the manual alphabet used in the United States cannot correctly be called English, because the two-handed manual alphabet of British Sign Language (BSL) is quite different.

As in the case of spoken languages, ASL and other sign languages are quite distinct from each other. Signers of ASL and BSL, for example, are no more likely to understand each other than are speakers of English and Chinese. What is called **Signed English** (or Sign English) should not be confused with any of the naturally occurring sign languages like ASL. Signed English is actually an artificial signing system combining the signs of ASL and the grammatical structure of English (see discussion later in this chapter). Although it is taught to deaf children around the country, Signed English is not normally used in day-to-day conversations among deaf adults. It is possible that with improvements in the reading and writing skills of deaf children, the mingling of English and ASL someday might make Signed English far more conventional and accepted than it is now, but that remains to be seen.

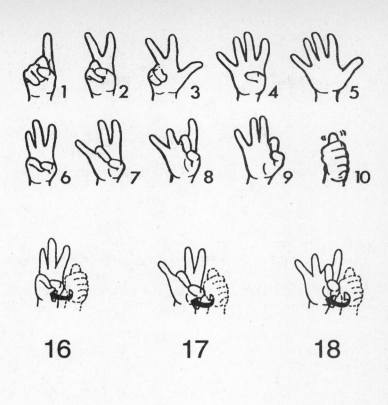

Figure 3-1 ASL number signs

Figure 3-2 ASL manual alphabet

The goal of Signed English and other hybridized forms of English/sign language is clear enough: They seek to facilitate signed communication for deaf children while also encouraging acquisition of the English structure necessary for reading, writing, and possibly speech. After many years of debate concerning whether deaf children should be taught signed or spoken communication, a new educational debate is whether deaf students should continue to be taught using systems like Signed English or taught in ASL instead. Teaching ASL would contribute to the preservation and extension of Deaf culture, and some authors claim that learning ASL can also facilitate deaf children's learning to read and write. This argument may seem to have some credibility, because sign language is more accessible to young deaf children than spoken language if their parents know it and use it consistently. Because ASL bears no resemblance to English or any other written language, however, it should not contribute to reading English any more than would the learning any other language. At the same time, the artificial nature of Signed English may make it less effective than other alternatives as a foundation for natural language development.[5] While the jury is still out on this issue, normal development clearly demands the availability of some early language. ASL and similar sign languages clearly are excellent alternatives to spoken language, even if they do not contribute directly to children's English literacy skills (see Chapter 7 for a detailed discussion). At the same time, early learning of ASL provides deaf children with proficiency in at least one language, and with that comes access to information that will contribute to subsequent development. Acquisition of ASL or another natural sign language also gives children a sense of mastery and control that is important to subsequent academic success.

A BRIEF HISTORY OF SIGN LANGUAGE

From both practical and educational perspectives, it is difficult to understand how any informed observer could claim that a sign language like ASL is anything but a true language. Historically, extensive vocabularies of signs appear to have existed in Spain as early as the sixteenth century, but it was not until two hundred years later that signs were combined with grammars, and sign language moved into the classroom. This shift, and the accompanying changes within the Deaf community, also moved signing from a gestural system to a full-fledged language.

The distinction of being the first to take the important step of combining signs with a signing grammar is usually ascribed to the French educator Abbé Charles Michel de l'Epée (1712–89). Some years later, it was Thomas Hopkins Gallaudet (1787–1851) and Laurent Clerc (1786–1869) who brought Abbé de l'Epée's sign language to America and opened the first public school for deaf children, in Hartford, Connecticut. At that point, de l'Epée's sign system was blended with many of the signs that were already in common usage by American deaf people, and ASL was born.[6] One suspects that the resulting change in education of the deaf and in the communication between deaf children and their parents must have opened new horizons of interpersonal contact not much less dramatic than the classic scene in *The Miracle Worker* in which the deaf and blind Helen Keller first grasps the meaningfulness of fingerspelling.

Although ASL is sometimes compared to Native American "sign languages," the comparison is a faulty one. The truly *manual* communication systems of Native Americans did not replace spoken language, and as far as we know there were no silent tribes. Rather, Native American signs were used primarily to allow communication among different tribes having different spoken languages when they gathered for festive, political, or commercial purposes. Interestingly, some of those signs have near-identical counterparts in ASL, including the three signs seen in Figure 3-3. Presumably, such commonalities are coincidental, and I have only found them to occur for signs that are relatively **iconic.**

Over the last two hundred years, signed languages have become both more conventional and more rule-governed in their use by deaf people and more accepted by hearing educators. Until the late 1960s, however, signing was still thought by many hearing people to be a relatively primitive communication system that lacked extensive vocabulary and the means to express subtle or abstract concepts. This impression remains in some countries, but in North America the language status of ASL and other signed languages has been well documented by linguists, psychologists, and educators. Beyond naturally occurring sign languages, several alternative systems have been developed, and these will be described after considering some of the mechanics of sign language. Those readers not interested in the linguistic details of ASL might want to skip directly to the section on artificial speech and sign systems.

COMPONENTS OF SIGNS

Modification and Inflection

A glance at the Everyday Signs section at the back of the book will reveal that signs can be described in terms of three primary characteristics: the shape of the hand or hands, the place at which the sign is made or where it begins, and the movements involved in making a sign. Signs also can be distinguished by whether they are made with one or two hands, by the orientation of the hands relative to the signer, and whether they involve a stable "base" hand or not. As can be seen in Figure 3-4, any one of the primary sign characteristics is sufficient to change the meaning of a sign (for example, EGG versus NAME, MOTHER versus FATHER)[7] just as such small differences can change the meanings of words (*load* versus *toad*, *beet* versus *beer*). Most signs, in fact, can be defined in terms of a combination of

coffee

draw

boat

Figure 3-3 ASL signs that were the same in early
Native American sign systems

egg

name

mother

father

Figure 3-4 Changes in hand movement and placement that change signs' meanings

components from a set of eighteen handshapes, twelve places of articulation, and twenty-five different movements. By comparison, there are forty-four different sounds and twenty-six letters that make up all English words.

Changes in the movement, place of articulation, or handshape of a particular sign also can be used to modify the number or tense of a sign, just as words in English can be **inflected** by adding particular beginnings or endings: *dog* to *dogs, jump* to *jumped, important* to *unimportant,* and so on. In ASL, the sign DOGS is made by repeated signing of DOG, and JUMPED is made by adding a FINISH past-marker to JUMP or letting context specify the past. Only the sign UNIMPORTANT is made by the addition of a simple NOT marker, although there are other ways to sign the concept as well. More extensive inflections also occur in ASL. For example, the movement in the sign COMPLAIN can change to communicate COMPLAIN CONSTANTLY or COMPLAIN VEHEMENTLY, and the sign CHAIR can be altered to mean COUCH or ROW OF CHAIRS. The ability to make such changes, represents one of the properties that distinguishes sign language from gesture. A true language must have a mechanism for modifications of this sort in order to be efficient and allow a full range of communication. Similarly, new signs, like new words, are constantly being invented (within acceptable grammatical rules), and signs can be used in metaphorical ways or as puns.

Classifiers

One central component of signs is what is referred to as a **classifier.** Most simply, classifiers in sign language are particular handshapes that have general-purpose meanings. For example, rather than using the normal, literal signs in the context of a sentence, an upright 1-hand (see Figure 3-1) can be used to indicate a person; a bent, downward V-hand (Figure 3-2) can be used to indicate an animal; and a rotated 3-hand can be used to indicate a car or other vehicle. Classifiers typically are first assigned to a particular person or thing and then are used to indicate actions or directions taken within an episode. Figure 3-5 presents two simple examples of classifiers. In the left panel, the person classifier is used in the sign MEET, and in the right panel, the vehicle classifier is used in the sign PARK. More complex uses of classifiers also occur, and one can easily imagine classifiers used to describe a person (1-hand) who gets into a car (horizontal 3-hand) and weaves down a hill before hitting an animal (bent V-hand) which dies, with "feet" turned upward (two inverted, bent V-hands).

There is also a class of less specific classifiers that function more like

meet   **park**

Figure 3-5 ASL classifiers for PERSON and VEHICLE in MEET and PARK

adjectives than nouns. These are most often used for indicating either shape or size. For example, F-hands or C-hands moved vertically or horizontally are used to denote the size of cylindrical objects, and I-hands can denote thin filaments or lines (the I-hand also is involved in signs like STRING and SPAGHETTI—see Everyday Signs). Note that although both these general classifiers and the more specific nounlike classifiers make use of alphabetic and numerical handshapes, their meanings are completely arbitrary and are not tied to the letter-meaning of the handshape. Similar characteristics are found in spoken classifier languages like Japanese and Thai.

As one might suspect by this point, sign languages have their own accents, dialects, and idiosyncratic signs.[8] Signs can be limited to particular regions, schools, or even individual families. **Home signs,** for example, are signs used in much the same way as some special words and names are used in hearing families. Both are most common in homes with small children, often originating from mispronunciations or missigns. Some such words seem to live on into adulthood, like the words *grabbers* and *bazuter* in my family. Dialectical differences in sign language, like some differences in spoken language, can make for some difficulty in communication (for example, at a convention of the National Association of the Deaf). These differences also can make for some funny incidents, as when I first discovered that one commonly used sign I had learned in Canada was indistinguishable from a common four-letter signed profanity in North Carolina.

COMBINING SIGNS

Sign language sometimes gives the impression of not having very strong requirements about the order of signs within sentences, occasionally leading people to assume that it has no grammar. This appearance occurs primarily because of the contrast with English, which happens to be a language with relatively rigid word-order rules. Other spoken languages, like Italian or Japanese, have more flexibility in word order and are closer in this respect to ASL.

There are a variety of grammatical rules within sign languages operating at several different levels. Most signs, for example, must be made within a particular **signing space**, a roughly square area from the top of the head to the waist and about one foot to either side of the body. Signs made outside of this space might be seen as ungrammatical or as having some kind of special extended or metaphorical meaning. There are also rules about the positioning of "base" hands, the ways in which signs and classifiers are combined, and symmetry of movement. One example of the latter is the sign SIMULTANEOUS COMMUNICATION shown in the top of Figure 3-6. Because the two hands have the same movement but different handshape, the sign is technically ungrammatical even though it has been used for years. SAME-TIME COMMUNICATION, in the bottom of Figure 3-6, thus has replaced the old sign for SIMULTANEOUS COMMUNICATION. As in English, however, some ungrammatical forms continue to stay in the language despite our best attempts to purge them (for example, nonwords like *alright, irregardless,* a whole *nother* issue). When I recently took a sign language examination (on which my job depended!), I made sure that I used the sign SAME-TIME COMMUNICATION. But when I used the same sign later that week in a meeting of deaf and hearing colleagues, one of the deaf people said "huh?" Luckily, another deaf person interjected, "Oh, he means SIMULTANEOUS COMMUNICATION," using the more common sign.

USING SPACE

One of the most salient grammatical characteristics of signed languages is their use of the signing space to communicate both time and location. Time is indicated by positions moving from behind the signer (the PAST), through the here and NOW, and out in front of the signer (the FUTURE). The sign WEEK (see Everyday Signs), for example, is normally made out in front of the body. When the basic sign is finished by moving the right hand

simultaneous
communication

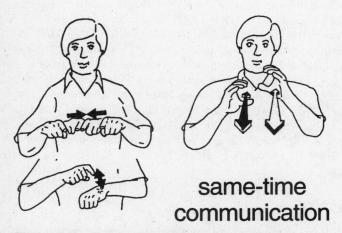

same-time
communication

Figure 3-6 ASL signs SIMULTANEOUS COMMUNICA-
TION and SAME-TIME COMMUNICATION

backward toward the right shoulder, it means LAST-WEEK; finishing it with a forward arc means NEXT-WEEK. Signs for YEAR and MONTH can be similarly modified.

The space in front of a signer also is used to establish the location of people, objects, and places that are part of an ongoing conversation. When first mentioning particular individuals in an event, usually via a **name-sign** or fingerspelled name, those people can be placed in different locations in the signing space, to the right, to the left or in front of the signer. Later, they can be referred to just by pointing at the location in which they were put, without having to rename them. Sign language novices might have some difficulty keeping their signing spaces organized, but it is only a matter of practice before the utility of locating signs is appreciated, and both production and comprehension are made much easier. As with any language, regular use in many contexts is essential for the acquisition of the signs and rules of sign language. Being hearing does not make sign language any easier or harder to learn. As a second language, it takes just as much effort as any foreign language. You do not have to learn to read and write it, but most signers will tell you that good fingerspelling is a real challenge.

Beyond constraints on the form of individual signs, sign languages like ASL have rich varieties of rules for sign combination that had gone unnoticed until relatively recently. For example, although ASL has considerable flexibility in sign order, the subject-verb-object ordering of English is most frequently used, probably because of the immersion of ASL within a culture in which the host language is English. Still, the fact that all of the rules and structures of signed languages do not necessarily conform to those of their host languages should not be surprising. That lack of correspondence would only be worthy of wonder if signed languages mapped directly onto their host spoken languages, and we have already seen that this is not the case.

Artificial Speech and Sign Systems Taught to Deaf Children

In addition to ASL and Signed English, there are several other communication systems for deaf children that have been around for some time. These language alternatives fall into two categories: modifications to sign communication, typically intended to make it more English-like, and modifications to spoken communication.[9] None of these formally developed systems has caught on to the degree of Signed English, primarily because no one has provided any firm evidence about their effectiveness (but see the discussion of Pidgin Signed English below). Nonetheless, each alternative has its proponents, and anecdotal evidence concerning the successes of particular children with particular systems is not hard to find. This is not to say that one of these alternatives, or another yet to be invented, might not prove effective in facilitating the education and interpersonal communication of deaf children as a group or for particular deaf children. As with ASL and Signed English, however, we will not be in a position to decide which way of expressing language is best for which children until appropriate, scientific evaluations have been made. Meanwhile, there seems no reason why any one mode of language need be used in isolation, and various combined methods are possible. Most importantly, it is essential that deaf children begin to be exposed to language as early as possible and that parents and other family members be fully involved partners. If there is no one to communicate with outside of the classroom, language experience in any mode does little good. With this in mind, let us briefly survey some of the available language alternatives for deaf children.

SPOKEN COMMUNICATION AND CUED SPEECH

Up to now, this chapter has included relatively little discussion of spoken language, although it will be considered below. The primary reason for this approach is that the focus here is on deaf children with greater hearing losses, those who are less likely to benefit from exposure to spoken language. The claim is not that these deaf children cannot learn to speak; surely some of them can. Rather, the point is that in the absence of hearing (especially during the critical periods of language learning), spoken communication is rarely viable as the primary means of communication for deaf children or deaf adults. With extensive speech training, some deaf children reach the point where family members can understand some of their speech, but that does not mean that they will be understood by others outside the family or that they will be able to understand the speech of others.

Still, there are exceptions. We have all seen deaf people on television or elsewhere who appear to have excellent, or at least pretty good speech. In many cases, these are individuals with lesser hearing losses or people who had better hearing when they learned to speak and then experienced progressive or acute hearing losses. Others have improved their speech as older children or as adults. Often, this shift occurs only after using sign language early in life, at the point where an individual has the motivation and ability to benefit from spoken language methods. And still, there are exceptions like several of my deaf colleagues and Heather Whitestone, Miss America 1994, who were raised with intensive speech therapy and have very good speech. There are several schools and programs in this country offering education exclusively in spoken language and claiming varying degrees of success. Still to be determined is whether the children who succeed in such programs are representative of all deaf children or whether they have particular characteristics that make them most likely to benefit from such exposure in the first place. In any case, the argument for exclusive exposure to spoken language has never been supported in any broad sense and thus, for the present, spoken language seems most likely to be effective when combined with ASL.

Cued Speech

One increasingly popular supplement to spoken language is **Cued Speech,** which supports spoken language with a set of sound-related handshapes. The motivation for the invention of Cued Speech lay in the fact that many speech sounds look the same on the lips when they are pronounced, especially in English, making speechreading difficult. For example, if you look in the mirror, and pronounce the names of letters *c, e, g,* and *z,* they look very similar on the lips. Speechreading of some other languages, like Italian, is somewhat easier because of greater regularity in the way in which sounds are combined and their unambiguous correspondence to writing. More of the language therefore can be "seen on the lips," and one therefore might expect that deaf children in such countries would have relatively better speech skills, and perhaps reading skills, than deaf children in the United States. Preliminary findings appear to support this prediction.

The idea behind Cued Speech is that if deaf children could be given cues sufficient to distinguish sounds that look alike on the lips in English, they would be better able to learn to lipread and reproduce those lip movements, themselves, in spoken communication. Cued speech thus maintains an "oralist" approach to language, while providing a manual means of overcoming the limitations of oral ambiguity. Overall, it uses thirty-six different cues to clarify the forty-four different sounds in English. Cues for vowel sounds are produced by placing the hand at one of four different locations on the face in the area of the mouth (plus two location combinations). Cues for consonant sounds are provided by making one of eight alternative handshapes and combining them with the vowel locations. The handshapes of Cued Speech thus play a very different role from the handshapes of ASL, which carry information about meaning rather than about sound. Accordingly, Cued Speech is not technically a language, but is a support for spoken English—providing, of course, that everyone involved in a conversation knows how to read and produce the cues.

Although the effectiveness of Cued Speech is still under investigation, there are some encouraging research findings related to its effects on reading ability. Dr. Jacqueline Leybaert and her colleagues in Belgium have shown that deaf children who are consistently exposed to French Cued Speech during the preschool years *both at home and at school* learn to read faster and show enhanced subskills in reading relative to deaf children exposed only to spoken language (see Chapter 7). Still to be determined is how reading skills of children learning Cued Speech compare to children learning sign language or some hybrid, like Signed English. Meanwhile, we need to recognize that Cued Speech alone will not give younger deaf children access to speech. Some parents have found it effective to expose their children to ASL first, and then bring in Cued Speech during the school years. One former colleague of mine followed this route, teaching her son Cued Speech when he was about eight years old. The problem, of course, is that if you are using your hands for vowel and consonant cues, you cannot be signing at the same time. Therefore, Cued Speech may be most effective in situations where a story or situation is first described in sign language and then, when it is fully understood, retold with Cued Speech. This combination may help to convey the link between speech and the printed word, but the necessary research has yet to be done.

ALTERNATIVE FORMS OF SIGN COMMUNICATION

Earlier, I noted that artificial hybrids of sign language and English are intended to help children learn to read and write. These combination forms of signing are collectively known as **manually coded English,** because they present English on the hands rather than the lips.

Pidgin Signed English

Most people who learn to sign as adults do not really use either ASL (for which it may be hard to find classes) or Signed English (for which we have little need). I was in that situation myself when I started learning to sign in North Carolina. My sign teacher there was the son of Deaf parents (or a **CODA,** a child of deaf adults) who insisted that ASL could not be taught, only learned naturalistically. What he taught, therefore, was a hybrid sign language known as **Pidgin Signed English** or PSE. Pidgin languages, in general, are those that develop when different languages mix together, typically through the immigration of language groups into new locations. In this manner, English mixed together with French in Louisiana to produce Cajun, and English mixed with several African languages in South Carolina to produce Gullah. When a pidgin is passed on to a second generation as their first language, it evolves into a more rich, complex language called a *creole*. It is via this mechanism that a more complex form of Signed English may become more common in the future.

PSE combines the signs of ASL with a mixed grammar of English and ASL. It also includes a variety of initialized signs. Initialized signs typically involve a single sign made with various letter handshapes that give it several different but related meanings. Examples include a cluster of signs containing SITUATION, CONTEXT, ENVIRONMENT, and CULTURE and one containing GROUP, CLASS, DEPARTMENT, and TEAM (see Everyday Signs). In ASL, all four signs in each group are made with the same handshape, and the precise meaning must be derived from context. In PSE, like other forms of manually coded English, they are all different.

Signed English

As noted earlier, Signed English is the form of signing most frequently taught to deaf children in the United States. Like PSE, Signed English combines English grammar with the signs of ASL, but it goes beyond the use of initialized signs and English word order. Signed English also includes a set of fourteen markers that are combined with signs to communicate English structure. Consistent with its purpose of helping deaf children learn to read and write, these structural markers refer to important grammatical features of English. The fourteen markers correspond to the following structures, all but one occurring at the end of a sign:

regular noun plural (duck**s**)
irregular noun plural (child**ren**)
possessive (Simon**'s**)
regular past tense verb (jump**ed**)
irregular past tense verb (**wro**te)
third person singular (writ**ten**)
present progressive (jump**ing**)
past participle (**gone**)
adverbial -ly (slow**ly**)
adjectival -y (funn**y**)
comparative (funn**ier**)
superlative (funn**iest**)
agent (person or thing)
opposition: not, un-, im-, in- (**im**polite)

Although potentially an important aspect of language used in the classroom, the grammatical markers of Signed English are unnecessary when signing is in the hands of an expert.

Seeing Essential English (SEE1)

SEE1 was developed during the early 1960s as a way to express English literally using the hands. Every English word is supposed to have a basic (ASL) sign in SEE1, and signs are produced in English word order. Additional signs are used to represent English grammatical structures, as in Signed English, but SEE1 goes farther, using a different sign for each meaningful unit of English rather than for each concept. Thus, for example, while ASL and Signed English use single signs for compound English words that represent a single concept (*butterfly* or *sweetheart*), SEE1 uses two signs, one for each component unit. *Butterfly* is thus signed by combining the signs BUTTER and FLY, and *sweetheart* is signed by combining the signs SWEET and HEART—combinations that make spelling sense but not conceptual sense.

SEE1 retains those ASL signs that conform to a "two-out-of-three" rule. A single sign is used for an English word with two or more uses, as long as each pair shares two of the following: sound, meaning, or spelling. Thus *bow* as in *bow and arrow* can have the same sign as *bow* as in *tie a bow* or *violin bow* because they share sound and spelling. *Bow* as in *bow from the waist*, however, would have to have a different sign because it shares only spelling with the previous two *bows*.

Signing Exact English (SEE2)

SEE2 was a spinoff from SEE1, the consequence of a difference of opinions among the developers of SEE1 about their goals rather than any agreed-upon improvement in the system. SEE2 uses the same general rules as SEE1, but has a one-to-one correspondence between signs and meanings (it is more "exact"). In SEE2, therefore, the word *bow* has four different signs, and SEE2 thus has more signs than SEE1. SEE2 also makes considerable use of initialized signs.

Among the several alternative communication systems available for deaf children, it would seem that the systems that are likely to be most effective are those that combine as many sources of information as possible. Indeed, this is precisely the philosophy behind Simultaneous Communication and Total Communication. These artificial sign systems, however, do not lead deaf children to fluency in either sign language or in English. If they do not facilitate learning to read and write, there does not seem any good reason to use them. At present, it is unclear whether the limited benefits to deaf children's English skills after learning a hybrid sign system are significant enough to offset their failure to become fluent in ASL. Until more work has been done, this issue will continue to be a problem.

Speech Training and Speech Assessment

Speech training and speech assessment should be thought of as a whole, not as two different endeavors. Assessment of a child's skills and needs are essential to effective teaching of spoken language, and the progress of teaching requires regular assessments both of progress in speech skill acquisition and possible changes in young children's hearing. Both assessment and training therefore have to take into consideration the goals and capabilities of the children and their families, not just abstract principles about the importance of spoken language. Indeed, it is the intense adherence to the primacy of speech by some advocates of oral approaches to education that drives many deaf individuals away from its potential benefits.

The goal of speech and speechreading training should be to allow deaf children to take advantage of the most information possible and have access to the full range of opportunities offered to hearing children. As indicated in the quote by Robert Davila at the beginning of this chapter, the ultimate decision to use speech, sign, or some combination of them rests with the individual. Parents and educators will find themselves—and their children—best positioned if they make all resources available to children until such time as the children themselves are able to make their own decisions.

Speech training can take a variety of forms, depending on the needs of the individual child. Different programs focus on different levels of spoken language, from individual letter sounds, through syllables, to whole word pronunciation methods. Syllable methods, for example, involve repeated practice with single consonant-vowel pairs such as *pa, pa, pa* or sets of pairs that vary in the vowel's place of articulation, such as the set that would sound like *pee, pa, peh, po, pu*, where you can feel the tongue moving farther and farther back in the mouth. Examples like this are not visible on the mouth (look in the mirror again) and are extremely difficult for deaf children to learn; hence the potential usefulness of Cued Speech. Alternatively, speech training can focus on the pronunciation of whole words. This is often done with words in isolation, although their presentation within meaningful contexts can also contribute to reading as well as speechreading skill.

Regardless of its level, speech training usually involves one-on-one interaction with trained speech therapists over relatively long and repetitive sessions in which students model therapists' behavior. Parents are given exercises to work on at home with their child when the therapist is not around, but this is rarely sufficient. There are also a variety of technological tools available for professional and home use for speech training. Several computer software companies, for example, market interactive computer software in which young children's productions of correct sounds lead to interesting visual events, such as a monkey climbing a tree. Older children might be shown speech patterns on the computer screen and work to match them with their own productions. These and other methods serve to help coordinate motor movements of the tongue and mouth and appropriate inflow and outflow of air as well as establishing rapport and comfort between the child and the speech training enterprise.

As with speech training, speech assessment can take various forms. At the level of individual sounds, speech therapists evaluate vocal intensity, duration, and pitch, in addition to the correctness of the articulation. As individual speech sounds come into a child's repertoire, they have to be expanded, combined, and regularly maintained or they frequently will "degrade." Some speech skills that are acquired at the level of individual sounds are not easily integrated into syllables and words, so that there must be a constant monitoring and correction of the full repertoire. Clearly, this relatively intense focus can be difficult for younger deaf children, many of whom will never master the basics well enough to engage in spoken conversation outside of the family. At the same time, because of positive responses from many hearing adults, spoken communication successes can add to a child's feelings of accomplishment, as well as facilitating communication within the home and school.

Speech training must be coupled with appropriate amplification, so that children can receive some feedback in addition to what they can see on the lips. If they also have sufficient residual (aided) hearing and speechreading skills to comprehend the spoken language of others, spoken language can be a valuable tool. Unfortunately, there is relatively little research available to parents and professionals on the effectiveness of different speech training methods, and each method has its own adherents and success stories (parents usually will not hear about the failures with any method). Without good information on which to evaluate the appropriateness for any given child, parents may be at a loss in deciding how to proceed. In such cases, information can be obtained from *experienced* speech pathologists and audiologists within the school system, avoiding, perhaps, new graduates who may not have had as much experience with diverse methodologies or others who have entrenched biases (check with other parents). For more general information, there is a list of local and national information sources at the back of the book.

Summary

Language is an essential component of normal development. Because the vast majority of deaf children are born to nonsigning hearing parents, however, most of them will be denied access to many parts of the world until they have passed the most critical ages for language acquisition, the first three to four years. All available research indicates that for children with greater hearing losses, exposure only to spoken language usually fails to give children all of the linguistic tools they need for academic and social purposes, although some children will benefit. While access to English may be essential for English literacy, it is most important that deaf children, like hearing children, be able to communicate with their parents from the beginning. Following chapters will show the various ways that early communication affects social and cognitive development, while the present chapter has focused on demonstrating that signed languages are as complete and rich as spoken languages and can fill all of the same roles.

Almost every country has its own sign language, and some countries have more than one, corresponding to their multiple spoken languages. Parts of American Sign Language, especially the grammar, actually came from France, but ASL differs dramatically from the sign languages used in Quebec (La Langue des Signes Quebecoise) and England (British Sign Language). True sign languages are characterized by the same kinds of features as spoken languages, including rules for formation, modification, and combination of signs. Signs are generally characterized by several clearly defined characteristics such as handshape and movement. They are combined in grammatically defined ways using three-dimensional space and a variety of grammatical devices such as classifiers, used like pronouns, and linking movements. Like spoken words, most signs are arbitrary and combine with a manual alphabet, facial expression, and body movement to yield a full and natural language taught by deaf parents to their deaf children.

A variety of hybrid systems have been developed in an effort to provide deaf children with early access to language via signing while simultaneously giving them access to English. Some of these, such as Cued Speech, are spoken language systems that include manual movements that disambiguate sounds (and hence words) that are made similarly on the lips. Other systems, such as Signed English, include ASL signs combined through English grammar. Research to date suggests that such artificial combinations do not result in children being fluent in two languages, and most often they are fluent in neither. The variety of difficulties encountered by children who learn artificial sign systems may be offset by advantages in learning to read, at least relative to children who are exposed only to spoken language, but research on this point is not conclusive (see Chapter 7).

Regardless of its method—signed or spoken—consistent access to a natural language is essential to deaf and hearing children if they are to have the tools they need to become literate and get a comprehensive education. Whatever system a deaf child might experience at school, language learning cannot stop there. Unless deaf children can bring language home with them and use it during play, to get help with schoolwork, and to communicate with their families, they cannot be expected to reach their full potentials. If deaf education is not yet producing high school graduates who are fully literate (see Chapters 6 and 8), the blame cannot be placed wholly on the schools. The basic underpinnings of learning and education begin at home, years before the young deaf or hearing child goes off to school. We therefore now turn to consideration of deaf children's development from birth through adolescence. By this point, the reader should have some understanding of deafness, which will help us to examine social, language, and cognitive development more closely. Thus armed, we will be able to see the implications of early hearing losses for growth throughout childhood and make some fairly good predictions about how and when we will need to compensate for those losses.

Notes

1. Deaf parents who use spoken language as their primary means of communication typically do not teach their deaf children to sign.

2. Perhaps it is their lack of recognition of the full richness of sign language that leads many "oralists" in this country and in others to assume that a manual language is insufficient for deaf children to be successful.

3. Saying that signs are arbitrary means that, like words, they bear no relation to the things they represent. A few words do sound like what they represent (onomatopoeatic words like *gurgle* or *swish*) and a few signs look like what they represent (iconic signs like CAMERA or FISHING). These are exceptions, however. Most units of language mean what they do only by social agreement, and therefore they are different in each language.

4. The linkage of a sign language like ASL to fingerspelling may seem rather odd, because a language that is explicitly not English is combined with an

English back-up system. This may be an indicator of the merging of ASL and its English "host," although the necessarily linguistic studies have not yet been done to demonstrate this.

5. Research has shown that even when parents use imperfect ASL, their deaf children still become fluent signers. The same cannot be said for artificial English/sign language systems, which lack the full internal consistency of natural languages like English or ASL.

6. The origins of ASL in French Sign Language means that a deaf person from the United States would be more likely to understand a signer in France than in England! I recently experienced this when a deaf friend and I visited the French National Institute for the Deaf. We could converse in sign fairly well with hearing and deaf people there, even though our French left much to be desired.

7. Throughout this book, English gloss (translations) of signs are indicated by capital letters.

8. For an interesting collection of signs from a variety of dialects in this country, see *Signs Across America*, listed in the suggested readings.

9. Note that I used the word *communication* rather than *language* here. That is because such hybrids are not really languages in the technical (linguistic) sense of the word. They also differ from true languages in terms of their acquisition by children.

4

Early Interactions:
The Roots of Childhood

My son isn't handicapped. He just can't hear.

Mother of a graduating college student

Descriptions of deaf children written in the 1950s and 1960s often painted a bleak picture of them as living isolated and empty lives filled with emotional troubles and behavioral problems. Since then, investigations have provided a much better understanding of the psychological functioning of deaf children and deaf adults, and many of the earlier misconceptions and biases have been swept away. Intervention programs have been developed to provide young deaf children with a variety of social and educational experiences and to provide their parents with much-needed information and support. Such programs now begin early and play a much more proactive role in preparing for schooling, with particular emphasis on the importance of early exposure to language. Thanks in large part to the Deaf community itself, many hearing people have now come to realize that once one gets beyond the appearances of sign language, deaf and hearing children are much the same. In the end, they grow up to have comparable roles and responsibilities in society.

These similarities notwithstanding, notice that I use the word *comparable* rather than *identical*. I think the difference is important. Deaf children's lives do not have to be identical to those of hearing children in order for them to be happy, intelligent, and successful. Deaf and hearing children have many of the same external forces acting on them, and they all respond more or less in the same ways. Most children therefore follow a similar course of development regardless of their hearing status. That course may be followed by different children at different rates, and it may have some rather different characteristics depending on the hearing status of the children and their parents. Such differences are not necessarily bad, however, and may reflect very good adjustments by children to various aspects of their family and social settings. What is essential for adults in a deaf child's world is to recognize the child's strengths and weaknesses—to build on the former and to work to overcome the latter. All of this begins essentially at birth.

Origins of Social Relations

During the earliest stages of social development, mothers and children develop **synchrony** with each other through a variety of shared experiences. Eventually, their actions become intertwined in a way that both simplifies their day-to-day routines and teaches the child about successful (and unsuccessful) strategies for social interaction.

Consider a typical and almost universal routine: An infant cries or fusses; his mother attends to him, touching and caressing him, talking to him, and perhaps picking him up. The infant temporarily ceases to fuss; looks at his mother, who is now speaking or smiling; produces some vocal sounds; and is answered by her with more sounds, more handling, and so on. Although relatively inexperienced at such things, the infant is clearly playing an important role in this interaction. Unwittingly, he is giving his mother cues that partially determine her behavior, including the passing of cues back to him for the next part of the interaction (called **reciprocity**). Over time, both sides become better at this socialization game, developing better timing, more variety, and greater complexity. True conversation is still a long way off, but in the meantime, these back-and-forth interactions teach the child about taking turns both vocally and behaviorally (for example, by waving hands or smiling) and about being part of a social relationship.

But consider the situation when the mother or the infant, or both, are deaf. A deaf mother may first be alerted to her child's fussing by a visual signalling device if she is in another room (see Chapter 2). From that point, the interaction is essentially just like that of a hearing mother with a hearing child, with gestures and signs replacing speech. Ultimately, sign language will provide a means for mother and child to interact at a distance, as long as they can still see each other, allowing both of them to turn their attention to other things while still maintaining contact.

The situation is probably quite different in the case of deaf infants with hearing mothers, especially in the great majority of cases, in which the mother does not recognize or even imagine that her child is deaf. One potential source of difference stems from the possible medical causes for the child's hearing loss in the case of nonhereditary deafness. Even if there are no direct, health-related consequences beyond hearing loss, there may be indirect effects on mother and child, such as continuing maternal stress or differences in child temperament that could affect the frequency or the quality of their interactions. Unless there is some reason to expect it, hearing loss often is not noticed early by parents and pediatricians. For one thing, the loss might not be complete, so that deaf children may be able to hear some things—like the yelling of parents or siblings—but unable to hear normal speech. With greater hearing losses, deaf children will still be sensitive to the vibration and pressure changes caused by loud noises, and reactions to clapping behind their heads or the slamming of doors might incorrectly be interpreted as signs of normal hearing.[1] Further, the multitude of mutual cues that mother and child have developed over the first weeks and months of life may give the impression that nothing is amiss. Sometimes, delays of more than a year in language development are overlooked as signals of hearing loss, or, even worse, they are taken as indicators of mental retardation, autism, or incompetent parenting.

EARLY INTERACTIONS HAVE FAR-REACHING EFFECTS

To understand how the personalities and social relationships of deaf children develop, we need a feel for what happens between deaf infants and their parents during the first months at home. It is through their mothers, in particular, that infants have their first contact with the world, through feeding, cuddling, bathing, and, in most cases, hearing their mothers' voices. These earliest experiences do not *determine* the course of development, but they will have ever widening implications for growth in learning, exploration, and social interactions. Humans are social creatures, and even diaper changing and bathing are social events for infants and mothers. What the infant learns from these experiences through synchrony and reciprocity will affect the building of more complex social relationships with others in the family and, eventually, with those beyond the family. Within these earliest experiences, language typically plays a central and ever increasing role (see Chapter 5). Even before birth, it appears that sounds in a hearing child's environment may indirectly affect the course of development. During the last three months of pregnancy, the fetus usually rests with its head against the mother's pelvis. At this point in development, most fetuses have developed to the point where they can hear and even react to human speech. This means that for those mothers who speak and are carrying babies who can hear, the fetus can now hear its mother's voice, in addition to her heartbeat, as those sounds are conducted through her bones.

The fact that the fetus experiences its mother's voice before birth is not a matter of dispute among scientists, but the possible effects of that experience on later development are still unresolved. At the very least, we know that auditory experiences before birth can affect later learning and perception in both humans and animals, and they can play a role in the early bonding of mothers and infants. Working with humans, for example, Anthony DeCasper and his colleagues have demonstrated that infants less than three days old can learn to suck on a nipple in a particular pattern (either fast or slow) in order to turn on a tape recorder that allows them to hear their mothers' voices. In one study, DeCasper found that two-day-old babies were "willing and able" to adjust their sucking patterns in order to hear their mothers' voices rather than the voice of another woman, indicating that the newborns could tell the difference between the voices and that they had a clear preference. Perhaps most impressive of all were the results of a study in which mothers regularly read a particular passage aloud (for example, from *The Cat in the Hat*), during the last six weeks of pregnancy. Later, their babies showed a preference for that passage over a different one within hours after they were born (due to the particular rhythmic structure of the sounds, not because they liked the story). Interestingly, fathers' voices, which cannot be heard by fetuses in the womb, do not show any sign of being especially attractive to newborns.

These results suggest that hearing mothers' speech both before birth and soon thereafter might play a role in early social interactions by making the mother familiar to the newborn. But just as infants are likely to respond positively to the familiar sound of mothers' voices, so mothers are likely to respond positively, in turn, to an infant who smiles, gurgles, and looks at her mother's face in response to her voice (reciprocity again). Building on this original relationship, mother and child gradually become more attuned to each other and expand on their early "conversations."

This typical scenario does not mean that early mother-infant relationships require vocal or spoken communication, and we already have seen that there are a variety of other forms of interaction between deaf babies and their mothers. Most obviously, there are visual, tactile, and other cues that serve to identify familiar people and objects to infants within the first few days of life. In the early relationships of infants and their parents, in fact, smiles and rhythmically patterned touching and stroking seem to be just as soothing as familiar voices. Maternal touch, in particular, has powerful effects on both deaf and hearing newborns. Deaf mothers tend to touch their infants more than do hearing mothers, but hearing mothers who are aware of their children's hearing losses also are likely to touch their infants more, to use more exaggerated facial expressions, and to try to keep objects and themselves within their infants' line of sight. Parents who have not yet discovered that their children are deaf also might unknowingly compensate for the lack of hearing with other means of communication, but there are not yet data available on this possibility. Nevertheless, it is clear that there are multiple, sometimes unnoticed cues involved in the early social interactions of parents and their deaf children, and that these cues will contribute to mother-child attachment and other relationships.

Unlike some animals, such as birds, which depend on maternal and sibling vocalizations to keep them safe, deaf children may not be at any particular disadvantage because they cannot recognize their mothers' voices at birth. As compared to hearing infants, deaf infants and their hearing mothers may simply begin their relationships interacting in somewhat different ways that have somewhat different consequences. When we watch the interactions of deaf infants with deaf parents, they look very much like hearing infants with hearing parents. By the time they are a year old, both deaf children of deaf parents and hearing children of hearing parents can tell when others are happy, frightened, or sad, just by looking at their faces. At that age, deaf children show as much affection to their parents as hearing children, and they clearly know how to get attention by tapping people on the arm or waving to them rather than calling. Deaf infants and their deaf mothers thus have quite normal early relationships. The only way in which they look different is the use of signed rather than spoken communication.

Accepting Childhood Deafness

Discovering that one's child is deaf or handicapped in some way is not easy for many parents. Pregnancy is an exciting but anxious time for parents-to-be. Still, most pregnancies are unplanned, and even those couples who want to have children are often nervous about whether the decision to do so at a particular time is a wise one. Parents-to-be wonder about how their child will be supported and cared for, about its impact on their lifestyle and their relationship, and about whether it will be healthy and happy. How must it feel to discover that your child cannot hear?

In the case of deaf parents, some of them may hope that their children will be deaf or not care one way or the other.[2] Recently, for example, my wife and I were out to dinner with some Deaf friends. Near the end of the meal, an acquaintance of theirs came by the table with his wife and three-month-old son. At the end of the introductions, the fellow introduced his young son, finishing with the proud statement "DEAF!" Without even thinking about it, I congratulated him—later thinking about how much different the situation was than it would be for hearing parents.

Hearing losses in children of hearing parents typically are not diagnosed until the third or fourth year of life (age two to three), with thirty months being fairly close to the national average in the United States. Most deaf mothers of deaf children, in contrast, claim that they can recognize whether their children are deaf by at least six months of age simply by the way their infants behave and react to them. Our acquaintances from the restaurant may have either figured out for themselves that their son was deaf, or they may have had him tested while still in the hospital (see Chapter 2). Hearing parents, of course, would wait much longer. Radiologists looking at X rays of advanced changes in the body often can see their development in earlier X rays that they previously had pronounced normal. Similarly, hearing parents of deaf children, after hearing loss is discovered and confirmed, often are able to recollect having seen—but not recognized— some of the early signs. When these clues first appear, they are not so obvious. Sometimes, the fear of finding that something is wrong can lead parents to convince themselves that they are overly concerned and just nervous with their status as new parents. It may be more comforting to believe grandmothers' and pediatricians' (correct) claims that many children are slow to talk, that some are louder criers and harder to soothe than others, and that some simply do not respond as warmly as parents might like. The fact that a baby sleeps through many loud noises and yet seems to respond to others when she is awake is perplexing, but at least it suggests that she is not deaf, and perhaps she really does have partial hearing. Suggestions from concerned friends and relatives about the possibility of early hearing loss thus are often shrugged off.

Eventually, the uneasy, troubled feelings win out. A deaf infant is not as quick as a hearing infant to notice people coming into a room. Crying does not stop, or even pause, when mother calls to her baby. Gentle words do not seem to be very soothing. As the months go by, hearing parents come to realize that their child's behavior is varying more and more from what is considered normal. Parents may feel rejected, guilty, or anxious about the apparent lack of a mutual relationship with their child. Some parents begin to think that their child might have some undetermined psychological problems. Others put emotional distance between them and their child. Ultimately, all parents of deaf children recognize that it is the child's hearing that needs to be evaluated. For those families lucky enough to be near a university or a medical center with an audiology clinic, an informed diagnosis can then be obtained relatively quickly. For those in more rural areas or without medical insurance, an audiologist or otolaryngologist may be difficult to find.

Beyond blaming pediatricians for not recognizing their children's hearing losses earlier, perhaps the most common complaint of parents who receive a diagnosis of deafness in their child is the lack of information and support from professionals involved in their children's care. Recent changes in public awareness about hearing loss may make such complaints less common, but many people retain distorted and simply mistaken ideas about being deaf, sign language, and deaf education (see Chapter 1). Coupled with the need for more accurate information is the need for sympathetic understanding for parents who are making the psychological adjustment to having a deaf child. The discovery that their child is deaf may be greeted by some parents with relief and the positive realization that "it wasn't anything worse." Other parents have a very difficult time adapting to the idea of having a child who is labelled *handicapped*. In either case, there is likely to be a period of grieving that is both natural and helpful.

Parents' grief after receiving a diagnosis that their child is deaf may not be so much over the loss of hearing, as over the loss of a "perfect" child and a "normal" life for the child and the whole family. Such grief has a natural course that serves a variety of psychological functions for us. Typically, the first stage of the process is denial. Especially in cases of profound hearing loss, hearing parents may feel that the diagnosis must have been a mistake, that the error will be found, that the dream will end. Alternatively, hoping for cures that do not exist, parents may take their young deaf child from one specialist to another, or, as a last resort, visit quacks or faith-healers.[3] There can be pain and worry about the child's welfare and future, together with concerns about the stability of the marriage and of the family. These feelings are often accompanied by a period in which parents "negotiate" with themselves, with fate, with God. Somehow, there is a feeling that by changing one's ways, by taking on a child's supposed suffering, his hearing will be miraculously restored.

But most of the time, the situation does not correct itself. Parents' bargaining is often replaced by anger—again toward themselves, toward fate, toward God. There may be a time of despair, when all hope seems lost; it must be someone's fault! Although the anger is always misdirected (except perhaps for that aimed at fate) this emotional upheaval can make matters worse, as interactions within the family and especially with the innocent but offending child become more strained. Anger thus eventually gives way to guilt over one's own poor behavior toward the child and others in the family. It is not the mother's fault that a child is born deaf, and yet for a time she is willing to take the psychological blame and, for a time, the father (lagging behind emotionally as men often do) is willing to let her.

Only after a child's hearing loss is truly accepted can parents start to appreciate their child for who she is. Only then will they be able to begin a constructive rearrangement of their lives to accommodate their child's needs and their new status as parents of a deaf child. The adjustment of hearing families to the arrival of a deaf child will have a variety of practical, emotional, and financial ramifications, and the effects of such changes are felt by each member of the immediate and extended family. Although it might not seem possible to parents who are at their low points, most families with a deaf child function quite normally after a period of adjustment. With relatively little disruption to regular family routines, aside from the need to learn and use sign language consistently, life goes on quite naturally. Some professionals suggest that such families nevertheless should be considered "at risk" as a result of having a continuous source of potential stress. Hearing parents of deaf children, in fact, generally do report more stress than do parents without deaf children. Perhaps the most significant factor in their adjustment is the amount of social support they receive from others. When family and friends provide positive emotional and practical support, for example, helping with the many special trips to doctors, schools, and clinics, parents adjust surprisingly quickly. Because mothers are the ones who typically take on most of the added responsibility, they are also the ones who need the most support.[4]

In our concern about parents' abilities to cope with the responsibilities of having a deaf child, we should not lose sight of the fact that their attitudes about their child's being deaf will also have important effects on later school success and on social and emotional development. The home is the place where any young child should be able to feel safe, understood, and loved. It is the place that should provide deaf children with the emotional strength and resources they need to handle a world that is not entirely able to deal with them. Most deaf children will grow up to be just as emotionally well adjusted as hearing children, but they need the same kind of parenting and the same kinds of experiences as their hearing peers. To achieve this equivalence, parents will have to adjust the quantity and quality of interaction they have with their young deaf child. Let us therefore consider the nature of those relationships and the emotional bonds that develop between parents and children.

Attachment: Mother and Child Reunion

Attachment refers to the emotional bond that develops between young children and their mothers or other caregivers. Psychological attachment is not something that can be seen, but is inferred from what the infant does. In many mammals, including humans, youngsters initially attempt to stay close to their mothers and other companions. When separated from these significant others, toddlers of many species may wander around aimlessly, stop playing, or, in most species, indicate their distress through crying. This kind of behavior, and the attachment it reflects, are normal and important parts of early childhood.

In human infants, the early phases of attachment can be seen during the first months of life. They are reflected in the way in which children focus their attention and are most likely to interact comfortably with just one or two adults, usually either the parents or a parent and some other caregiver. By eight months of age, infants obviously and intentionally attempt to stay close to their primary caregivers when confronted with new situations or new people. Although there are special laboratory techniques involved in scientific studies of attachment, there are also fairly regular behaviors that can be taken as signals of relatively stable or unstable attachments between mother and child. In particular, it is not unusual for children between eight and eighteen months of age to show some signs of distress if they are left either in a strange room or with a strange person (behaviors known as separation anxiety and stranger anxiety, respectively), although there is much variability in these phenomena both within and across children. When they are reunited, children who have warm and secure attachment bonds with their mothers generally will greet them and seek comfort from them. In contrast, children with less stable or secure attachments will not approach them when they return; will begin to do so and then turn away; or they will approach their mothers but refuse to be comforted, possibly throwing temper tantrums or reacting negatively in other ways.

In the case of young children of deaf mothers, we need to recognize at the outset that there may be cultural factors in the Deaf community relative to the hearing community that affect maternal attitudes toward mother-child interactions, just as hearing mothers' conceptions of appropriate attachment behaviors differ in various countries and cultures. For hearing mothers of deaf children, there is also the possibility that when viewed from outside, differences in the way they interact with their children, out of real or perceived necessity, may lead to erroneous conclusions about the nature of their emotional bonds with their children. Hearing mothers of deaf preschoolers, for example, frequently are described as playing a far more active role in their children's day-to-day behaviors than mothers of hearing children, often bordering on being intrusive (see below). When a mother's attention to her deaf child is withdrawn, say, when she leaves the room, the change therefore may be greater from the child's perspective than in the case of a hearing child, and the child might appear more surprised or distraught than would a hearing child of the same age. Alternatively, less control might be welcomed by some children, who thus might appear less distraught than a hearing child in a similar situation.

Although we do not yet fully understand the dynamics of interactions between hearing mothers and their deaf children, it is sometimes claimed that deaf children generally are likely to be less securely attached to their mothers, as compared to hearing children of hearing parents. That characterization has *not* been verified by psychological research. What we do know is that those mothers who have good communication with their deaf children tend to have more stable and warm relationships with them, regardless of whether they themselves are hearing or deaf. Those mothers who have less efficient communication with their deaf children tend to have less securely attached children, who may exhibit unacceptable behaviors in preschool or day-care settings as well as at home. These differences, however, are not entirely a function of communication fluency, even if communication is an essential ingredient for normal development. In situations where mothers lack the knowledge and communicative skill to deal competently with their children's behavior, they are more likely to have to depend on direct, physical means. This method might be effective in the short term, but usually does little to teach children what is expected of them in the future. Those mothers who have established an effective channel of communication with their deaf children have less need for such control and are less likely than others to be overly directive or to use physical means of restraining their children. Generally, hearing parents of deaf children use more physical punishment than hearing parents with hearing children or deaf parents with either deaf or hearing children. This difference is most pronounced when parents and children do not share a common language. Apparently, when communication fails, punishment is a handy alternative.

Looking Beyond the Earliest Relationships

Let us now consider several components of early personality and emotional development in deaf children that relate to social interactions outside of the family. (Chapter 9 will discuss personality issues during the later school years.) Keeping in mind the continuity in social development from the very earliest parent-child relationships, we should be able to gain some insight into links between these early interactions and later social functioning during the preschool years and beyond. In this context, it is important to note again that young children's social behavior with peers is not determined by the nature and quality of their attachment with mother or any other single aspect of the mother-child relationship. Despite the lack of a strong *causal* relationship between security of attachment and subsequent social behavior, children who have better social relationships with their primary caregivers also tend to be those who develop good social relations with peers and higher self-esteem. Children who are good socializers probably have several personality characteristics that make them better able to get along with other children and hence more popular. Most of these qualities are acquired early in life through interactions within the family, but others may come as part of their natural temperament. Some deaf and hearing children, for example, simply are more sociable than others, a quality that is seen early by parents and appears to carry on through the school years. Some children are better at social problem-solving, figuring out how to play successfully with other children and who they can turn to for emotional or practical support. Part of this ability seems to lie in the fact that some children appear more sensitive to the social cues given off by other children and adults, and thus they are better at responding appropriately to both positive and negative overtures.

It is not surprising that children's social behavior and their emotional stability are affected by the quality of parent-child relationships. For example, controlling or overprotective behaviors on the part of hearing mothers are likely to affect their deaf children's interactions with peers and other adults because they lead the children to expect those kinds of behaviors from others. Parents and teachers who are constantly rescuing deaf children from awkward situations will prevent them from developing their own strategies for solving problems. At the same time, we have to recognize that some maternal actions that might appear to be somewhat overbearing may be necessary in order to ensure their children's safety, cooperation, or obedience. What appears to be intrusiveness simply may be part of getting their children's attention, and some of their directiveness might reflect attempts to overcome communication barriers rather than any desire to control their children's behaviors. We thus have to be sensitive to differences in behavior that can be interpreted in more than one way.

In considering the earliest parent-child relationships, we saw that parents and infants develop synchrony and reciprocity in their interactions. Hearing parents and their deaf children establish such mutual signals, even if it sometimes takes longer than in the cases of deaf children of deaf parents or hearing children of hearing parents. Deaf children, however, may find that these signals do not work as well outside of the family unless they involve a standard form of sign language. Many of the skills involved in later child-child interactions are quite different from those involved in mother-child interactions. Young deaf children may behave toward peers in much the same way as young hearing children, but without a shared communication system, they may not get or give as many social cues as hearing children. This situation is made more complex by the fact that, as compared to hearing age-mates, young deaf children are likely to have interacted socially with fewer other children and other adults.[5] The growth of early intervention programs have been particularly helpful in this regard, exposing deaf children to considerable diversity in social and communicative interactions.

Research conducted within intervention classrooms has shown that the stability of friendships among deaf preschool children is similar to those of hearing children. Both groups, for example, show similar patterns of playmate preference. Although younger deaf children (of hearing parents) do not use much formal language in interactions with either deaf or hearing playmates, they do use a variety of nonlanguage communication in those interactions. Older deaf children appear to use more language and gestural communication with other deaf children than they do with hearing children. Their interactions with deaf playmates also tend to be more social and less object-centered than are their communications with hearing playmates. Finally, deaf children who have better language skills are more likely than children with poorer language skills to play with more than one child at a time, to interact with teachers, and to use language during play. When one looks at children enrolled in early intervention programs involving both sign language and spoken language instruction, they also tend to show more cooperative play with peers than do children who receive spoken language instruction only. Children enrolled in speech-only programs, meanwhile, have been found to be more disruptive and aggressive in their play than children in settings that include sign language. These findings suggest that special programs for deaf children provide a variety of language and nonlanguage opportunities that would not be otherwise available. It seems likely that the availability of more diverse experiences enhances the ability of young deaf children to deal with later social interactions and the necessities of growing up in a largely hearing world. At the same time, early intervention provides support for par-ents who, as a result, are better able to accommodate their children's special needs.

It should now be clear that the emotional and academic lives of young deaf children are enhanced by parents who are sensitive enough to their needs to pursue (1) early diagnosis of their children's hearing losses, (2) intervention and education programs for themselves and their children, and (3) communication instruction. There is also strong support for a relation between early parent-child communication, attachment, and later social ability: Those children with stable and secure attachments early in life tend to be more socially competent during the school years than are children with less secure attachments. At this time, there is no evidence to suggest that there is any benefit to the use of spoken language over sign language, or the reverse, in the establishment of early parent-child bonds, at least when parents and children share the same communication modality. Signing can fill *all* of the roles normally filled by parents' speech and is often indicated as the best route to follow with young deaf children. Still, some parents do not understand the importance of early communication and frequently do not know what sign language is all about. Some of them view signing as a foreign and perhaps dangerous step that might impede the development of speech. Other parents are eager for their children to look and act as "normal" as possible, and sign language clearly does not fit that requirement. Little do they realize that early acquisition of sign language might be the best way to nurture a child who approaches their "normal" ideal, and that the denial of that opportunity starts their child off at a distinct disadvantage relative to other children.

Summary

Early childhood is a time of rapid learning for both deaf and hearing infants. In addition to learning about things and people in the environment, they also learn a lot about how to learn and how to interact both with language and in nonverbal ways. When mothers ask their month-old babies questions in baby talk, they are not really expecting answers, except perhaps through smiles and other facial expression. When parents and infants share a language, either signed or spoken, those games can be important language-learning episodes. These interactions teach infants about social interactions and support the development of a reciprocal emotional relationship between mother and child in which they each have their own roles. Eventually, an attachment bond will form, as children seek out their mothers and other familiar figures and use them as safe bases for exploration of places and other people.

Adjusting to having a deaf child is not an easy experience for many hearing parents. Periods of grieving, depression, and guilt are normal and will eventually give way to concerted efforts to determine the needs and services available for their children—and for themselves. Mothers tend to take the greatest emotional and day-to-day responsibilities for deaf children, as they do for most children with special needs in most cultures, and they sometimes will feel overwhelmed. Those mothers who receive more social support from friends and family are the ones who are best at coping with their new situation, and the effects of that support are seen in better behavioral interactions and greater sensitivity to their children's communication needs.

Normally, language plays a continuing and expanding role in early social interaction, both through explicit communication with children and through their observation of relations between communication and behaviors of caregivers. As far as anyone can tell, signed and spoken communication are equivalent in their potential to supply all of the information and experience necessary for normal social development. That equivalence requires that parents be competent language users in whatever modes are most accessible to their child. One way in which hearing parents can gain the language skills they need, as well as emotional and practical support for their needs, is through early intervention programs. Such programs, described more fully in Chapter 6, include communication instruction for both parents and children in sign language, spoken language, or both. They also expose children (and parents) to others who are similar to them. Together with explicit and implicit instruction within the home, such programs foster the early development of child-child social interactions. As deaf children move out of the home environment into the larger community, they gain much-needed diversity in their experience. Multiple social partners help to offset the tendency of hearing mothers to be controlling and perhaps overprotective of their deaf children and contribute to cognitive and language development as well as to social development. Communication with those inside and outside of the home now takes on even greater importance, and we therefore turn to considering language development in some detail.

Notes

1. One example of this occurred when a well-known televangelist and faith healer visited Greensboro, North Carolina, while I was living there. During a revival, he brought a deaf boy and his hearing parents up on the stage to "cure him of his affliction." The preacher fired a pistol (with blanks) behind the boy's head, and when he jumped, the boy was declared "healed." The child left the stage just as deaf as when he stepped onto it. If every window in a house would vibrate to a gunshot, why would the child not be expected to feel it?

2. Deaf parents' hoping for deaf children is obviously a controversial issue. For some interesting perspectives on the topic, see "Beyond the Envelope— Weirdness" in the July, 1995, issue of *Deaf Life* magazine.

3. According to recent advertisements in *News of the World*, an expensive mixture of garlic and honey is an effective cure for hearing loss. While I would like to joke about it, people actually buy such products, even though *they do not work*.

4. In fact, social support for hearing mothers with deaf children has implications far beyond the family functioning. Mothers who have such support dur-

ing the early months tend to have greater visual and tactile responsiveness to their infants, and their infants appear better able to cope with stress factors. This provides added evidence of the importance of early mother-child reciprocity.

5. Differences in the number of adults with whom children interact can have implications far beyond social interaction. Research on hearing children's language development, for example, has shown that the variety of their experience with adults is a better predictor of vocabulary size than the variety of experience with other children. This relation primarily reflects the fact that adults are better language models than children.

5

Language Development

*I knew how to sign because my grandparents and an uncle were deaf.
But when my son was born deaf, I was afraid that signing would
prevent him from learning to speak. . . . It wasn't until Tim was
fourteen that we started signing at home. I can't believe I waited so
many years to get to know my son! It's really sad.*

Kathy, a hearing mother

The basic question of this chapter is: How do deaf children learn language?
or perhaps more specifically, Do deaf children acquire language in the same
ways as hearing children? In order to answer either question, we have to
look at both how children go about learning language and exactly what it is
that they learn that allows them to communicate with others—that is, what
they have to know in order to be able to use the language. (Chapter 7 deals
with expression of language skills in reading and writing.) As a starting
point, let us consider the very beginnings of communication, when a child's
spoken, signed, or gestural productions first begin to have what I call "communicative consequences" for mothers and fathers. This is the point, during
the first year of life, when both deaf and hearing children are beginning to
make regular vocal sounds and are using simple gestures.

With both hands and voices available to young children, many researchers believe they should be equally able to learn either a signed or a
spoken language. Although both kinds of language require small but accurate muscle movements, such agility develops at different rates in different
parts of the body. In particular, coordinated hand movements generally develop before coordinated mouth movements. This manual priority has been
taken to indicate that children should be able to produce sign language earlier than they can produce spoken language, a possibility that we will consider later. At this point, it is sufficient to note that a biological preference

for signed over spoken language is also consistent with the belief that in the history of humankind, manual communication was used before spoken communication.[1]

Most of the evidence concerning the development of spoken communication in humans, as a species, comes from historical studies of brain development and anthropological findings concerning our distant ancestors. Closer to home, some relevant evidence comes from studies concerning the early use of signs and words by young hearing children of deaf parents and some hearing children of hearing parents who use sign language with their children for other reasons. Although these findings are far from conclusive, they suggest that sign languages can be acquired just as early as spoken languages, and perhaps somewhat earlier. In order to set the stage for discussions of the emergence of the first words and the first signs, let us consider what often appears—at least to parents—to be even earlier approximations to communication.

Do Deaf Babies Babble?

Babies come into the world with the potential to learn any human language. Not all languages, however, consist of the same basic elements. In Italian, for example, the pronunciation of a longer or shorter s sound can make for two different words. I discovered this fact—to the delight of my Italian audience—when I once confused the word for "to marry" (*sposare*) with the word for "to be worn out" (*spossare*) in describing my relationship with the woman who is now my wife. This difference is one that native English speakers do not hear without considerable practice, just as native Japanese speakers cannot easily hear the difference between *rice* and *lice* and hearing students of American Sign Language (ASL) initially are unable to see the difference between I AM ALWAYS SICK and I FREQUENTLY GET SICK (see Chapter 3). It is only with time and exposure to many examples that children learn the range of elements, either sounds or sign components, in their native language. Meanwhile, they gradually lose the ability to discriminate and produce language elements with which they have no practice. This process may explain, in part, why it is easier to learn a second language in early childhood than in adulthood, regardless of whether that language is spoken or signed: Children's "sensory software" has not yet become exclusively tuned to the repertoire of only a single language.

Infants who can hear appear to start homing in on the sounds relevant to their native language during the first few weeks or months of life, when they start producing the simple sounds we call babbling. There are at least two ways in which the babbling of young infants might be related to later language acquisition. One possibility is that babbling actually is a direct precursor to language. From this perspective, babbling is seen as babies' exercising their language production equipment (the diaphragm, tongue, lips, and so on) in preparation for language, even though they are not really trying to talk. A second possibility is less concerned with the particular sounds or gestures that an infant might produce than the effects of those productions on other people, and especially the parents. We will consider both of these possibilities in asking two related questions: Do deaf babies vocally babble in ways similar to hearing babies? and Do deaf babies do anything with their hands that resembles the babbling that hearing babies do with their voices?

VOCAL BABBLING BY DEAF INFANTS

Although it might not seem that way to an untrained ear, hearing children's babbling actually follows a fairly regular course of development. During the first two months of life, for example, infants produce what appear to be simple vowel sounds: *ah*, *ee*, and *oo*. From two to three months of age, these vowel-like sounds are joined by consonant-like sounds, made for the most part in the back of the mouth, producing sounds like *ka*, *coo*, and *goo*. This stage is thus called the cooing stage, although it usually sounds more like a "gooing" stage. Over the next three months or so, these vocal sounds are further expanded to include a variety of other sounds like grunts, growls, and squeals, as well as clearer vowels and consonant-vowel combinations. Typically, it is not until seven to eleven months that hearing infants start to produce the well-formed syllables needed for babbling. This is the stage in which sounds are repeated to form the first vocalizations that excited parents might interpret as words: *mama*, *dada*, *kaka*, and so on. This type of babbling is important for two reasons. On the technical side, such repetitive babbling is the first time that infants produce the syllables which will be the building blocks of words. On the social side, it is at this point that parents start responding to their children's apparent attempts at communication, leading to a new form of parent-child interaction and reciprocity.

In many books and articles written about deaf children, the question of whether deaf babies babble *vocally* appears very complicated. The confusion arises for the most part from informal observations of deaf babies made by parents and other untrained baby watchers. That is, it seems to make sense for deaf babies to babble early on, perhaps up to the point when hearing babies start to produce words, even if they cannot hear what they babble. This pattern of early vocalization would suggest that babbling is an innate, natural behavior that occurs regardless of a baby's early environment or hearing status. However, this sequence is not what generally occurs. When it comes to early vocalizations like crying, fussing, grunting and cooing, deaf babies really do sound much the same as hearing babies of hearing parents. Then, after the first few months, their vocal babbling usually shows a steady decrease both in frequency and variety. These declines contrast with the babbling of hearing babies, which increases steadily in both quantity and variability over the first year of life. Even when hearing losses are discovered early and children have received hearing aids and intensive early speech therapy, deaf children's vocal babbling diverges from that of hearing children. Repetitive babbling may still occur; but it appears later and less frequently than in hearing children. Some investigators have reported vocal babbling in two- to five-year-old deaf children, but these vocalizations clearly differ from the babbling of hearing children, who would have moved on to using words and phrases at that age.

The lack of complex early babbling by deaf children means that at the age when parents and siblings should be beginning to respond to their grunts and babbles, deaf babies already may be at a disadvantage both socially and communicatively relative to hearing children. As we will see in the next section, deaf and hearing children of deaf parents at this stage will be making and seeing signs and gestures that may function in the same ways as vocalizing and hearing do for hearing babies. For the vast majority of deaf children, however, it is still too early for their hearing parents to suspect their hearing losses. It will be one to two more years, on average, before those children are recognized as deaf and some form of early language intervention can begin. The lack of spoken communication between hearing parents and their deaf children is thus a real and potentially important factor in development, with implications even at this early age for later cognitive and social development as well as for language development and day-to-day functioning. There are, of course, other modes of communication available for hearing families with deaf children. Hearing mothers and their deaf infants presumably have developed regular patterns of interaction through physical contact at this point, and they soon will begin to use gestures and body language to communicate just as deaf mothers do with their deaf and hearing infants. Often overlooked by hearing parents are the beginnings of nonvocal communication, beginnings at least as important as vocal babbling is for hearing infants. This topic has received far less attention than has vocal babbling, but it is an exciting one that may hold considerable promise for understanding and facilitating language development in deaf children.

MANUAL BABBLING?

Whereas vocal babbling consists of the combined vowel and consonant sounds that make up language, there are various forms that manual babbling (which I call "mabbling") could take. One of these would be the simple production or repetition of components of signs, such as isolated handshapes or movements. Some of those movements actually will constitute complete signs that are made by repeating simple handshapes and movements. For example, the sign MILK is made by opening and closing of the hand into a fist, as in milking a cow (see Everyday Signs), and the sign MOTHER or MAMA is made by touching an open hand to the chin (see Figure 3-4). Mabbling of this sort is likely have social consequences when seen by deaf parents, just as babbling by hearing infants ("mama") might get reactions from hearing parents. Another form of mabbling would resemble the combination of sounds seen in babbling. Some young deaf children of deaf parents, for example, produce individual and repeated sign components without any apparent attempt at communication. This form of mabbling has only been documented in a few children, but it may well be a more general phenomenon. There is a relatively small set of about a half dozen hand configurations that frequently are seen in deaf infants who are learning sign language as a first language. These handshapes comprise the primary stuff of later signs and, like the basic vowel and consonant sounds in spokenlanguage, are general enough to be found across all documented sign languages.

Just as importantly, mabbling provides a motivation for deaf parents or signing hearing parents to engage in "conversations" with their deaf infants in the same way that babbling prompts hearing parents to talk to their hearing infants. Eventually, the language-relevant parts of mabbling will become incorporated into communication along with meaningful gestures, and deaf children will be well on the way to acquiring language. Mabbling is thus different from gesturing, because gestures are meaningful while mabbling is not. Nonetheless, early gestures play a vital role in early learning and communication and are worthy of consideration in their own right.

Gestures and Signs

The focus of most research on deaf children's early manual behavior has been on their use of meaningful gestures. My own research has shown that gestures accompany the speech of hearing children in much the same way as they accompany the signs of deaf children. When hearing children use gestures, however, we can easily distinguish them from words. The distinction is somewhat harder to make when deaf children mix gestures with their signs, because the two forms of communication share the same channel of communication—from hand to eye. Deaf children's gestures nonetheless may give us some insight into their language development and, later, into their cognitive development and the thoughts that underlie their behavior. We therefore need to look more closely at the relations among early gestures, early words or signs, and children's knowledge of the things to which they refer.

Observers and investigators of young children's early gestures generally assume that their use paves the way for hearing and deaf children's eventual use of words and signs, respectively. When children are at the point of using only single words or signs (ten to sixteen months) and also when they move to using combinations of two words or signs (sixteen to twenty-four months), gestures continue to play an important role in the language development of hearing children. In Chapter 3, I argued that this fact makes it odd and likely disruptive for language development to deny deaf children the opportunity to use gestures in interpersonal communication. Of course, we would not want deaf children to depend on gestures to the exclusion of signed or spoken communication, but there is no evidence that this ever occurs when a more regular form of communication is available. Rather, for both deaf and hearing individuals, gestures are an essential component of communication from the first year of life through adulthood. The questions of interest are how deaf and hearing children use gestures and how they eventually come to be supplemented by language. In fact, there appear to be several shifts in the frequency and purpose of gestures at various points of development. Among young deaf children of deaf parents, for example, there is a noticeable change in use of pointing from its immature use as a gesture showing or requesting something to a mature form in the personal pronouns of ASL like ME, HER, and YOU.[2] At around nine months of age, both deaf and hearing children use pointing as a *showing* or *requesting* gesture. Then, at around twelve months, deaf children stop using pointing to refer to people, although it still can refer to things and places. Six to twelve months later, person-pointing comes back into use, but this time, those motions are used in the context of sign as personal pronouns. Such shifts indicate that gestures and signs are distinct, even if they look the same.

In terms of their form and frequency, most of the gestures of young deaf and hearing children appear to be the same until about age two. During the school years, deaf children tend to use more gestures with their sign language than hearing children use with their speech, although my own research has shown that this difference disappears by the time they reach adulthood. In terms of their function, it is during the earliest stages of parent-child communication that gestures are particularly important because of the role they play in social interactions. That is, both gesture and language initially develop in children largely because of the need to communicate their wants, needs, and desires. Even deaf children who do not have the benefits of early language input therefore show spontaneous and regular use of gestures to communicate with those around them.

First Signs, First Words

The ages at which deaf children first begin to use signs and words vary considerably. There have been occasional claims of deaf children using simple signs like MILK and MAMA as early as five or six months of age! One problem with such observations is that they almost always have been made by parents, who might read more into their child's behavior than would unbiased witnesses. Several investigators, meanwhile, have reported that deaf and hearing children who learn sign language naturally from their deaf parents produce their first recognizable signs at around nine months of age. Hearing children, by contrast, tend to produce their first words around their first birthdays, regardless of whether they have hearing or deaf parents and regardless of whether they are already using some simple signs. That is, signs do *not* slow the emergence of speech.

Deciding when the first words occur has never been easy, even with hearing children. Between nine and twelve months of age, hearing children make some sounds that are similar to adult words. These protowords often, but not always, are produced in the correct context and so they tend to sound like real words, at least to parents' ears. At the same time, the fact that protowords are also produced in contexts that are not correct, in which case they are less likely to be noticed by parents, suggests that children in this stage do not understand the "language" they are producing. Protowords simply may be attempts to imitate sounds made by adults and may have no more meaning for the child than babbling.

In the context of dealing with a young child at home, as opposed to in a research study, it probably is not too important to decide which early sounds are protowords and which are true words. What is important is that whatever they are, these vocalizations lead to responses from listeners. As a result, protowords either get used more often and more correctly, gradually

becoming or being replaced by real words, or they drop out of a child's vocabulary. For this to occur, it does not matter whether the "words" are real,
baby talk, or even babbles, as long as there is some kind of social agreement
between the child and her listeners that particular sounds have particular
meanings. Some of these baby words will remain with children if they continue to be used in the family.[3] Such home words are paralleled by home
signs in deaf families (see Chapter 3).

A parallel scenario presumably develops for deaf children who are ready
to produce their first signs. As with the appearance of the first words, it is
difficult to know how seriously to take reports by parents of signs being
made as early as six months of age. Like first words, first signs tend to be
rather simple approximations that, at least initially, could be entirely unin-
tended by the child. The sign MILK is a good example, here. Is it because
milk is so important for infants (from whose point of view?) that MILK is
most frequently reported as children's first sign? Or is it because the sign is
so simple, being made by the simple opening and closing of a 5-hand (see
Figure 3-2)? Flexing of the unformed hand occurs frequently in both deaf
and hearing infants, and it seems only a matter of time before it is produced
in an appropriate context and interpreted as a sign by enthusiastic parents.
Similarly, the signs MAMA and DADA or some simplified version of them
(see Figure 3-4) seem likely to occur occasionally just by chance. As it happens, MAMA generally occurs earlier and more frequently than DADA. Is
this because mama is more important to the child than dada? Is it because
mama is more likely to be around and *see* early MAMA signs? Or is it because DADA is made on the forehead, outside of the infant's line-of-sight,
and thus is more difficult to repeat correctly once it has been seen by an excited father? Probably it is some combination of all of these factors.

Examples of this sort suggest some caution in attributing intention or
meaning to the very early signs produced by young deaf children. Nevertheless, the social implications of those early signs and protosigns are exactly
the same as those created by the first words and protowords of hearing children. Once again, it seems that deciding exactly when early spoken or
signed productions should be considered language may be less important
than identifying their roles in social communication. The earlier appearance of signing over speech by up to three months does seem to be a real
phenomenon, however, regardless of how long it lasts. This early sign advantage is seen in both deaf and hearing children who are learning to sign
and is consistent with what we know about the maturation of the hands before the vocal system. Whether or not this early advantage gives deaf children who sign a long-term edge over nonsigning, deaf or hearing peers remains at issue.

GROWING VOCABULARIES

Consider now the relation between the number of words a young hearing child knows at any particular age and the number of signs that a young deaf child knows at the same age. Some children learning to sign have been reported to have larger vocabularies during the first year or two than hearing children learning spoken language only. This finding could be taken as support for the suggestion that signed languages can be acquired earlier than spoken languages, but in almost all cases where such advantages have been documented, the children have been hearing rather than deaf. Hearing children of deaf parents who use ASL are able to benefit from a much wider range of language experience than deaf or hearing children who have only spoken language available to them. It thus is unclear whether the advantage in early vocabulary size should be attributed to the language or to the context in which these bilingual children are learning language.

In any case, the difference does not last long. Typically, any sign language advantage disappears by age two, when the ability to combine signs and words becomes important in the two-word, **telegraphic speech** stage (e.g., "want milk"). In other words, when we remove the head start that signing (deaf or hearing) children have over speaking (hearing) children, signs and words appear to be learned at about the same rate. As far as I can tell, the spectacular exceptions in this regard—children who have been reported to have vocabularies that increase much faster than is normal—have not only been hearing, but they also have been children of university professors who are fluent in ASL and specialists in language development, which is why they are studying their children in the first place! This observation suggests that under special circumstances signs *can* be acquired at a faster rate than words, but this does not seem to be the case under more natural circumstances (but see the last two paragraphs of this section).

Hearing children of hearing parents generally use about ten different words when they are fifteen months of age and fifty words and about ten phrases at around 20 months. Of course, these numbers are rough averages, and particular children may be faster or slower in their rates of vocabulary growth. Those averages, however, also appear to hold for the sign vocabularies of deaf children with deaf parents learning ASL in the U.S. and Canada as well as those learning La Langue des Signes Quebecoise (LSQ), the sign language of French-speaking Canada. Children learning to sign and those learning to speak also seem to have a lot of overlap in the particular words and signs that they use. This consistency makes some intuitive sense in that we would expect that regardless of their language, deaf and hearing children likely would have similar things to talk about.

One aspect of signed languages that people expect to affect early learning is the fact that some signs look like what they mean. As mentioned in Chapter 3, signs actually fall along a continuum, from looking very much like what they mean (GOLF, BOWL), to having some association with what they mean (BOY, DOG), to being completely arbitrary (NUT, CHURCH).[4] It would not be surprising to find that the signs acquired earliest are those falling toward the "obvious" end of the continuum, and naive observers, including both parents and scientists who are unfamiliar with sign language, often claim that this is the case. But those observers are wrong. Such claims frequently are based on the incorrect interpretation of signs: The observer thinks that a sign means what it looks like, when it actually means something quite different.[5] Alternatively, they may only notice the few obvious signs that occur in a signed conversation and assume that most of the language is like that.

More important than the fact that there are not really very many transparent or iconic signs is the fact that the obviousness of a sign actually has no effect on how likely it is to be learned by young children. Transparent signs are easier for hearing adults to remember when they take sign language classes, but that is a function of experience and learning strategies that young children do not yet have. Either deaf children do not understand the "obvious" bases of such signs (any more than they understand words like *submarine* or *antiseptic* from analyzing their component parts) or they may have less use for them. If you look at the list of Everyday Signs at the back of the book, it should be apparent that most of the signs likely to be important for young deaf children bear little resemblance to their meanings.

Before moving on to more complex language, a note seems in order concerning the early language of deaf children in speech-only programs. Regardless of the rate of early sign acquisition by young deaf children in sign language settings and hearing children in spoken language settings, there is little doubt of the contrast they provide with the rates of language learning by deaf children exposed to spoken language. Among children with severe to profound hearing losses, even the best pupils of the best spoken language programs have extremely limited early vocabularies, rarely beyond ten words at two-and-a-half years of age. The language of deaf preschoolers in speech-only programs generally is at least two to three years behind the language of hearing children, even after more than a year of intensive speech therapy as part of early intervention programs. Beyond the extent of their hearing losses, part of the difference in language development by deaf children in speech- and sign-oriented programs may be related to differences in the ages at which their parents become aware of those losses. Recent surveys indicate that children who attend speech-oriented programs generally have had their hearing losses discovered considerably later than children who attend sign-oriented programs. Further, parents who notice their children's hearing losses very early may have been initially more sensitive to their children's language needs or might have less time and emotion invested in attempting exclusively spoken language instruction before trying the route of Total Communication. Whatever the reasons, most severely and profoundly deaf children who receive early exposure to sign communication are more competent in their early language development (and later, reading) than those children who receive only exposure to spoken language.

Does Learning to Sign Affect Learning to Speak?

One of the longest-running debates within deaf education has been whether teaching young deaf children sign language will impair their ability or motivation to acquire spoken language. As I indicated earlier, there is no evidence to support that claim. Although it has been observed that ASL grammar sometimes intrudes into deaf children's speech and writing, this phenomenon is a common one among children and adults learning a second language, and it has nothing at all to do with sign language per se. What seems to be neglected in most prospeech arguments is the importance of early linguistic stimulation of children, in *any* mode. Regardless of how language acquisition occurs, it requires regular input and feedback during the first two to three years of life. Spoken language communication does not work well for very young deaf children because they lack the abilities and motivation available to older children and adults, not because spoken language is in any way inferior to sign language. Later, some deaf children will develop speech that is well-enough understood by others and sufficient for the practical purposes of day-to-day life. Other children will not reach those levels of proficiency. Most importantly, speech ability does not confer any advantage on the receptive part of language—speech and speechreading are not the same skill. I do not mean to suggest that language learning in sign language is a cure-all, but the consistency of the available evidence clearly tells us that it is potentially an important tool in childhood as well as later.

SIGNS AND WORDS IN THE SAME CHILD

During the first two years of life, young hearing children, as a group, tend to have considerable overlap in the ideas that they express, although some children communicate them via gesture and others via words. Looking at individual children, however, we see that any particular child generally has either a gesture or a word for a thing, but not both. Similarly, it appears that deaf children either have a gesture or a sign for a thing, but not both, even though their gestures and signs are in the same modality. One family I know, for example, includes a mother who is deaf and a father and one child who both have normal hearing. As in many such families, the hearing daughter has grown up a bilingual, using both spoken English and ASL (neither the parents nor the girl use Simultaneous Communication). This girl started signing before she started talking. During her early childhood, when her parents kept careful records of her language progress, the girl acquired signs and words at about the same rate. In this natural setting, well over three-quarters of all of the signs and words she used occurred in only one of her two languages. That is, she had either a sign or word for a concept, but not both. Only about 15 percent of the concepts in her vocabulary were expressed in both signs and words (although not necessarily at the same time).

Beyond this frequently reported tendency to have a label for a thing in only one language at a time, there is also an inclination in later childhood to use only one mode of communication at a time, that is, not to use Simultaneous Communication. Deaf preschoolers, for example, tend to prefer signed communication over spoken communication even when both languages are available. This preference results from the simple fact that signed communication is more likely than spoken communication to be successful for these children, independent of the extent of their exposure to speech. In both later childhood and adulthood, some deaf individuals are more comfortable with spoken language than others, and some are more comfortably and competently bilingual than others. Deaf children's bilingual balance—that is, their relative fluencies in the two languages—will depend in part on the age of onset and degree of their hearing losses. Other factors, such as parental language abilities (signing by hearing parents, speech and signing by deaf parents) and the quality of early education and exposure to language (for example, in a **bilingual-bicultural** program) also will make a difference.

Finally, for children who are initially exposed only to spoken language, later learning of sign language does not affect how often they use their voices, and parental concerns that sign language will replace early speech are unfounded. Rather, speech and sign skills may become increasingly intertwined in these children, improving both speech production and comprehension.

Putting It All Together

The preceding sections have focused on young children's use of single signs, words, and gestures. We now move beyond those early vocabularies to the ways in which signs and words are put together into what really looks like, and is, language. In considering the learning of sign language and spoken language, we need to recognize that languages vary in the ways that particular ideas are expressed, and one cannot always translate word-for-word from one spoken language to another, even though we can translate the meaning of what is said. This situation also holds when it comes to ASL and English, and that is why ASL and Signed English are not identical.

The ability to translate fully between signed and spoken languages is important to note because some observers of deaf children's early language learning have claimed that their signing tends to be more concrete and more tied to the "here and now" than the speech of hearing age-mates. We have seen that deaf and hearing children follow essentially the same course of early language learning in terms of their ability to express various meanings, but this claim concerns *what* young deaf and hearing children talk about. For example, the vocabularies of deaf children of hearing parents generally have a greater percentage of words that refer to people, places, and things as compared to hearing children of hearing parents or deaf children of deaf parents. At the same time, their vocabularies have fewer signs or words that allow them to refer to more abstract concepts like time or the existence of things. A major contributor to this difference is undoubtedly that their parents differ in what *they* talk about. The majority of deaf children learn to sign from hearing parents who themselves are only beginning signers and thus are less able to communicate at a complex or abstract level. To make this more obvious, we need only think back to the ways in which we were taught foreign language in school: Generally, we learned about practical things, about going to a restaurant or to the doctor, about travelling on a train, and about visiting museums or other historical places. I do not ever recall having learned how to talk about abstract things like religion, politics, or the meaning of life in a foreign language. If parents are able to sign or speak only about food, toys, and simple social situations, their children are likely to have similar limitations, at least early on. At the same time, as noted above, parents' imperfect use of ASL is not an impediment to their children's eventual ASL fluency (see Chapter 3, Note 5).

To the extent that slow growth in deaf children's vocabularies is a consequence of the context of their early language learning, we would not attribute the observed lags to anything inherent in the children. After all, deaf children of deaf parents have no trouble becoming fluent in ASL and have vocabularies just as large (or larger) and just as abstract as hearing children of the same age. Rather, parents' shortcomings in the language domain are often passed on to their children, who may not yet have sufficient vocabulary to function in social and academic settings. Unless deaf children *and* their hearing parents receive additional language instruction, the children will continue to fall behind hearing age-mates. That is why deaf children of hearing parents often enter school already at a language disadvantage relative to hearing age-mates, and some may never overcome that lag.

As deaf children move into preschool and other settings outside of the home, they usually have more varied sign language experiences with more signing partners, and the language learning context becomes more complex. One interesting aspect of this situation is that young deaf children of hearing parents often learn sign language at a faster rate than their parents. There are at least two factors that contribute to this situation. One of these is the fact that once they enter a preschool program, those youngsters are exposed to far more sign language, and more natural sign language, than are their parents. It would be a rare parent indeed who had the time to spend four to six hours a day in a room where signing was the primary means of communication.

A second factor affecting the rate of sign language learning is that deaf children are far more dependent on signing than are their parents. For many deaf children, sign communication is essentially the only way to express their needs, desires, curiosity, and creativity. Their parents, in contrast, have a full range of spoken language at their disposal. This situation is unfortunate in some ways, because parents and teachers of deaf children often do not realize that they are saying far more in their speech than in their signing. The problem is not that the signs cannot express the same information. It is just that greater fluency in speaking seems to overpower one's signing ability. It therefore is not at all unusual to see people who think that they are using Simultaneous Communication (SC) omitting signs from over half of their sentences. One of the more glaring examples of this I have seen occurred when I introduced an older deaf gentleman to a hearing friend who worked at a school for the deaf. Although I had signed my introduction, my friend began an animated conversation with the man in spoken English. When I interrupted and pointed out that the fellow was deaf, my friend paused and then said, "So you're deaf are you?" while signing only "YOU." He then waited for an answer, while the deaf man walked away, unaware that he had been asked anything, and it was probably just as well that way.[6]

Language ability varies, of course, but the available evidence indicates that even in the classroom, at least one-quarter of a spoken message may be omitted from the signed message by teachers who honestly believe that they are using SC. Even more troubling are cases in which people say one thing and incorrectly sign something else. Not only is there no real communication, but the child is faced with erroneous information about which signs mean what.[7] Many deaf children thus not only start learning language later than peers who share a language with their parents, but they are confronted with less consistent and less useful language experience when they do start. Is it any wonder that they often lag behind those other children in the quality and complexity of their language skills?

LEARNING TO USE SIGN EFFICIENTLY

During the preschool years, ages two to five, deaf children who are naturally exposed to signing in the home rapidly increase the frequency with which they use conventional signs to communicate about objects and actions. When signs begin to fill out the vocabulary, they do not necessarily replace gestures. As with the words of hearing children, they often fill other roles in communication instead. In addition to the accumulation of new signs, modifications of existing signs also enhance the preschooler's ability to communicate with others. Deaf two-year-olds exposed to ASL, for example, appear to understand conventional sign modifications, such as verb inflections (see Chapter 3), and by age three they are modifying signs themselves. The early modifications produced by those children generally do not conform fully to the rules of ASL until they are closer to five years old. Nevertheless, deaf three- and four-year-olds clearly know that signs can be altered to modify their meanings. Most of their invented modifications make sense, and, like the spoken modifications of words produced by hearing children, there is remarkable consistency across children.

One common example of such approximations to ASL occurs with **directional signs.** Directional signs (LOOK-AT, GIVE, INFORM, and so on) are those signs that include a movement component that indicates the *from* and *to* of the action, as shown in Figure 5-1. Prior to their understanding of the directional quality of signs, deaf children often use sequences of several signs linked together to communicate the same information. For example, because GIVE is a directional sign, an older child can sign YOU-GIVE-ME as a single sign, as shown in Figure 5-1. Two-year-olds, in contrast, are more likely to use the three sign sequence YOU GIVE ME containing two personal pronouns and a verb. From about two-and-a half to four years of age, pointing and other gestures are used together with signs instead of using more grammatically complex, if formationally simpler, verb inflections. These replacements are most common during the latter half of

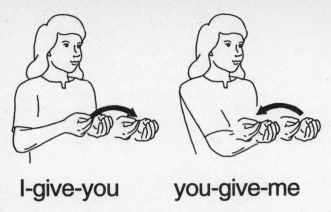

I-give-you   you-give-me

Figure 5-1 The sign GIVE is a directional sign that can be inflected to mean I-GIVE-YOU, YOU-GIVE-ME, and so on.

that period, although many deaf children continue to use them occasionally until they are near five years old. Interestingly, this seems to be a common phenomenon in language learning, and I still find myself doing exactly the same thing in Italian, even though I have all of the pronoun forms in my repertoire (and I do not use the child forms in ASL).

During the second half of their fourth year, when deaf three-year-olds begin to modify verb signs, they tend to use them first to communicate directions and locations. They begin to include qualitative and quantitative information in their signs, indicating how big, how good, how bad, or how fast something is. They also modify signs and their meanings through conventional ASL facial expression to indicate subjective meaning. For example, I WANT THAT becomes I REALLY WANT THAT A LOT! when signed with vigor and appropriate expression, and THERE'S A WORM similarly becomes THERE'S A YUKKY WORM with correct changes to the face and orientation of the head. By the time they are four, deaf children exposed to sign language are able to express how things occur, why things occur, and their intentions.

As with hearing children, deaf three- and four-year-olds, also use some signs incorrectly in what are called overgeneralizations. Hearing children of this age, frequently overgeneralize irregular verbs and nouns that they previously used correctly. Thus, *fell* becomes *falled* and *children* becomes *childrens*, presumably because they have learned the general rule (for the past tense and the plural in these examples) and attempt to make all similar words conform to that rule. Deaf children similarly are seen to overgeneralize, for example, by adding direction to nondirectional verbs such as TOUCH or DRINK, giving them understandable points of origin and conclusion. Overgeneralizations of this sort are as well understood by others when they occur in deaf children's signing as when they occur in hearing children's speech and may be laughed at, responded to, or corrected by others around them. Whatever their reaction, parents and teachers should recognize the importance of such "errors." They indicate that the child is making sophisticated guesses about the grammar of the language and acquiring its component rules.

In deaf three-year-olds, we also see the beginnings of demonstrative pronouns such as THAT, THERE, and THIS, and possessive pronouns such as YOUR, MINE, and OUR. Both types of pronouns appear to occur somewhat later in deaf children than in hearing children, who begin to use them by the middle of their third year (age two-and-a-half), but there is very little evidence on this subject. In fact, there is surprisingly little research on the development of sign language in deaf children between the ages three and six years, regardless of whether they have deaf or hearing parents. We know that the order in which new aspects of language are learned by deaf children of hearing parents is consistent with that of hearing children of hearing parents and deaf children of deaf parents, even if it tends to lag some months behind. Beyond that general conclusion, however, there is relatively little information available to parents, teachers, or researchers, as most of the available research has focused on younger or older children.

DEAF CHILDREN'S EXPOSURE TO SOCIAL LANGUAGE

In general, deaf parents show greater awareness of the communication needs of deaf children than do hearing parents. This awareness results in part from their own experiences, but they also are likely to be more sensitive to visual signals from their children, and they clearly will have a better channel of communication with them via sign language. Some hearing parents also are very aware of cues from their young deaf children about the success or failure of communication. Most, however, lack competence and confidence in their signing abilities, and these attributes can make it more difficult for them to adapt to the needs of their children. For their part, hearing fathers tend to have even poorer sign skills than hearing mothers—presumably one reason (and perhaps a partial cause?) for mothers taking on a proportionally greater caregiving role than they do with hearing children.

Given this greater responsibility of hearing mothers of deaf children, it is important that we consider the language that they use in communicating with their young children. A moment of reflection or observation will reveal that the language that adults use with children frequently is modified to be appropriate for the presumed language capabilities of the young listener. Sometimes called Motherese, such modification is seen regardless of whether a child is hearing or deaf and regardless of whether signed or spoken language is used. When directed to young children by either deaf or hearing mothers, language tends to be slower, simpler, and more likely to include shortened versions of words or signs than the language directed to older children or adults. Because language development in deaf children of deaf parents occurs in a natural manner, we would expect that deaf mothers' use of Motherese in communicating with their young children would begin just as early as it does in hearing mothers of hearing children, and this turns out to be the case. When their babies are as young as three months of age, deaf mothers use primarily single signs with their babies, frequently with the same kinds of repetition as we see in hearing mothers speaking to their hearing babies. Deaf mothers' signing also tends to be accompanied by smiles and numerous mouth movements, and they use exaggerated facial expressions with their babies even more than hearing mothers. "Baby talk" thus clearly occurs in signing as well as speech.

Speech makes language available to hearing babies regardless of whether they are looking in the right direction. Frequently, however, it appears that a deaf child is not watching his mother, and many hearing mothers are reluctant to sign at those times. Deaf mothers also sometimes report they resist signing to their children unless they have made eye contact, but they commonly move their hands out in front of their babies, rather than moving a child's head or physically changing their position, so that the children will see their signs. Over time, this strategy teaches infants to attend visually to cues in the environment, and deaf babies become remarkably good at picking up on mothers' visual cues across a much wider range of positions than one would expect from a hearing child. In fact, there is now some evidence that deaf children actually are better at detecting visual events in the periphery of their vision than are hearing children. This ability does not result from their being deaf, but from the fact that for them, there *are* important things happening on the edges of their visual range. Their eyes and brains thus adjust accordingly, with important implications for social and language development. The same phenomenon is seen in hearing children of deaf parents, because such children must also rely on visual cues from their parents.

The ways in which parents accommodate to the language needs of their deaf babies as well as their hearing babies seem to play an important role in determining the effectiveness and interest in communication on both sides of the conversation. It therefore would not be surprising if a lack of sign language flexibility and fluency on the part of hearing parents were to reduce the quality of their social and educational interactions with their deaf children. In fact, when they are signing to their deaf children about a common object of attention, hearing mothers often tend to oversimplify and end up producing language that carries far less information than the language they use with hearing children in similar situations. Similarly, parents often oversimplify language for younger hearing children, using constructions well below their comprehension levels. Such limitations are not unexpected given that most hearing mothers have little more than beginning competence in sign language. When they are extreme, however, lack of parental sign skills can have significant implications for subsequent development.

Summary

This chapter explored the contexts, capabilities, and components of language learning by deaf children. From vocal and manual babbling, to first words and signs, to more complex language, normal language development depends on frequent and regular communication interactions between deaf children and those around them, regardless of whether it is signed or spoken. Deaf children initially babble like hearing children, making sounds that may be responded to by overzealous parents, even if they bear no relation to later language ability. Unlike hearing children, however, their vocal babbling decreases in quantity and variety over the first year of life. Manual babbling (mabbling) also seems to occur in deaf children, although its function and characteristics are not well understood. In any case, babies' vocal and manual babbling appear to have important social roles for hearing and deaf parents, respectively, and lead to conversations that contribute to social and cognitive development as well as language learning.

In young deaf and hearing children, gestures serve practical functions of identifying, requesting, or showing things in social situations. In the case of hearing children, those gesture are obvious and distinct from ongoing spoken language. In the case of deaf children, the fact that gestures and sign language use the same modality (hand to eye) makes the two difficult to distinguish. Actually, the gestures used by deaf and hearing children are remarkably similar. Deaf children use more of them than hearing children, but that difference disappears by the time they are adults. As both deaf and hearing children develop, their vocabularies grow and their gestures are replaced with conventional language. This and other evidence suggests that although gestures may have a special role within American Sign Language, they are natural and normal for both deaf and hearing children. There is no evidence that preventing their use by deaf children has any positive impact on their spoken language skills, and it may even work to their disadvantage.

There also is no evidence that early sign language learning impedes or prevents spoken language learning. Sign language may provide a bridge to spoken and written English (see Chapter 7), and different children will excel in and prefer different modes of communication. Overall, exposure exclusively to spoken language tends not to be as successful for language learning in young deaf children. There are certainly exceptions, and the extent to which speech instruction, or any language instruction, will be successful depends on a variety of factors within the child (e.g., extent of hearing loss), within the parents (e.g., acceptance of the child), and within the language-learning context. My concern is that many deaf children spend years in intensive speech therapy—often to the exclusion of sign language—while missing the critical first years of language learning. This and the previous chapter therefore have raised a variety of issues that need to be taken into consideration before any decision about "the language of choice" is made by parents.

A variety of investigations have suggested that children learning sign language might even have an advantage over children learning spoken language due to differences in the maturation rate of the fingers, hands, and arms relative to tongues, mouths, and vocal tracts. This benefit appears to maintain through the one-word/one-sign stage, but as children start combining words into longer strings, the difference disappears. Increasing complexity and skill in signed and spoken language subsequently follow the same course in deaf and hearing children, even if a lack of early language experience creates a lag in development for some deaf children. If normal language development, whatever its form, requires early and consistent input, hearing parents of young deaf children will most often find it useful and important to learn sign language. If their skill remains limited and their vocabularies concrete, they should not be surprised to see this reflected in their children's language skills, at least temporarily, until the children are exposed to more and better language models. Children with full access to natural languages such as ASL or English will eventually gain fluency. The same cannot be said for artificial languages constructed by committees, such as SEE1 or Esperanto. Most importantly, parents and professionals have to address the needs of each child, as an individual, in the context of the family and educational system.

Notes

1. One of the more convincing lines of argument for the pre-eminence of manual communication is that the human (or prehuman) brain developed to the point of controlling the fine muscle movements involved in use of the hands before those necessary for spoken communication. Most likely, the earlier development of hand coordination was for use in grasping and tool use, but eventually the predominance of tools required that the hands be freed, and manual forms of communication were replaced by simple oral forms. (Mouth tools would have been a bit harder to develop than hand tools!)

2. Pointing gestures remain in deaf children's vocabularies after they learn language, just as they remain in the vocabularies of hearing children. The important issue here is that there are two different kinds of pointing available to sign language users, one (a sign) within the language and one (a gesture) that supplements language.

3. Parents who complain that their children use baby talk at an age when they should have already grown out of it usually have only themselves to blame. If children continue to hear baby talk, they will consider it an accepted part of language, and it will persist.

4. Examples given here are from ASL. Other sign languages may have signs for these same concepts that are more or less related to what they represent. In British Sign Language, for example, the sign CHURCH is made by showing the movement of pulling a bell-ringing rope—quite different from the more arbitrary ASL sign (see Everyday Signs).

5. Readers can see how easily such errors might occur by doing a short experiment. Turn to the Everyday Signs in the back of the book and cover the English translations of them with a card or dark piece of paper. Then try to guess what each sign means simply by looking at it. Because of the nature of this book, all of the signs listed are relatively simple and no attempts have been made to include or exclude "obvious" signs. My guess is that there will be far more wrong than right guesses.

6. When meetings involve both deaf and hearing people who use sign language, it may be useful to have them be silent. Not having spoken language available levels the playing field for deaf and hearing participants, and having to understand each other's signing helps to demonstrate to hearing signers some

of their communication weaknesses. Personally, I find such meetings preferable to those using Simultaneous Communication.

7. Unfortunately, the phenomenon of saying one thing and signing another due to incorrect sign selection is not limited to children or inexperienced signers. I still see it happening in my interactions with hearing people who sign often, and deaf friends complain that some of the people they interact with most frequently leave them wondering if they missed something important.

6

Going to School

In the dormitories [of residential schools], away from the structured control of the classroom, deaf children are introduced to the social life of Deaf people. In the informal dormitory environment children learn not only sign language but the content of the culture. In this way, the schools become hubs of the communities that surround them, preserving for the next generation the culture of earlier generations.

Carol Padden and Tom Humphries

After deciding which language they want their deaf child exposed to during the preschool years, deciding what kind of school they want for their child is perhaps the most difficult decision parents have to make. As this chapter will make clear, the choice of schools often locks in the language decision until children are either able to learn a second language or until parents abandon one system that does not meet their child's needs and attempt to start over with another.

With the exception of several bilingual-bicultural programs, which emphasize both English and American Sign Language (ASL), most deaf students enter schools that focus on either spoken language or sign language as the primary means of communication and instruction.[1] As at other critical milestones, some parents of deaf children find the information available to them in making the decision about which school their child should attend confusing and contradictory. Recent federal legislation has been aimed at making access to education easier for deaf children and their families, but, as is often the case, the laws have been interpreted and bent in so many ways that the results are often more rather than less baffling. The present chapter, therefore, will try to make some sense of this issue, while avoiding any *a priori* judgments about what is best. Looking ahead, there will not be any single answer to the question, What kind of school is best for my deaf child?

Rather, different children will have different needs, and different programs, as well as different kinds of programs, will be better suited to them. The two conclusions of which we can be sure are (1) there needs to be a broad range of educational options available to deaf children and their parents and (2) the choice of a school program will have long-term implications for personal and career goals as well as academic achievement. In order to help the reader wade through the many relevant issues, we therefore will first examine the kinds of educational options available for deaf children, and then look at their academic and psychological implications.

Educating Deaf Children

Over the past hundred years or so, the educating of deaf children has changed dramatically both in the number of children it reaches and in its content. From 1850 to 1950, for example, enrollment in **residential schools** for the deaf (see below) and other special programs rose from just over 1,100 to over 20,000. By the early 1970s, that number had more than tripled, largely due to the rubella epidemic of 1962–65 that led to as many as 40,000 children being born deaf. By the mid-1970s, over a third of all deaf children attended residential schools, and another third attended special school programs.

More recently, the number deaf children in residential schools has been decreasing, especially at the elementary school level. One survey, for example, indicated that of the more than 46,000 deaf and hard of hearing children in special schools or programs in the United States, only about 9,400 (25 percent) were enrolled in residential schools during the 1993–94 academic year.[2] Another 11,700 were enrolled in day school programs administered by either residential schools or local school authorities, and over 22,000 were enrolled in local school programs in which they received at least some academic classroom instruction with hearing students. These changes are largely the result of changes in federal and state laws mandating the education of handicapped children in the "least restrictive environment," and the related emergence of mainstreaming and **inclusion** movements. Several issues involved in these movements are far more complex than many people have assumed, and so I will deal with them in some depth below.

In terms of content, the two most dramatic changes in the education of deaf children have been the introduction of sign language into the learning environment and the movement away from purely vocational training to a more inclusive academic agenda comparable to that offered to hearing children. At the same time, the greater involvement of the federal government in ensuring appropriate educational opportunities for deaf children has had a profound impact on their education, primarily through a series of laws passed between 1973 and 1990. These laws are often misinterpreted or, perhaps better said, interpreted in a variety of ways that often leaves parents and educators frustrated. Therefore, before we consider the variety of school programs available for deaf children, a brief overview of the primary legal issues is in order.

Legal Issues Confronting the Education of Deaf Children

The powerful role played by the United States Congress in changing the face of education for deaf students started with the Rehabilitation Act of 1973, especially its Section 504, and the 1975 Education for All Handicapped Children Act (PL 94-142). These laws combined to assure free and appropriate public education **(FAPE)** for children with disabilities. PL 94-142 was amended by the Education of the Handicapped Amendments of 1986 (PL 99-457) and the 1990 Individuals with Disabilities Education Act (PL 101-476), known as **IDEA**. Since then, the abbreviation IDEA has come to be used to refer to entire PL 94-142 package. Among other requirements, these laws mandate early identification of hearing losses in school-age children as well as appropriate and unbiased evaluation of deaf children using a variety of alternative communication methods, including sign language.

This extraordinary congressional action resulted from the realization that only about 50 percent of children with disabilities attending public schools were receiving the support necessary for academic success, and that over one million disabled students were excluded from public school classrooms. Although the laws did not specify the nature of the education school boards would have to supply, they did require (1) that all children from age three to twenty-one years be educated in the **least restrictive environment** (LRE) as close as possible to a child's home, (2) the availability of a continuum of placements from hospitals to regular classes, (3) the development of **individualized education plans** (IEPs) for each child requiring special educational programming. The laws also required the inclusion of parents in educational decisions affecting disabled children for the first time.

The confusion surrounding IDEA primarily concerns the definition of an LRE and the intent of the law's requirement that disabled children should be educated with nondisabled children "to the greatest extent possible." Perhaps more than anything else, it was this language that led to the mainstreaming and inclusion movements. The primary goal of the law was to eliminate discrimination in education by preventing the exclusion of children with disabilities from programs in which they could favorably compete with nondisabled peers. Unfortunately, the lack of detail in the law and the fact that it was an unfunded mandate led to conflict at state and local levels. The intent of IDEA was clearly to integrate children with disabilities into public school classrooms whenever appropriate, but it did not actually use the term *mainstreaming*. While allowing all children, including deaf children, to participate in regular public school classrooms, the law was not clear on whether putting children into mainstream environments was a requirement or an option. Nor was it clear how deaf children and other students with special needs were to obtain access to the support services necessary for their educational success.

Both proponents and opponents of PL 94-142 applaud the outlawing of educational discrimination against deaf children and others. Opponents fall into two categories. Some parents have complained that the presence of disabled children in the public school classroom—especially those with behavioral problems—impede their "normal" children's opportunities for academic success.[3] Many such situations result from overly broad interpretations of the law itself, placing some students in inappropriate contexts in the interests of satisfying vague legal jargon. Other complaints reflect the kinds of continuing discrimination that the law was intended to eliminate. At the same time, many parents—especially those who have deaf children—argue that the law requires mainstream classrooms as an available educational option, not as the only option. For those parents and many educators of deaf children, it is important to maintain a variety of educational alternatives for deaf children that allow for optimization of their potentials. One aspect of this position is the need to recognize deaf children as a linguistic minority with the right to receive their education via sign language. Consistent with this argument, the Bilingual Education Act of 1988 provided legal definitions for the terms *native language* and *limited English proficiency* that are frequently used in educational legislation, and it included deaf students and sign language under bilingual terminology for the first time.

In 1992, a "Notice of Policy Guidance on Deaf Students' Educational Services" was published in the U.S. *Federal Register*. Written by the director of the U.S. Office of Special Education within the Department of Education, this clarification of IDEA emphasized that the overriding concern in determining the appropriate and least restrictive educational environment for a child who is deaf is that it be made on an individual basis (to ensure

FAPE) in a manner that addresses students' communication and socialization needs as well as their academic needs. It listed five considerations that local and state education agencies are required to take into account in determining appropriate educational placement and IEPs for deaf children:

(1) linguistic needs
(2) severity of hearing loss and potential for using residual hearing with or without amplification devices
(3) academic level
(4) social, emotional, and cultural needs, including opportunities for interaction and communication with peers, and
(5) communication needs, including the child's and family's preferred mode of communication.

The Secretary of Education later re-emphasized this point in a statement published in the newsletter of the American Society for Deaf Children, when he noted, "We do not advocate a 'one size fits all' approach in making decisions about how students should be educated. Educational placement decisions for students with disabilities are made at the local level and should be based on individual student needs and address the issue of adequate resources for both students and teachers." The question remains, however, of how best to ensure that deaf children and school systems have the resources necessary for educational success. Coupled with the Americans with Disabilities Act (ADA), laws aimed at preventing educational discrimination against deaf children have improved their access to diverse educational options and a "slice of the budgetary pie." More recently, with shrinking local, state, and federal dollars, unfunded mandates like ADA and IDEA offer a glimpse of educational opportunities, but they often leave children, parents, and schools without any real way to achieve them. Bickering among various parent groups about the single right answer to these problems does not help the situation, even if it is understandable given the diverse and often contradictory arguments confronting them.

Educational Program Alternatives

Legal questions are not the only issue that confront parents trying to find the best educational placements for their children. Concerns about facilitating social development, academic achievement, and giving deaf children equal access to all of society clearly enter into the decision. In order to understand fully the dynamics and consequences of changing educational op-

portunities for deaf children, we therefore need to consider the several kinds
of programs available.

PRESCHOOL PROGRAMS

Previous chapters have already touched on the importance of preschool intervention programs for deaf children and their parents. Like other preschool programs, early intervention programs for deaf children are intended
to give them the skills necessary to succeed when they enter formal schooling, usually kindergarten. In the case of deaf children, they usually are designed to accommodate youngsters from birth to four years. Such programs
are run by public school systems, state health and human services depart-
ments, residential schools for the deaf, and some private organizations.
Many school systems also offer the opportunity of home-based preschool
education in which itinerant teachers work with parents, children, siblings,
and other family members at home. In providing services for parents as well
as children, preschool programs focus on language development, parent-
child communication, social skills, and appropriate support for any residual
hearing children might have through testing and possible fitting for hearing
aids. Teachers generally provide parents with strategies for enhancing their
children's development, including instruction in sign language, speech training, or both, depending on the particular program. Because of the small
numbers of children in each class and the number and variety of programs
available, these programs are readily available for children in both metropolitan and rural areas.

The educational impact of various kinds of preschool programs has not
been fully investigated, but there is broad agreement that they are important
in helping children function socially both in later school settings and within
the family. In Chapter 4, it was noted that friendships and playmate preferences among deaf preschool children are just as stable as those among hearing children, and deaf preschoolers tend to initiate more interpersonal interactions than children who do not attend such programs. At least one
recent study also has shown a strong relation between social functioning and
the kind of preschool program that deaf children attend. In that investigation, children who were exposed to Simultaneous Communication (SC)
showed higher levels of social play and more frequent dramatic play, usually
taken as an indicator of cognitive development, than children in speech-only
preschool settings. The speech-only children, meanwhile, were found to be
far more disruptive in their play, exhibiting many more aggressive acts like
pushing, hitting, and pinching than those in SC classrooms. While it is difficult to unravel the many factors that might make for such differences, there
seems to be fairly consistent evidence that early exposure to sign communi-

cation facilitates deaf children's social interactions with peers as well as with their parents. Although studies involving older deaf children with and without preschool experience still lie ahead, it seems likely that the availability of more diverse social, language, and educational experiences can only enhance the flexibility of young deaf children in dealing with later social interactions and the necessity of growing up in a largely hearing society.

RESIDENTIAL SCHOOLS

The term *residential school for the deaf* elicits a variety of reactions in hearing people. Parents and teachers who have never visited one should reject the exaggerated image of an institution with green walls, stark rooms, and "lost" children. Residential schools have a long and venerable history in this country, even though they may be scorned by people who are opposed to either the teaching of sign language or to any kind of special education programs for deaf children. (A recent book written by one such an individual, for example, listed "residing in a broken home" as the first reason why a residential school might be selected for a deaf child!) Residential schools are at the heart of the Deaf community. They are places where lifelong friendships are formed, where language and culture are learned, and where teaching can occur directly without the need for intermediaries such as interpreters.

As the quote at the top of this chapter indicates, it is often in the dormitories and after-school activities that deaf children acquire the knowledge and skills that make them feel a part of Deaf society, or any society. Looking up to older, fluently signing and socially competent deaf children (especially those of deaf parents), younger deaf children discover role models and an environment in which they are on an equal footing with their peers.

Residential schools traditionally have drawn children from all parts of every state into settings specially designed to fit their needs. They serve deaf children of both hearing parents and deaf parents, and the latter group typically has a strong preference for this setting for their children. During the 1970s and 1980s, as a result of the rubella epidemic, these schools multiplied and expanded. With the more recent decline in the population of deaf children since the development of a rubella vaccine, some of the newer residential schools have closed, and most of those that remain now offer **day school programs** in addition to residential schooling. Others now accept deaf-blind children or children with multiple handicaps in order to keep their doors open.

Different kinds of school programs are more or less beneficial for children with different strengths and different needs. Fueling current disagreements about the appropriateness of residential versus public school placement, there is conflicting evidence supporting each as leading to better educational outcomes for deaf children. A variety of reports through the years, for example, have called for more deaf teachers and more hearing teachers who are better trained in sign language for residential schools. At the same time, there is considerable evidence that deaf children lack adequate access to classroom information in public school settings. Educators and parents who advocate for the availability of the residential school option point out that the presence of deaf adults who are well educated and fluent in sign language has a significant, long-term impact on young deaf children's educational and personal well-being. Deaf adults also can serve as models for the development of appropriate social behavior, sex roles, and moral reasoning in deaf children. Consistent with this argument, deaf children who attend residential schools tend to be better adjusted and more emotionally mature than deaf children enrolled in public schools programs, as will be discussed in a section later in this chapter. In the absence of such models, deaf children from hearing families occasionally have been reported to believe that they will either regain their hearing when they get older or die as children. After all, they never see any adults who are deaf.

Proponents of residential schools for the deaf point out that without such opportunities, only the 10 percent of deaf children with at least one deaf parent would be expected to know about American Sign Language (ASL) or Deaf culture. While preschool programs provide some of this for younger deaf children, the concern here is with providing a social, cultural, and academic context that gives older deaf children a supportive learning environment. The maintenance of the cultural hub of the Deaf community is not an insignificant part of the argument to preserve residential schools, but it is separate from the consideration of their educational impact (considered below). The variety of factors related to initial school placement—degree of hearing loss, early intervention experience, parental factors, and so on—makes it difficult to draw any general conclusions about the utility of residential versus public school programs. There are, nevertheless, several domains in which consequences of residential schools appear fairly clear, and these will be discussed at various places in this and subsequent chapters. In any case, the primary goal should be to identify the individual educational needs of each child in choosing the appropriate educational environment. For this to occur, there must be alternatives available that provide different kinds of programming.

DAY SCHOOL PROGRAMS

Day school programs for deaf children can be housed in public schools, on residential school campuses, or in other educational centers. These programs typically employ some deaf teachers and teachers' aides and expose deaf children to others who are deaf or hard of hearing. Unlike children in residential schools, the children in day schools live at home and are exposed to deaf models, children and adults, primarily during the school day in the context of the academic curriculum.

The benefits of day school programs relative to residential schools lie primarily in the fact that children can remain at home while still having teachers and staff who are specially trained in educational methods designed to optimize educational opportunities for deaf children. When parents are involved in their child's language learning, take the time to work with their children after school hours, and participate in extracurricular activities, day school programs can be an excellent compromise between residential schools and mainstreaming. As Chapter 8 will show, parental involvement of this kind is an important ingredient for academic achievement, and day school programs can provide very effective environments for deaf children by meshing home-based and school-based support. The primary drawback to such programs is their scarcity. Day programs are available at most residential schools, where children attend the same classes but do not stay in the dormitory, and can found in most metropolitan areas, but they are less frequent in suburban areas and rare in rural areas.

PUBLIC SCHOOL MAINSTREAMING AND INCLUSION

In the absence of day programs, mainstreaming and inclusion are the dominant educational alternatives to deaf children's attending residential school. Both involve placing deaf students or others with special needs in regular public school classrooms for the entire school day. The primary difference is that mainstreaming typically involves attendance of some special classes and some regular classes, whereas inclusion entails students being fully included in all aspects of public school setting. Mainstream programs also typically involve the availability of a special resource room with appropriately trained teachers or aides, while inclusion often does not. In some cases, a child's IEP calls for partial mainstreaming, where the child spends part of the day in a residential school setting and part of the day in a public school.

One common complaint about mainstreaming programs is that they do not provide the quality, "regular" education that their supporters claim. Deaf students are often placed in regular classrooms only for nonacademic courses, while taking their core curricula either in separate classrooms or at other schools to which they have to commute during school hours. Beyond sometimes being misled about the academic integrity of such programs, students with such partial segregation may acquire the same kinds of stigma that students in their parents' or grandparents' generations once experienced when they went off to remedial education classes in their schools. Indeed, the available evidence suggests that deaf children who receive such dual-track educations have more difficulty with both social integration and academic achievement than those who are consistently taught in one setting or the other. One hears stories of children who have made a successful transition from special programs to partial mainstreaming to full mainstreaming, but I have heard just as many stories about children who found success by going the other direction.

Mainstream settings need not suffer from the problems of programs that only provide superficial integration. For some students, a mainstream classroom with appropriate academic support services can provide excellent educational opportunities. Mainstreaming is not for all deaf students, but then no one type of program is. The key is to try to identify the right kind of program for a child in the first place *and* closely monitor academic and social progress for signs of the program's appropriateness or inappropriateness. Now that parents are involved in establishing IEPs, they have a greater role in determining the course of their children's education, consistent with the 1992 "Notice of Policy Guidance on Deaf Students' Educational Services" cited earlier.

This discussion should not be taken to imply that the support offered by mainstreaming is universally desired by parents of deaf children. There are a number of parents, especially among those whose children have lesser hearing losses, who advocate full inclusion. *Mandatory* inclusion does not seem an appropriate response to either the needs of deaf children or the legal requirements of IDEA and ADA. Such a policy fails to recognize that different children, whether they are deaf, hearing, mentally retarded, blind, or whatever, have different needs that may be best served by different educational options. Some parents prefer that their children sink or swim in the public school (full inclusion) setting. In my view, sinking is not a viable alternative, and not all children have the tools necessary to swim in that environment, especially when support services are insufficient to allow them full access to classroom activities. Perhaps if mainstream programs in elementary, middle, and secondary schools were fully equitable, the full inclusion movement would not gave gained the momentum it has. For now, one can only hope that innocent children will not get caught in the undertow of politics and run the risk of being overwhelmed.

POSTSECONDARY EDUCATION FOR DEAF STUDENTS

The days when deaf children were trained primarily in vocational schools for careers in manufacturing or manual labor are now gone, as are many of the jobs for which they once were trained. There is a now full array of educational opportunities available for deaf students in community colleges and in four-year colleges and universities. At least there should be. Passage of the ADA guaranteed deaf students, as well as others, full access to public and private services, including the college classroom, and the following section describes the kinds of academic services that should be provided under the ADA and other laws.

At present, there are over 15,000 deaf and hard of hearing students enrolled in postsecondary educational institutions in this country, roughly 93 percent of them at the undergraduate level. That number is most likely an underestimate, as many students and colleges still are not aware of their rights to obtain support services. Nevertheless, almost 50 percent of all two- and four-year institutions have identified themselves as serving at least one deaf or hard-of-hearing student and among larger colleges and universities this number rises to around 95 percent. The most recent *College & Careers Programs for Deaf Students*, published jointly by Gallaudet University and the National Technical Institute for the Deaf (NTID), listed 136 colleges and universities that provide special programs and services for deaf and hard-of-hearing students. Included in this number are four federally funded, regional Postsecondary Education Programs for Deaf Students and the two national programs, NTID and Gallaudet, which deserve special mention.

In 1965, the National Technical Institute for the Deaf was established as one of eight colleges of Rochester Institute of Technology, founded in 1862. In a unique, fully mainstreamed setting, 1,100 deaf and hard-of-hearing students at Rochester Institute of Technology are able to earn degrees at several levels in a variety of technical fields such as engineering, computer science, applied art, and photography, and there is also an interpreter training program for hearing students. Courses in the college of NTID proper are taught by faculty who use ASL or Simultaneous Communication, depending on the communication preferences and needs of their students. Courses taught in other colleges of the university are supported by sign language interpreters and note takers whenever there are deaf students in a class. At present, NTID provides over 65,000 hours of interpreting and over 45,000 hours of note-taking services each year in support of deaf students cross-registered in one of the other seven colleges. The job placement rate for NTID students is about 95 percent, with approximately 80 percent of graduates finding work in business and industry.

Gallaudet University offers a wide array of undergraduate and graduate programs to its 1,600 deaf and hard of hearing students. Graduate programs are also open to hearing students. Established in 1864, Gallaudet is the only free-standing liberal arts college for deaf students in the world and, like NTID, it also serves as a research center and public service center for issues and information relevant to deafness. In a bilingual (ASL and English) setting, Gallaudet students can select from a diverse array of majors. Like NTID, Gallaudet is supported primarily by the federal government and places almost 95 percent of its graduates either in jobs or graduate education programs.

Students who attend NTID or Gallaudet have graduation rates between 50 percent and 60 percent. Deaf students who attend other colleges and universities have a much lower graduation rate, around 35 percent from two-year programs and 30 percent from four-year programs. This compares to graduation rates of 40 percent at two-year programs and 70 percent at four-year programs among their hearing peers. Although there have not been many studies conducted to determine the precise reason for these differences, discussions with students who have transferred from other schools to NTID or Gallaudet indicate that some students come for the culture—to be around other deaf people and enjoy unhindered social and academic communication while getting a quality education. At the same time, these colleges provide a way to avoid the access problems of "regular" colleges and universities. Even when academic classroom support is provided at such schools, deaf students may be tacitly denied access to advising, public lectures, and other campus activities. Further, deaf students may have special needs related to their educational progress prior to the college years or to multiple handicaps. Many institutions still do not know their responsibilities for providing such educational support under the ADA, and others simply are unable or unwilling to do so. Until this situation changes, special college programs for deaf and hard-of-hearing students will remain an important means of leveling the playing field.

Academic Support Services

Research has shown that deaf students tend to have higher academic achievement than hard of hearing students. This finding might seem contradictory to those who assume that more hearing is always better than less hearing. One factor that is likely involved here is the level of special support that the two kinds of students receive. Students who have lesser hearing losses may not be identified as easily as those with greater hearing losses, they and their parents may not know that they qualify for special services, and older students may not apply for such services for personal reasons (see

Tucker's *The Feel of Silence*). Even when services are requested, hard-of-hearing students and even some deaf students may not be able get them if they are judged "not disabled enough" by school administrators who desire to avoid costly support for only one or two students.

The primary academic support services needed by deaf students are both communication related: interpreting and note taking. There are also other issues involved, including the effective use of classroom space, teaching strategies, and the sensitivity of teachers and counselors to the communication needs and learning strategies of deaf students. There is also the need for technologies discussed in Chapter 2: visual fire alarms, TTYs, caption decoders, and so on.

INTERPRETING

Students with mild to moderate hearing losses can often follow classroom instruction fairly well by sitting in the front row. Nevertheless, communication can be disrupted in several ways: the teacher may talk while facing the blackboard or wandering around the room, thus reducing both the volume and the availability of mouth and other facial cues; there may be multiple conversations going on during questions and answers that require rapid switching of attention; or teachers and other students may not speak clearly enough for a deaf student to follow.[4] With greater hearing losses, following a speaking teacher is almost impossible. Even when speechreading skills are sufficient for one-on-one conversations about specific topics, that strategy can quickly become swamped in a classroom for all of the reasons cited above. True, some students with more severe hearing losses use spoken language as their primary means of communication and are able to succeed in such settings without communication support. They are few and far between, however, and often report succeeding *despite* going to class, through the assistance of their parents, friends, and supportive teachers. Other deaf students have speech skills good enough to lead teachers to assume they have comparable abilities in speechreading—usually an erroneous assumption.

Deaf students who are unable to survive schooling with spoken communication alone, must depend on sign language interpreters. A real sign language interpreter in a school setting is someone who has received extensive training in sign language and its variants, in special aspects of educational interpreting (as opposed to legal or medical interpreting), is certified by their state or the national Registry of Interpreters for the Deaf (RID), and is bound by a clear and detailed code of ethics. Unfortunately, it is common for schools to try to make use of lesser-trained individuals who can be paid less than professional interpreters but also are less skilled. Just knowing sign language does not make someone competent to interpret in the classroom. Nor, for that matter, is such a person competent to interpret for parent-teacher meetings when one of the parties is deaf. Nevertheless, I have heard stories about deaf parents going to a school meeting and requesting an interpreter, only to find that a teacher's aide or other person who has some knowledge of sign language is "interpreting" for the meeting. These meetings are usually doomed from the outset and do not really do any good for the child, parent, teacher, or the school. One of the best outcomes is the scheduling of another meeting with a qualified interpreter, but in some cases even that may not be appropriately communicated. Some schools simply refuse such requests in the erroneous belief that they have met their legal and moral obligations.

Chapter 3 described some of the variety of communication systems available to young deaf children, from ASL to Signed English to spoken language. Similarly, there are interpreters for each of these, although only the first two would properly be called sign language interpreting.[5] In all cases, the goal of the interpreter is to communicate faithfully everything that the teacher and other students say and everything that the deaf students says (the sign-to-voice direction is referred to as *reverse interpreting*). Usually, this occurs with the interpreter standing near the teacher, so that the student can watch both people and take advantage of the teachers' movements, facial expressions, and demonstrations.

Most interpreters will provide the deaf student with additional class-related information that they normally would be denied, such as the context of discussions, noises coming from inside or outside the room, and the tone of communications if they are not clear. Interpreters are not teachers' aides, and they should not have responsibilities outside of interpreting per se. Most certified interpreters, in fact, are reluctant to step outside of their interpreter role at all, and some will deflect questions directed at them to the person for whom they are interpreting. For example, an interpreter might respond to a hearing student's question of "Who are you?" by simply signing WHO ARE YOU? and allowing the deaf student to answer the question. I once saw a similar example in a university meeting involving two deaf faculty members and about ten hearing faculty, some of whom could not sign for themselves. When we went around the room introducing ourselves, the interpreter was inadvertently left out (although I understand from interpreter friends that this is not unusual). In order to recognize the interpreter, a deaf colleague in the meeting joked, AND WHO IS THAT FAT

GUY UP THERE WAVING HIS HANDS? The interpreter accordingly voiced, "And who is that fat guy up there waving his hands?" to the laughter of those who understood what had happened and the puzzlement of those who did not. (The interpreter then did introduce himself.)

NOTE TAKING

At first glance, a reader might wonder why deaf students should have the benefit of someone to take notes for them in class—after all, hearing students do not receive such services. A deaf student has to rely on visual communication. When hearing students look down to write in their notebooks, they are able to continue to follow the lecture or classroom conversation because they can hear it. I have taught some hearing students who spend almost all of the class looking down and taking notes, but still following what is going on. Deaf students who rely on signed communication do not have that luxury. Each time they look down to write something, they miss part of what is being said. The alternative of not taking notes at all puts the deaf student at a clear disadvantage, and so many of them depend on classroom note takers. As deaf children move into later grades, where notes become more important in class, hearing students are often asked to volunteer to share their notes with deaf classmates.[6] As an alternative to note taking, teachers may copy their class notes or overhead transparencies for deaf students. Hearing as well as deaf students benefit from such opportunities, and once teachers have prepared them for a deaf student, many will continue doing so for future classes.

OTHER SUPPORT CONSIDERATIONS

A variety of other support functions can be useful for deaf students, both inside and outside the classroom. Within the classroom, deaf students' reliance of visual information makes the frequent use of overhead transparencies, video projection, and similar teaching tools indispensable. In addition to the assistive listening devices described in Chapter 2, classrooms designed to be user-friendly to the deaf student allow unhindered view of the instructor and blackboards, offer good acoustics for those students who make use of residual hearing, and avoid "visually noisy" walls in order to make visual monitoring of the classroom more comfortable. Unfortunately, these last two characteristics can sometimes conflict in classroom designs. I have seen a whole series of classrooms that were designed with vertical wood slats on a sound-absorbing wall. The goal was to support spoken language communication through better acoustics, but the visual noise of the walls created significant eyestrain in the deaf students for whom it was intended. (The solution was painting the wood and walls the same color.)

Outside of the classroom, deaf students often benefit from the availability of tutors (either students, off-duty teachers, or staff hired specially for that purpose). Personal, academic, and career counselors also serve an important role for deaf students, who will be less likely to get such advice from hearing parents, teachers, and peers. In programs with larger numbers of deaf students, there are frequently resource rooms, advising centers, or technical assistance centers. Counselors, hearing aid technicians, and audiologists may be physically housed within these sites, or students may be directed to them by individuals who are. In many schools, electronic bulletin boards and computer "notes conferences" are increasingly popular, and users have no way of knowing which students are deaf and which are hearing (or blind or physically challenged).

Taken together, the array of support services described above helps to give deaf students equal access to the educations they have been promised under Section 504 of the Rehabilitation Act of 1973, IDEA, and ADA. But education is not simply a matter of sitting in a classroom. Effective teaching and learning requires clear communication between students and instructors and the opportunity to ask questions and interact with other students. In addition to providing effective educational and career information, academic support services allow deaf students to be integrated into their schools and communities to an extent that would otherwise be nearly impossible. Differing school programs and differing levels of academic support therefore can lead to considerable differences in academic, social, and personal success.

Educational Implications of Alternative School Placements

A variety of investigations have examined the educational outcomes of various kinds of school programs for deaf children. In all such studies, there is a potential source of bias, and the rule of *caveat emptor*, buyer beware, is important here. A truly fair comparison of two programs or different types of programs would need to include students who are comparable in terms of hearing losses, communication skills, academic backgrounds, family support, and so on. This kind of control happens in laboratory research, but it is not likely to occur naturally in the real world. It is therefore difficult to determine the extent to which observed differences between programs are due

to anything about the programs themselves or the possibility that they at-
tract different kinds of students in the first place. This is an important issue
because depending on how one views those results, they can be used to support one philosophy of schooling or another. Rather than providing hypo-
thetical examples of this problem, let me put it in the context of actual research findings.

In light of the legal and educational issues described earlier in this chapter, there have been several recent studies comparing the academic success
of deaf students attending residential school programs versus those attending mainstream programs. In general, these studies have indicated that students in regular school programs are likely to perform better in reading
comprehension and mathematics computation—two areas that traditionally
have given deaf students considerable difficulty (see Chapters 7 and 8).
When family and student characteristics, such as parental education and
early school experience are taken into account, that difference becomes relatively small, but it still holds for students who are fully mainstreamed (although not for those who are partially mainstreamed). This finding suggests
that a mainstream education setting can provide benefits for deaf children,
but there are several factors that obscure the true relation between the kind
of school program and student achievement. One is that children who attend one kind of school or another may be better students to begin with,
even before they go into such a program. This could result from many
things, such as differences in their hearing losses or spoken language skills,
more parental involvement in their education, or just because they are
smarter. Any of these characteristics (or some combination of them) might
actually be responsible for differences observed in academic success, but no
one would know if these variables were not independently evaluated. A second possibility is that exposure to both signed and spoken communication
in the mainstream classroom could be more beneficial than the exposure
only to spoken language or sign language in separate schools. Finally, it may
be that teacher and parent expectations are higher for children in mainstream settings.

I suspect that, on average, better students are more likely to attend
mainstream schools in the first place, but there is still no good evidence in
this regard. Meanwhile, on the basis of all of the studies I have seen, it appears that the other two factors definitely affect student success in alternative school programs. Consider for example the second factor, individual
differences among deaf students. Among deaf children who are enrolled in
separate school programs, there tend to be more students with greater hearing losses and more who have either physical or emotional problems than
there are among students who are in mainstream settings. This finding does

not mean that it is better to enroll any particular deaf child in a mainstream program than a special school program. What it does mean is that students who enroll in mainstream programs are more likely to come from advantaged backgrounds, have lesser hearing losses, have fewer physical challenges, and are doing better in school. Which of the first three, if any, is a cause of doing better is school is not clear. Importantly, the "mainstream advantage" is already present by age seven, and does not change much through the school years. This finding suggests that the difference in achievement between students in mainstream and special school programs is not caused by the school programs themselves, but by something that happens before children enter school. Either mainstreamed students are brighter or are better prepared in the first place, or perhaps they are more likely to have benefited from early intervention programs.

Another interesting finding is that the *amount* of mainstreaming can make a significant difference in academic achievement. One recent study found only small differences in reading and mathematics achievement between students who were instructed full-time in either mainstreamed settings or in special school programs designed for deaf children. However, comparing deaf students who attended five to ten hours of school a week in local public schools (one to two hours per day) to those who attended more than sixteen hours a week in those schools (over half of each school day), students in the latter group performed consistently better. The most surprising finding was that by age fifteen or so, students who attended local public schools for only one to two hours per day showed a marked drop-off in both reading and mathematics scores. By age seventeen, these students had fallen below students who were instructed fully in either mainstreamed or separate settings.

There are several potential explanations for such findings. One of the most obvious possibilities is that spending one to two hours a day in a public school does not provide much time for real academic experiences, especially when traveling between schools takes up some of that time. It also is not clear whether the children receiving fewer mainstream class hours in that study were receiving reading and mathematics instruction during that time. One to two hours a day in a public school seems unlikely to allow a deaf student sufficient time to become comfortable in that setting, in any case, a factor that may disrupt some of the potential for learning. Finally, it is important to emphasize once again that the students who might attend these alternative programs likely have different academic qualifications to begin with or may be differently motivated to succeed. In particular, because many parents and teachers may expect more from students in mainstream settings, there may be a self-fulfilling prophecy. In other words, those children might achieve just as much in other kinds of programs if the same demands were placed on them. We just do not know.

Psychological Implications of Alternative School Placements

Given the importance of factors like motivation for educational achievement and **self-esteem**, it will be worthwhile to consider possible differences in social and personality functioning as they relate to attending particular kinds of school programs. Earlier in this chapter, I described the 1992 "Notice of Policy Guidance on Deaf Students' Educational Services," which clarified some incorrect interpretations of PL 92-142 (IDEA). Part of that clarification called for the consideration of social, emotional, and cultural needs in determining the appropriate school placement for deaf children, including the opportunity for interactions and communication with peers. This provision came partly in response to the concern that deaf children placed in mainstream or inclusion settings would lose the normal kinds of social interactions typically available to hearing children in public schools and deaf children in residential schools.

Clearly, part of education involves acquiring the roles, rules, attitudes, and values of one's society. Peer relationships are thus an essential part of social development (see also Chapter 4), but the question of how best to foster the development of such relationships is not a simple matter. On the surface, one could imagine either that deaf children might benefit from being surrounded by hearing peers or that the lack of communication might result in their becoming socially isolated. In order to evaluate this issue, we have to consider deaf students' social experiences when they are in programs with hearing peers versus when they are in programs with deaf peers. Only then can we know how best to support deaf children's development of identity and integration with society. Keep in mind, however, that this is not just an issue of having friends or socializing at school. Students with positive social interactions in school tend to have higher academic achievement (see Chapter 8), better mental health (see Chapter 9), and are more likely to succeed in their careers. Children may not be not graded on it, but they do learn a lot about social functioning in school.

Advocates of inclusion programs for deaf children argue that placing deaf children and children with disabilities in regular classes will enhance their self-esteem and sense of control, as well as fostering the integration of all people with disabilities into society. Italy is currently experimenting with a similar concept, in which essentially all children with disabilities are placed in public school settings. As the program has been explained to me by one of its leaders, the hope is that after a generation or two of having all handicapped children in the same classrooms as nonhandicapped children, people with disabilities will no longer "seem different," and society will be more accepting of the equality of all children. While this is a laudable goal, there appears a rather basic problem with this wholesale inclusionist approach. The idea of putting deaf children or others with special needs into regular classrooms rests on the assumption that they are able to learn in these settings. It is by functioning smoothly in such classrooms that they would become part of the groups who are supposed to accept them. To support such efforts, Italy has a large number of special-education teachers who work within the public schools as resources for children with disabilities. In the case of deaf children, however, there are no sign language interpreters in schools, and few teachers know Italian Sign Language (LIS). In fact, some Italian teachers I have met did not know that LIS exists. As generalists, the special education teachers thus have little training in how to deal effectively with the special needs of children who cannot hear—or those with other impediments to full access. As a result, many deaf children are unable to benefit from the public school classroom and tend to be isolated from both peers and educators. In the interests of this grand experiment, a whole generation of deaf and handicapped children may be left out, unable to benefit fully from the school experience and with nowhere else to turn.

In the United States, several recent studies, conducted by both deaf and hearing researchers, have evaluated the social consequences of placement in mainstream versus special school settings. The results of these studies uniformly refute the claims of mainstreaming and inclusion supporters, demonstrating instead that many deaf children in such settings feel lonely, rejected, and socially isolated. Many deaf students find themselves frustrated in their attempts to relate to or interact with their hearing classmates and thus may focus more on relations with teachers and other deaf peers—not an unusual finding for students who are excluded by their minority status. In contrast, deaf students in both residential schools and in special programs within local public schools report having more friendships and feeling more emotionally secure and accepted by peers. Students who are in Total Communication programs also show higher self-esteem than peers in speech-only programs, as do students whose parents are better signers (see Chapter 9).

For students in partial mainstream settings, social adjustment generally is better in interactions with deaf than with hearing peers, given equal exposure to both. Increasing the amount of mainstreaming does not improve the amount of emotional security, a finding that contrasts with the finding in the preceding section indicating that increased mainstreaming is linked to greater achievement in reading and mathematics. Taken together, these results suggest that, contrary to the claims of inclusion advocates, there are no clear social or emotional benefits for deaf children who attend school with hearing peers. Quite the contrary: They tend to have more problems of self-identity, of emotional security, and in starting and maintaining friendships. When they do have personal interactions with hearing peers, deaf students report that their contacts are often less than positive. While it remains possible that such interactions may have some "sleeper effects" which will show up later in life, there is no way to tell whether such effects will be positive, perhaps allowing for smoother interactions with hearing society, or negative, perhaps making such students outsiders in both deaf and hearing cultures. At present, the risk seems rather high given that there are viable alternatives.

Summary

Although most parents of deaf children want a simple and straightforward answer to the question, What kind of school is best for my child? there isn't one. If there is one message to be taken away from this chapter, it is that there must be a continuum of placements for deaf children, and parents and teachers need to collaborate to determine which is best for any particular child. Following a series of federal and state legal decisions since the 1970s, there are now several laws that protect deaf children from discrimination in education and ensure that they are fairly and appropriately evaluated, placed, and academically supported. This is not to say that there is full agreement about the best educational system for deaf children, and even while the laws are being implemented, there is disagreement about what they mean and who will pay for them. Nonetheless, parents now have a central role in the planning of their deaf children's educational placement, and they need to be informed about their options and the implications of those options.

Early intervention (preschool) programs are available across most of the United States and in other countries. Normally funded by local school districts or residential schools for the deaf, these programs support the legal mandate for early testing and intervention for children who have significant hearing losses or other impediments to full educational access. Such programs provide communication instruction for both parents and children, and usually provide tutoring for parents in the special needs of their children as well. Deaf children benefit from these programs socially as well as in communication and in educational experiences partly because they are able to interact with deaf peers and adults, often for the first time. Children who attend such programs tend to be advantaged both academically and socially when they enter school, and there are no disagreements about the importance of those programs.

The kind of school program a deaf child attends varies with parental hearing status, geographical location, program availability, and a variety of other factors. Most deaf parents prefer that their deaf children attend schools for the deaf. Through these schools, children gain the same kinds of early social interactions and lifelong friendships that their parents experienced. In addition, they are exposed to many aspects of Deaf culture and a variety of deaf role models. Hearing parents typically are more confused and unsure about the alternatives, and they are pulled in both directions. The legal requirement is that there be alternatives available across a wide range, so that parents and school systems can develop the best education plan for each child. In practice, most parents lean toward regular public schools until such time as they might find their children unable to compete successfully or become integrated in the regular classroom.

Some deaf children clearly succeed in mainstream settings with appropriate academic support services such as sign language interpreters, note takers, and appropriate advising. Success without such services is rare. Is the frequency of success enough to warrant choosing mainstream placement? Although there is no good answer to the question, there are several factors that should enter into the decision. Perhaps most obvious is a child's degree of hearing loss. If children have good speech and speechreading skills, they are more likely to succeed in a regular classroom. If the school has good support services and is knowledgeable about the needs of deaf children, it is likely to help promote achievement. Preliminary evidence from research studies suggests that deaf students who are mainstreamed for half of each school day or more tend to show better academic performance. Mainstreaming for only one to two hours a day seems to result in good performance during the early school years, followed by a drop-off during the high school years. It remains unclear whether this downward trend reflects some cumulative effect of schooling or a change in programs. For example, deaf students might find themselves mainstreamed for nonacademic subjects early on before entering regular high school classes for which they are not fully ready. In any case, available research suggests that half-day mainstreaming may be linked to higher achievement than either full-time mainstreaming or full-time placement in a special program. The problem (and this is a big problem) is that it is still unclear whether fully mainstreamed students perform better because of something inherent in the programs, because better students tend to enter those programs in the first place, or because teachers and parents have higher expectations for children in those programs. Just because mainstreaming is related to better academic performance, it does not mean that sending deaf students who are unprepared for the public school classroom into such programs will make them better students.

For many deaf students, mainstream settings fail to foster social development in the ways that we know are important for normal, healthy development. Deaf children often are excluded from social interactions with hearing students by virtue of communication barriers and the fact that, whether we like it or not, they are different from their hearing peers. As a result, they often feel lonely, emotionally insecure, and isolated in public school classrooms. They also tend to have lower academic achievement.

While emphasizing that the choice of the right program for a deaf child depends on many factors relevant to that particular child and her family, I would be less than honest if I did not admit that from all of my knowledge in the area, I have a good idea of how I would try to place my own deaf child if I had one. First and foremost, I would find a quality early intervention program that emphasizes sign communication. Building on that base, I would closely monitor language development in both sign language and spoken language, seeking to support and optimize both, first through use of ASL and later adding speech therapy and Cued Speech, as appropriate, to help support her learning to read (see Chapters 3 and 7). For the school years, my own leaning would be toward a day program and extracurricular activities at a residential school if I lived near one, providing my child with the opportunity to interact with deaf children and adults, identify herself as a member of Deaf culture, and appreciate that she has a stimulating and sympathetic community to support her in addition to her hearing family. If the quality of programs, academic support services, and my child's communication skills permitted it, I would allow her to attend a mainstream program for a half-day or more, although I would never require it. Most importantly, I would plan to spend a lot of time in quality education-related experiences with my child and ensure that my sign language skills were as good as I could possibly make them.

Notes

1. Bilingual-bicultural programs do not just emphasize two languages, but encourage deaf children to embrace both Deaf and hearing cultures. Not all bilingual cultural programs are the same, however, and political issues within

the Deaf community have created some disagreement among schools that seek to adopt bilingual-bicultural orientations. The focus of the disagreement concerns the extent to which programs encourage balance in language and social choices or lean toward redressing previous imbalances, pushing children toward a stronger Deaf orientation. Such issues arise in other areas as well, but newer "bi-bi" programs, like the pilot program at the Texas School for the Deaf, are walking a fine line, trying to avoid a backlash created by more radical programs.

2. All of the numbers presented here are approximate and depend on the particular definitions and methodologies of the studies in which they were obtained (see Chapter 2). While the figures presented in the text are consistent with most of the data I have seen, Department of Education statistics from just two years earlier suggest that there were over 15,000 more deaf and hard of hearing students than I have indicated here, with about 20 percent in special schools, one-third in separate classes within public schools, and almost half in regular classes with hearing peers.

3. Of course, those parents do not mention the fact that there are "normal" children who are equally or more disruptive in the classroom.

4. Deaf and hard-of-hearing students who have had to deal with noninterpreted classes also suffer from related eyestrain and headaches, as well as severe bouts of frustration.

5. Interpreters for spoken language, called oral interpreters, provide clear and well-articulated mouth movements for students who might have reduced visual acuity or others who depend on clear and consistent oral cues for speechreading. Use of oral interpreters eliminates many potential problems in the classroom (e.g., teachers can move around more), but relatively few deaf students find them useful.

6. Some programs train and pay student note takers, which improves their utility for both deaf and hearing students.

7

Learning to Read and Write

I like reading what you write to me. Not because of what you write
about. It just that I'm learning how, like when I read how you write,
language, grammar. I learn and want to write like that. I hope you
understand what I mean? I can't explain it. It's the writing of yours,
not what you write about.

Cheryl, age 20, writing to her English teacher

This chapter is about literacy, specifically the kind of literacy of greatest interest to most parents and teachers of deaf and hearing children: the ability to read and write in English.[1] But there are different kinds and definitions of literacy. The original sense of the term was related to the assumption that anyone who understood the idea of combining letters of the alphabet—the basic building blocks of written language—could use it in a creative, appropriate way to get and use an education. Thus, we refer to people becoming "lettered" or acquiring "knowledge of letters;" and Doctor of Letters is considered a prestigious, if largely ceremonial title for the honorary college degrees conferred on politicians and celebrities.

We now use the term *literacy* in a variety of other ways as well. Educators, for example, refer to students as being computer literate or having mathematical literacy. These terms are related to the original definition of literacy in the sense of having "building blocks" that allow more complex and sophisticated use of the whole, but the content is no longer just language, at least in the literal sense. There is also cultural literacy, which allows an individual access to various aspects of their culture as communicated by others through art, literature, and history. Traditionally, no one was considered truly educated if they were not well versed in literature (a "collection of letters"), that is, in the documentation of knowledge within their language and culture. Of course, we could also talk about literacy within

American Sign Language either in the narrow sense, where the components of signs would replace letters (see Chapter 3), or in the broader sense of providing access to the cultural heritage of the Deaf community (see Chapter 2).

Although in this chapter I will be focusing on the more narrow sense of literacy as it relates to English, it will be important to keep in mind yet another distinction: having some basic level of reading and writing competence may be different from having language skills flexible and creative enough to support educational and personal success. Functional literacy is the term most commonly linked to basic reading and writing abilities; the student who is functionally literate has the minimum reading and writing skills necessary to function in society. Traditionally, that minimum referred to a fourth- to fifth-grade level of competence—usually good enough to get a driver's license but sometimes not good enough to understand the warnings on medications or cookbook recipes let alone the manuals that come with home computers. Given the demands of the information age, several educational researchers now argue that an eleventh- to twelfth-grade level of skill for functional literacy might be more appropriate.

The reason why I also referred to literacy "flexible and creative enough to support educational and personal success" is that fourth- to fifth-grade functional literacy may not be sufficient for deaf children to have true access to the free and appropriate education to which they are entitled. To most people, and certainly to parents, true literacy requires fluency in the language used by those who teach us, who write textbooks, and who tell us the news on television—that is, fluency in English. This issue brings us back to the education of deaf children: Do deaf children need to be fluent in English, in ASL, or both to be considered literate? If the question seems a difficult one, consider Hispanic children in the United States who are fluent in Spanish but not English. Unless they learn English, they might not receive adequate educations in many parts of the United States, but they would surely be literate: They would have access to world knowledge and Hispanic culture through Spanish. In addition, we presume that Spanish would provide a bridge to learning English, and we would expect that Hispanic students who are encouraged and motivated to learn English should not have much trouble.

Consider now deaf children of deaf parents who learned ASL as their first language. Like Hispanic children who learned Spanish as their first language from Hispanic parents, these children are certainly literate in all senses of the word. They understand the building blocks of the language (signs and sign components), they can use them in novel and creative ways, and they have access to much knowledge of the world as well as to knowledge of both Deaf and hearing cultures. In order to gain access to the full body of knowledge available to hearing peers, however, they will also have to be able read and write in English. This situation does not minimize the importance of ASL as a language, any more than it minimizes Spanish. It simply reflects reality: Fluency in sign language, or any minority language, is not enough for full access to the larger culture even if it is sufficient for many of the purposes of family, friends, and day-to-day life.

My reason for laying this groundwork about literacy is not to seek political correctness or claim that a deaf child can be literate even if they cannot read and write English, although that is technically true. Rather, it is to point out the fact that without special attention, most deaf children will not be fully literate in either English or in sign language. The preceding description concerned deaf children of deaf parents. As we will see in the next section, such children generally are better readers than deaf children of hearing parents, suggesting that they are bilingual—literate in both ASL and English.[2] But they represent barely 10 percent of deaf children in this country. What about the other 90 percent?

Compared to hearing children, most deaf children of hearing parents enter school already at a language disadvantage, because they do not have access to their parents' English, and their parents typically are not proficient in sign language. That lag in language skills tends to increase during the school years, as deaf children of hearing parents show slower growth in language development relative to hearing children, even if both show the same general pattern of development. The important question is how we can best use the language skills they have to build literacy in what will most likely be their primary language, sign language, and their second language, English. As the remainder of this chapter will show, I believe that the available evidence indicates that being bilingual, in ASL and English for children in the United States, is the optimal situation, at least as it relates to learning to read and write. (Note that being bilingual in ASL and English does not mean learning Signed English or any other English-sign hybrid.) Chapters 1 and 4 have already considered the importance of early exposure to sign language as a means of giving deaf children an understanding of what language is. The following sections, therefore, will focus on the practical issues of their learning to read and write, together with consideration of the role that sign language can play in that process.

What is Reading?

Current data indicate that on average, eighteen-year-old deaf students leaving high school have reached only a third-grade to fourth-grade reading level, and over 30 percent of them leave school functionally illiterate by the old standard. This compares to a functional illiteracy rate of less than 1 percent among their hearing peers. Accordingly, Gallaudet University recently reported that a large majority of their students do not read well enough to make effective use of first-year college textbooks. That finding did not surprise either Gallaudet students or faculty, and the majority of both groups urged that there be a greater focus on reading English in the curriculum.

Most hearing people take reading for granted only because they learned to read relatively naturally in their first language—much more naturally than they would if they tried to learn another language as adults. This learning seems natural because everyone around us uses the same language, and there is a one-to-one correspondence between words that people utter and what can be written or read in a book.[3] For this reason, parents' reading to their children is one of the most important facilitators of later reading skill, not just because it motivates children by making reading enjoyable, but because it actually teaches them to read at the same time. At a more general level, reading aloud seems like a literate society's equivalent to the tradition of storytelling, a natural behavior of humans that seems to run through all cultures and times.

Reading is a very complex process that is not fully understood. Consider some of the elements of reading that fluent readers typically do not have to think about. First, reading involves the ability to distinguish arbitrary marks on a background, whether stone, paper, or computer screen. Even before you know what the marks mean, if they mean anything, you have to be able to perceive the marks, for example, through the eye for print or the hand for Braille. Then you have to recognize writing as writing. Only after you discriminate one mark from another do you have to be able to discriminate one kind of mark from another (for example in @&##&@@&) and groups of marks from other groups (for example @&# from #&@ or @@#). Up to this point, you could be looking at Chinese, English, or symbols on your typewriter, and you are doing fine, but you are not reading.

At the next level, there are two possibilities: One is that individual marks can be linked to sounds, which can be built up into larger patterns that you can say to yourself and recognize as words. In this way, you can sound out new words that you may have heard but have never seen or discover new words that you can pronounce but do not know. It is through this process that most readers know what *fowtuhgraf* means, even if it is written strangely. If you do, it probably means that you learned to read by what is called the phonics method (from *phon-*, meaning "sound"): You sound out words according to what are called spelling-to-sound rules. If these phonological rules were not important, I could randomly rearrange the letters in a word, and you would know what it is anyway.[4] Some readers, however, will have no idea what *fowtuhgraf* means. Most likely, those readers learned to read through the whole-word method, either because that was the philosophy of a particular teacher or the school system in which they were educated, or because they had one of many reading disabilities that made letter-by-letter reading impossible. For them, *fowtuhgraf* bears no resemblance at all to *photograph*. They also are unlikely to recognize printed words that they have heard but not seen before and thus have to make use of dictionaries more than people who learned via the phonics method.

Assuming that a set of marks is recognized as a word, the next step is to link meaning to it by "looking it up" in some kind of mental dictionary. The hard part, especially for deaf students, is that words have many different meanings as well as different pronunciations, and the correct one cannot be determined solely on the basis of definitions. Depending on how I count them, for example, my *Oxford English Dictionary* has either 10, 40, or 67 different meanings or senses for the word *bow*.[5] These include the bow that shoots arrows, the bow in one's shoelaces, the bow one takes after a performance (which also demonstrates the variability in sound-to-spelling patterns), the bow at the front of a boat, and others. Surely I am not likely to use all of these meanings, and some, like "the stock of cattle on a farm," I have never even heard of. Nevertheless, I was able to read them in the dictionary and I would likely understand most of them in context. To do this, I have to make use of two kinds of rules.

One kind of rule that helps us select the right sense or meaning of words from our mental dictionaries and allows the construction of an infinite number of utterances in a language is a grammatical rule or (syntax). People who are fluent in a particular language have internal sets of rules (grammar) that allow them to combine words into phrases, clauses, and sentences. Those rules allow us to produce completely new utterances, so we can do more than just repeat things that others have said, and to understand new strings of words produced by others. If grammatical rules were not important, I could randomly rearrange the words in this sentence, and it would not affect your interpretation—sentences like "Harry chased Bonnie" and "Bonnie chased Harry" would mean the same thing (see Note 4).

The grammar of English not only allows us to use the language, but it also tells us when someone else does not know how to use it, that is, when they are not using acceptable English (meaning that they do not have the correct internal rules). For example, after several years of studying Italian and French, I know enough of their grammars to understood why people from those countries speak English the way they do: They often put English words into Italian or French grammatical structure the same way that Signed English puts ASL signs into English grammar. Even more interesting is the fact that when I am speaking English with Italian or French colleagues, I sometimes find myself doing the same thing! Whether this is an unintentional attempt to make myself clearer or some mixing-up of the languages in my own head, I do not know, but it does seem to improve their comprehension.

So much for understanding sentences. Next is the level of discourse structure. It is at this level that we can identify what pronouns refer to, we can combine ideas into meaningful series, and we actually understand what we read. If discourse rules were not important, I could randomly rearrange the sentences on this page, and it would not interfere at all with your comprehension. Discourse-level rules, like spelling rules and grammatical rules, tell us that order does make a difference to some extent. Just as they acquire grammatical rules, most children acquire discourse rules naturally by watching the correspondence between things and events and the way that people describe them.

With this brief sketch about reading out of the way, we can return to the issue of deaf children's reading skills. It is essential to keep in mind that the above language rules are learned *relatively* easily for *most* readers *most* of the time partly because they acquire them early. That is one of the beautiful, if still mysterious, aspects of both first and second language learning: As long as it happens early, before age four or so for first languages and through adolescence for second languages, it seems to occur with relative ease—even if it takes several years. In contrast, many adults who try to learn other languages find that the rules do not come so easily the second time around. Luckily, we are able to use what we know about our first language to help with the second language, and therefore languages more similar to our first language are usually easier to learn. Imagine, then, what it would be like if you did not really understand the rules of the first language when you tried to learn a second, if the letters and words on the page did not correspond to what people "said," and if you did not see the correspondence of words and events. That is the situation of the average deaf child trying to learn to read.

What Makes Some Deaf Children (but Not Others) Good Readers?

Perhaps more than any other area relating to being deaf, the reading and writing abilities of deaf children have been the focus of attention from educators and researchers for decades. Taken together, the results and conclusions of relevant studies provide an enlightening, if disappointing picture of deaf children's skills in this regard.

Many of the behaviors that deaf children exhibit in reading and writing are the same as those made by people learning English as a second language. Over the past twenty years, programs like the English Language Teaching Outreach Program (ELTOP) at the National Technical Institute for the Deaf therefore have been developed to instruct teachers of deaf children in methods like those used in teaching English as a second language. Although their reading behaviors and their writing look similar, we need to learn more about *how* deaf children learn to function in English. After all, English is a language in which deaf children will have to function if they are to receive appropriate educations and achieve their potentials in the work force and intellectual life of society. First, we have to take into account the variation among deaf children and the influences of early language environments, types of hearing loss, and factors like parent and child motivation. Unfortunately, a large portion of the effort devoted to improving deaf children's literacy has gone into trying to teach them the skills and strategies that work for hearing children, even though it is apparent that deaf and hearing children often have very different background knowledge and learning strategies. As a result, despite decades of concerted effort, most deaf children in this country still progress only about 20 percent as fast as hearing children in learning to read. This means that deaf students leaving school are at a relatively greater disadvantage, lagging farther behind hearing peers than when they entered! At the same time, there are clearly many deaf adults and children who are excellent readers and excellent writers. What accounts for the differences?

DEAF CHILDREN OF DEAF PARENTS

A variety of sources, including a recent report from the National Institutes of Health, suggest that deaf children of deaf parents are, on average, better readers than deaf children of hearing parents. Why? Deaf children's relative lack of early language experience when they have hearing parents clearly plays an important role in their reading difficulties, but earlier chapters have emphasized that there are other differences between the two groups. Deaf and hearing parents may have very different expectations for their deaf children in terms of academic achievement. They also may differ in their ability to help their children in reading-related activities, and we know that children whose parents spend time working with them on academic and extracurricular activities are more motivated and have greater academic success (see Chapter 8).

In an earlier book, *Psychological Development of Deaf Children*, I did an extensive review of thirty years of studies concerning the reading abilities of deaf children of deaf parents as compared to deaf children of hearing parents. The results were surprising, because I fully expected that deaf children with deaf parents would always come out on top because of their early exposure to language. But it's not really that simple. Deaf children of deaf parents generally are better readers than deaf children of hearing parents. One important factor in this situation is that deaf parents are more sensitive to their children's communication needs. Regardless of whether their parents are deaf or hearing, however, deaf children who are better readers turn out to be the ones who had their hearing losses diagnosed earlier, had early access to language (usually via sign language), *and* were exposed to English. At the same time, having a mother who is a good signer appears to be more important than whether she is deaf or hearing or the precise age at which a child learns to sign (as long as it is early). So, deaf children of deaf parents will tend to read better than deaf children of hearing parents, but mothers and fathers who learn to sign well can have a powerful impact on their children's reading abilities.

Regrettably, there is no single predictor of reading success that works in all cases, and the combinations of factors that positively and negatively influence reading development are not yet fully understood. It may be, for example, that different environments lead to different strengths and weaknesses (for example, big vocabularies but little grammatical knowledge) depending on when, where, and from whom children learn their first and second languages. For example, deaf children of hearing parents tend to have better speech and speechreading abilities than deaf children of deaf parents, but those abilities do not seem linked to better reading, even though they would seem to support the phonological part of reading. Although it is also tempting to assume that a deaf child's early exposure to language through deaf parents would provide a considerable advantage in learning to read, this advantage may be offset by the fact that ASL vocabulary and syntax do not parallel those of printed English. Consistent with the research findings thus far, this difference supports the suggestion that early exposure to both ASL and Signed English or ASL and Cued Speech might be most beneficial for the reading abilities of deaf children, giving them the advantage of both early exposure to language and English-relevant language experience.[6]

My inclusion of ASL in this language mixture comes from the clear social, cognitive, and linguistic merits of sign language use by deaf children, as described throughout this book. ASL gives young deaf children access to what is happening in the world and provides an effective means of parent-child and teacher-child communication. As I mentioned briefly in Chapter 3, my inclusion of Cued Speech as a possible English supplement in this mixture draws from some recent research showing that deaf children who are exposed to Cued Speech from an early age show impressive performance in a variety of skills involved in reading. Importantly, those results are most striking when children use Cued Speech consistently both at home and at school. When it was used only at school, gains were much smaller. Although the relative benefits of Cued Speech and Signed English for support of reading skills have not yet been evaluated, it is important to distinguish the potential of these methods from the way in which they might actually be used. That is, Cued Speech has the benefit of providing continuous information to a child, but comprehension may not be complete. Signed English has the benefit of a link to ASL and thus better support for comprehension; but we have already seen that teachers of deaf children who use Simultaneous Communication leave 20 to 50 percent of what they say out of their signing, without recognizing how much information is lost. Such confusion is often cited as one reason to support the use of ASL in educating deaf students, but the problem may be more the fault of Signed English users than Signed English itself. At present therefore, my highest recommendation is for more research and persistence and flexibility on the part of parents and teachers. Use whatever works!

In addition to research on combining ASL and English in teaching deaf children to read, we need to examine the effect of other factors such as motivation, exposure to reading, and the quality of teaching. The effect of early exposure to reading, via parents and early school environments, seems a particularly important area of study given findings indicating that children who read more become better readers, as well as the other way around. Taking a narrower rather than a broader approach to reading, it also is important to consider the various subskills involved in reading. Deaf and hearing children, or deaf children of deaf versus hearing parents, may differ in these component skills even when their overall reading levels are the same. Alternatively, they may be similar on particular dimensions that create overall differences in reading level. Accordingly, let us spend a little more time with the three primary components of reading—phonology and spelling, vocabulary, and grammar—as they relate to deaf children.

PHONOLOGICAL KNOWLEDGE AND SPELLING

One of the most central and interesting issues in this area concerns how deaf children, especially those who have greater hearing losses, can make use of phonological information in the absence of hearing, because *phonological* normally refers to the way words sound. Even though spelling-to-sound skills are enhanced in deaf children with better speech, we know that they are separate from speech skills and cannot be explained on the basis of articulation alone. Rather, the bases for phonological abilities seem to involve some combination of information drawn from articulation, speechreading, fingerspelling, residual hearing, and exposure to writing, no one of which is sufficient in itself.[7] Several studies have indicated that the ability of deaf children to decode spelling patterns emerges much later than in hearing children. Skill in the use of such information does not appear directly tied to amount of hearing loss, at least among children with severe to profound losses. Deaf children with this skill are able to make use of phonological information, especially when words follow regular spelling patterns, although they often depend on more global characteristics such as how the word looks on the lips or on the printed page. Interestingly, similar findings are seen in the understanding of fingerspelling within sign language: Although letter-by-letter analysis often occurs for new or unfamiliar words, fingerspelling is generally seen in terms of overall patterns rather than in terms of component letters for both deaf and hearing signers.

Phonological skill also may contribute to better grammatical skill and better comprehension, because internal speech has been shown to be more efficient than either visual imagery or internal sign language for the memory component of reading. At that level, information about words is held and accumulated until relations among words (grammatical information) and relations among events (discourse information) reveal the meaning of a phrase or sentence. We know that deaf children make use of both phonological and whole-word strategies during reading. When words are regular in their spelling, phonological strategies are most likely to be successful. The linkage of such reading strategies to writing is seen in the fact that deaf students sometimes produce phonologically accurate misspellings such as *sizzers*. Similarly, whole-word codes based on how words look may result in a greater likelihood of leaving out letters (writing *orng* for orange) and making letter reversals (writing *sorpt* instead of sport).

Proficient reading, then, in deaf children as well as hearing children, depends on some underlying knowledge of the characteristics of individual letters. Deaf children in Simultaneous Communication programs or in exclusively spoken language programs tend to show more frequent use of phonological information relative to children in more sign-oriented programs, perhaps explaining some of their early advantage in reading performance. By college age, however, these differences become smaller or disappear. While showing deaf children how words sound may be useful for speech and reading, what is especially important is showing them the link between printed words and their meanings. There is no better way to achieve this than sitting down with a child and reading and signing to them. Books for very young children are also easy enough that they will give hearing parents a lot of good practice in their signing. As one of my colleagues recently pointed out: "Parents of deaf children do not have to act like teachers or trainers; they just have to act like parents!"

VOCABULARY KNOWLEDGE AND KNOWLEDGE OF THE WORLD

Although it has been well documented that vocabulary knowledge is a primary component of reading, consideration of deaf children presents the issue in a somewhat different light. We already have seen that most deaf children come from hearing homes in which they have more limited exposure to language. These children accordingly have been shown to have fewer signed or spoken labels for things around them than hearing children of hearing parents or deaf children of deaf parents. They also are less likely to gain such knowledge from reading. In this context, it is worth mentioning again the fact that more reading makes for better readers, as well as the other way around. The two-way street between how much children read and how good they are at it suggests that we need to make special efforts to expand vocabularies to which deaf children are exposed through print, sign, and speech. The more vocabulary they encounter, the bigger their vocabularies will be, and the bigger their vocabularies, the better they will be able to deal with new vocabulary.

Compared to hearing children, deaf children are more likely to understand and use concrete nouns and familiar action verbs over more abstract or general words with which they may have less experience. This is not just limited to childhood. Several colleagues and I teach a popular course for deaf college students entitled "Strategies for Organizing Word Knowledge." Students enroll in the course because they recognize their weaknesses in understanding such things as the multiple meanings of words, the fact that there can be several words that *almost* mean the same thing, and the hierarchical organization of word meanings (e.g., living things, animals, farm animals, cattle, cows, Herefords). Apparently, many deaf children get caught up in a cycle of having smaller expressive vocabularies, smaller receptive vocabularies, and fewer opportunities to expand either. Therefore, I frequently urge teachers of deaf schoolchildren to move away from the practice of focusing primarily on practical and familiar concepts. While acknowledging that many deaf students have difficulty with basic vocabulary and related skills, parents and teachers often underestimate the language skills of children—both hearing and deaf. In the case of deaf children, it is especially important to avoid this pitfall, because the bias is even stronger than it is with hearing children.

Deaf children's vocabulary skills typically are better when words have only a single meaning or when they are presented in context rather than in isolation (the latter happens on many achievement tests). Still, their vocabulary abilities tend to lag about a year behind their other reading subskills. This mismatch may disrupt reading by interfering with the access to word meaning that is so important for comprehension. In fact, when we observe deaf children's apparent difficulties with grammar during reading, we cannot really be sure that grammar is the problem. It could be that some children have trouble attending to grammatical information because their cognitive resources are overloaded with word-finding. In either case, the result would be reduced comprehension and reading speed, as well as a tendency to remember disconnected portions of texts rather than the whole picture, especially when the material is unfamiliar.

UNDERSTANDING GRAMMAR

During the 1970s, a lot of attention was given to the grammatical skills of young deaf readers. A variety of programs tried to apply current theories of grammar (or syntax) to deaf children, with little success. Deaf students generally were far more variable than hearing peers in their performance and tended to have particular difficulty with constructions that depended on keeping track of meaning across multiple events and grammatical structures in texts. Pronouns (*he, her, their, that, it*, etc.), for example, can cause difficulty because the reader has to remember the activities or characteristics of nouns in order to later understand who or what is being referred to. Such findings suggest that more global factors such as concept knowledge, **cognitive style** (see Chapter 9), and memory also play important roles in deaf children's reading in ways that cannot always be distinguished from grammatical issues.

At least one research study has directly examined the influence of early language experience on deaf children's grammatical skill. In that investigation, two groups of deaf children who had hearing parents and were exposed only to spoken language were compared to groups of deaf children of deaf parents who communicated with them either via manually coded English or ASL. Overall, the children exposed to sign language consistently outperformed children who were exposed only to spoken English—a finding that is contrary to the expectations of those who support educating deaf children in spoken language only. On the other hand, children exposed to some form of manually coded English by their deaf parents showed better grammatical skills in English than the children who learned ASL. In fact, the ASL group and the intensive spoken language group were roughly comparable—a finding contrary to expectations of anyone who would advocate either approach alone in educating deaf children. As was the case in early vocabulary development, then, it appears that the best approach for optimizing the grammatical component of deaf children's reading is to expose them to both sign language and English, regardless of whether their parents are deaf or hearing. Again, this does not mean that parents need to be training their children. They need to make language available in meaningful and enjoyable ways that will lead children to want to learn to read for its own sake.

Deaf Children's Writing

The intimate relationship of reading and writing is such that it will not come as a surprise to discover that deaf children's performance in the "input" domain of reading is mirrored in the "output" domain of writing. As in reading, deaf students vary considerably in their writing skill, and different criteria for writing may well be deemed important by different teachers at the college level as they are at the elementary and secondary levels. In a recent study involving Gallaudet University students, for example, individual faculty ranged from 5 percent to 75 percent in their estimates of the number of students with "satisfactory" writing skills. Clearly, writing is a very complex skill and one that is difficult to evaluate.

Examinations of writing samples from deaf children show them to produce shorter sentences than hearing peers and to repeatedly use simple subject-verb-object sentences which give the appearance of concrete and literal writing. Sometimes, their sentences are not sentences at all, at least in the sense of being grammatically correct in English. Taken together, such findings have led to the general conclusion, similar to that for reading, that the average deaf eighteen-year-old writes on a level comparable to that of a hearing eight-year-old.

Earlier, I suggested that some characteristics of deaf children's reading and writing might be attributable to the relatively low expectations of parents and teachers. Recent research in classrooms and laboratories, however, suggests that something is missing in all of this. For example, analyses of deaf students' writing has amply demonstrated that it can be rich and creative, even if, as reflected in the excerpt at the beginning of this chapter, it suffers in ways that many English teachers might find unacceptable. Some of my own work similarly has demonstrated that superficial problems notwithstanding, deaf students' writing as early as elementary school is both creative and conceptually well-structured. At the level where events and actions in a story are laid out and interwoven, their writing is fully comparable to that of hearing peers.

Take for example the following story written by a deaf twelve-year-old. As part of a study I conducted with Victoria Everhart, students were asked to write a story about being picked up by a UFO, what would happen, and what the aliens would be like. The following is representative of what we got and fits well with the above description of deaf children's writing.

> When I get in ufo They look funny. They have long pointed ears and have round face They speak different from our. They brought strange foods and Purple beverage. When I taste it I spill [spit] and begin to cought [cough]. I [It] taste like dog food. But It was very pretty inside with many feather and clothes were very pretty. But one thing people in ufo stare at me because they never see large musclar [muscular] and can pick up Heavy thing like weight, people or table. They feel it and said wow and start to teach me how to talk but they speak Russian language. I hate to learn Russian language. So I stay in ufo for 5 hours so they stop to place where they take me and drop their and they sent me a dog with long sharp teeth and was very tame I egan [began] to cry and miss them.

Among the other typical characteristics of deaf children's writing, one of the most noticeable ones in this passage is the frequent omission of words. A variety of studies and surveys have documented the fact that deaf children use fewer adverbs, conjunctions, and auxiliary verbs than hearing age-mates, whereas the frequencies of nouns and verbs are about the same (note, again, the similarity to reading performance). This characteristic could be taken to indicate that they are patterning written language on ASL, although similar errors are made by many learners of English as a second language.

But now look again. If you ignore the spelling and grammatical errors in this story, something English teachers and many mothers have a hard time doing, you will see that there is a very clear and coherent story underneath it all. The author told us what the UFO and its inhabitants would be like, about their appearance, food, and clothing. She recounted the reaction of others to her, as well as her reactions to them. After an attempt to communicate (through spoken language!), the aliens gave up, dropped her off, and sent her a gift for her troubles. After all of these wonders, is it surprising that she missed them when they left? The point here is that when we evaluated these stories on their English characteristics, the deaf students (aged seven to fifteen were found to be writing well "behind" the hearing students. When we examined the conceptual structure of the stories, however, the two groups were functioning at comparable levels. Even if deaf children are not fluent in English spelling and grammar, they still can demonstrate creativity and competence in writing.

Available findings thus indicate the clear parallels between deaf children's reading and writing. Although there are few studies from which to draw conclusions about differences between deaf children of deaf versus hearing parents, it appears likely that the writing abilities of those groups would follow the same patterns as their reading abilities. Deaf college students with deaf parents, for example, show better performance than deaf peers with hearing parents on writing tests intended for people who learn English as a second language. Similarly, deaf college students who learn ASL early from their deaf parents tend to perform better on writing tests than those who learn to sign as adolescents or adults. On the basis of these findings, we would also expect that the writing abilities of deaf children whose parents provide early exposure to both ASL and Signed English or ASL and Cued Speech should surpass those of children who are exposed to only ASL or spoken English. Unfortunately, those studies have not yet been done.

The Impact of Social and Emotional Factors on Literacy

Before leaving the topic of reading and writing by deaf children, it is worth re-emphasizing importance of social and emotional factors, such as motivation and desire for achievement, to the development of literacy and to academic success in general. Look again at the excerpt from a student's journal at the beginning of this chapter. Despite its superficial errors, it is clear that Cheryl enjoys writing and finds it interesting to reflect on her attraction to it. In her writing about writing, she shows a motivation to succeed and reveals the importance of having good models. Having a written dialogue with a supportive teacher allows her to improve and learn about writing not by having it corrected, though that happens too, but by analyzing her own writing and the writing of others. To me, this is a true sign of academic achievement: pursuit of knowledge for the sheer joy of learning.

Studies involving hearing children have shown that parents' spending time with their children, facilitating their academic and extracurricular interests, and answering their questions in supportive environments foster academic excellence as well as psychosocial maturity. Regrettably, a language barrier sometimes prevents such interactions between deaf children and their hearing parents, although this varies from family to family. Lower levels of literacy achievement by deaf children also may be related to their relatively narrow orientations toward many academic subjects. This attitude is reflected in the fact that skills learned in one course are not used in other courses, so that, for example, the transfer of algebra to physics or biology to psychology may not occur spontaneously. The reasons for such narrow views are as yet unclear, although I believe they are partly related to the ways in which parents and teachers of deaf children tend to focus on the concrete and familiar rather than on exploration and discovery. Knowledge about language is very abstract, and not everyone finds language as fascinating as language researchers like me (a fact that my students have made painfully clear). Reading and writing also may be viewed differently from the perspectives of deaf and hearing children. As second language learners, deaf children may be less invested in achieving English literacy due to either their own values or those of their parents—or their parents may not be as good at communicating those values.

Summary

At several points throughout this book, I describe evidence of deaf children's sign language skills being superior to their reading and writing in English. Such findings suggest that writing skills are independent of deaf children's general intellectual abilities and should not be taken as indicators of any general language fluency or language flexibility (but see Chapter 8). Those findings also suggest that literacy should be within their grasp.

The most frequently cited academic difficulty among deaf children is reading. At first blush, one might expect that the hardest part of reading for deaf children would be the ability to decode the spelling patterns of words, a process that normally depends on knowing how letters sound. Many deaf children are surprisingly good in this regard, however, apparently making use of information combined from fingerspelling, residual hearing, speechreading, articulation, and exposure to writing. At the same time, deaf children are more likely than hearing children to use visual and whole-word strategies during reading, and the same pattern appears in comparisons of deaf children who are more oriented toward use of sign language than spoken communication.

The most well-documented areas of difficulty for young deaf readers are vocabulary knowledge and grammatical abilities. Limitations in their vocabularies reflect the influence of early nonlinguistic as well as linguistic experience, as deaf children tend to have access to fewer language models (who name things) than do hearing peers. Slower recognition of words also may affect the ability to make use of grammar in comprehension because the cognitive system may be so busy trying to find word meanings that it will have less "space" to devote to understanding the larger message. Factors like vocabulary and grammatical knowledge run on a two-way street in literacy development: As they improve, children read more and more complex material, which in turns contributes to more skill development. Similarly, deaf children's beliefs about their own abilities and their desires to succeed operate in a two-way manner just as they do for hearing children, so that success breeds success. One essential aspect of academic achievement is that children have to notice that their success in school work is the result of their own efforts. This relation is consistent with the finding that children higher in intellectual achievement tend to feel that they are more in control of their own lives.

Overall, deaf children's reading difficulties do not appear to be the result of any particular orientation in their early language experience. Exactly which variables are the most important ones for predicting their reading success is unclear. At this time, it does not appear that early exposure to sign language is sufficient to account for the observed differences. The best deaf readers appear to be those who receive early exposure to sign language and exposure to the language in which they will eventually learn to read. Finally, the available literature suggests that the sources of difficulty apparent in deaf children's reading performance are also found in their writing. Lags in the development of vocabulary and grammatical skill result in deaf children's writing appearing concrete and repetitive relative both to hearing children's writing and to their own signed productions (see Chapter 8). At the same time, their writing is clearly well ordered and creative, showing that fluency in English and intellectual ability are at least partially separate. Nevertheless, reading and writing form an essential link to the worlds of social and intellectual interaction, and the consequences of literacy or illiteracy will have increasing impact on all realms of functioning as deaf children grow up.

Notes

1. It is worth emphasizing again that *English* is used here only for convenience and refers to whatever spoken and written language is used by the community in which a deaf child lives. Similarly, most references to American Sign Language in this chapter could appropriately be replaced by any other sign language.

2. True bilingualism is rare, and most people who use ASL and English, or

any two languages, are really more proficient in one language than the other. That issue does not concern us here, and the term *bilingual* will be used in its usual sense meaning relatively competent in two languages.

3. Actually, there isn't a one-to-one correspondence between spoken and written words. The breaks between spoken words are often less distinct than breaks between written words, for example, making speechreading and the development of speech-to-print translation systems extremely difficult. Issues like this create interesting problems for psychologists who study language and language learning, but they can be ignored for the present purposes.

4. The major problem with arbitrary rearrangements is that because all languages have limited numbers of elements, rearranging them is the method used to create new words. Rearranging the letters in *tap* for example, does more than just change the way the word looks and sounds *(pat, apt, pta.)*. The same constraint holds for words in sentences and may hold for sentences in paragraphs.

5. The many dictionary meanings of words do not include the novel, figurative ways in which words can be used and still be understood by competent users of the same language. This topic is somewhat outside of the current discussion, but deaf children's use and comprehension of figurative language is described at length in Chapter 8. With regard to the literal meanings of words like *bow*, multiple meanings create additional problems for artificial English/sign language systems (see Chapter 3).

6. As noted in Chapter 3, one problem in combining ASL with either Signed English or Cued Speech is that you cannot be doing both at the same time. It therefore is important to carefully identify which contexts are better served by one way of communicating or another. Thus far, it appears that ASL is a better (and more natural) route for everyday communication during the early years, while Signed English and Cued Speech may be more helpful later as bridges to reading and writing. Unfortunately, research into these issues has not yet yielded many firm conclusions.

7. Phonological skill is also related to the "inner voice" that we sometimes notice when we are reading. A friend who lost his hearing as a teenager tells me that he still hears his inner voice. Although this issue has been investigated with regard to young adults who are deaf, there have been no studies relating to deaf children or its role in reading.

8

Intelligence, Achievement, and Creativity

The education of children born deaf is essentially a war against cognitive poverty.

R. Conrad, *The Deaf School Child* (1979)

For some readers, this chapter will be the "bottom line" of the book, and I suspect that a few may have skipped forward to this point seeking an answer to the question, Are deaf children as smart as hearing children? Those who have read everything up to this chapter, however, will suspect (correctly) that the question is really a very complex one. Perhaps a better question would be, How much weight should we put on intelligence tests and achievement tests for deaf children? In any case, we first have to be clear about the kinds of characteristics we are talking about and how they are measured. Then we can try to deal with the question and make an attempt at some answers.

Understanding Intelligence

To understand children's intellectual growth and their eventual successes and failures in school, we have to consider both cognitive development and **intelligence.** Cognitive development refers to the increasing knowledge and mental abilities that are seen in children as they get older. Over time, the mind grows both in its contents (that is, knowledge) and in the ability to understand, remember, and use those contents. Such growth results from interactions among maturation, learning, and an increasingly analytic or problem-solving approach to the world. As more complex thinking develops, mental abilities become increasingly interlinked and children are able to use them with increasing flexibility.

Thinking is only one of many cognitive skills, even if the term is often used generically. Before reading the next sentence, take a minute and try to put into words or signs what thinking is, and you will see what I mean—but don't just think about thinking, try to define it. As I look out of my window while writing this paragraph, I can "think" about the scene before me: trees, a birdhouse, a pond, and so on. At the same time, because I am continuing to type while I look outside, I am also thinking about what I am writing. Both of these are conscious levels of thinking, meaning that I am aware of them. I am not really aware of the perceptual and memory skills that allow me to see in three dimensions, to recognize the trees as trees and the geese as geese, or to hit the right keys on the keyboard without looking at them. When we go about our everyday activities in the world, the majority of our thinking is at this unconscious level. Thinking usually is brought into awareness only when we have to solve a new problem or when we do what apparently only humans, of all animals, can do: reflect on our own thought processes.

By the time children are seven years old, they begin to think about their thinking. This level of sophistication might be related to literacy, as reading and writing may allow children to recognize the existence of realities separate from the one they themselves experience. Writing thus can provide a window onto the thinking of others, although people who cannot write nonetheless have very complex thought processes.

Most adults normally do not think about the development of children's thinking, but about the development of more specific aspects of cognition like memory, problem solving, mathematical skills, creativity, and language comprehension. Alternatively, some people think more globally about children's intelligence or IQ. As we take up this topic, it is important to make clear that intelligence and IQ are not the same thing, even if the terms are used that way by most people. For psychologists, the people who invented and are the sacred guardians of intelligence testing, IQ is defined in a seemingly circular fashion as whatever is measured by intelligence tests. Intelligence meanwhile is defined a little more helpfully as the repertoire of abilities that allow an individual to deal flexibly with novel information and situations at a particular age.

These definitions become somewhat clearer if we remember that IQ stands for *intelligence quotient*, a number obtained by dividing a child's mental age, as measured on an IQ test, by the child's actual, chronological age. Of course, we would not judge the intelligence of a five-year-old by the same standards as a twenty-five-year-old, and the intelligence quotient allows us to judge the age level at which someone is functioning in terms of the age level at which they should be functioning using standards obtained from testing large numbers of people at each age. For example, if a child obtains a score exactly at the average for his or her age, and we divide it by the child's age in years (and multiply by 100 so we do not have deal with decimal points), we arrive at an IQ of 100: the average IQ. Scoring at a level of older children, meaning that the mental age is higher than the chronological age, will yield an IQ greater than 100, and scoring at the level of younger children will yield an IQ less than 100.

Finally, it is important to note that IQ is only an *estimate* of intelligence, one that depends of the soundness of the test, the skill of the tester, and the child's understanding and following of the directions. We are now ready to reconsider the issue of intelligence and deaf children. Keep in mind, however, that the ultimate question in all of this should not be what kind of scores deaf children make on intelligence tests, but what they can achieve. I suggest this because it is not at all clear that intelligence tests are tapping the same things in deaf and hearing children—a topic to be discussed below.

Language and Thought

When I think of intelligence in deaf children (or hearing adults or porpoises, for that matter), I think about their ability to take what they already know and apply it in new ways in new situations. In this sense, intelligence depends on—or is—all of the aspects of cognitive development mentioned above: thinking, memory, problem solving, quantitative skills, and communication/language. It is the last item on this list, language, that creates the most complexity for understanding deaf children's intellectual functioning, and we need to deal with it directly. After all, most people assume that intelligence is directly related to language. How can you be intelligent without having language?

For the better part of this century, deaf children, and sometimes deaf adults, were a favorite testing group for educators and psychologists interested in intelligence, precisely because they were presumed to be "without language." The general expectation was that deaf children, or anyone else without language, would be clearly deficient in intelligence or in various aspects of intelligence. One major problem with this assumption is that those investigators typically equated *language* with *spoken language*. Even now, I have met teachers and researchers who, although they deny that language and speech are the same, nevertheless do not believe that sign language is sufficient to allow normal intellectual functioning and therefore assume that deaf children who cannot speak must be intellectually inferior. They are wrong. Readers who have finished the preceding chapters are aware that the equating of language and speech is an error, and that there is no reason to believe that spoken language is qualitatively better than sign language for the purposes of intellectual pursuits. These two ways of expressing language do have somewhat different characteristics and different fortes, but both can communicate essentially the same information. This statement means that children who are fluent in a spoken or signed language should have comparable intellectual abilities. *Fluent* here is meant in an age-appropriate way: Younger children generally are less fluent than older children, but hearing children of hearing parents and deaf children of deaf parents are equally fluent in their native languages at the same age (see Chapter 5).

A more complex situation arises for young deaf children with hearing parents. Such children frequently do not share a common language with others in the family. They do not benefit much from spoken language and their parents do not sign. Therefore, they may not be fluent in any language. The raw material of intelligence will be there, but they will not be fully proficient in using language for acquiring and manipulating facts about the world. It thus becomes important to distinguish between cognitive abilities that do and do not depend on language and decide what it all means in the case of deaf children.

During the early 1900s several studies involving deaf children showed them to lag behind hearing peers in educational progress by about five years. About 40 percent of that lag was seen as due to differences in "intelligence," because deaf students scored about two years behind hearing peers on intelligence tests. The remainder of the educational difference was presumed to result directly from the lack of language experience. During the 1920s and 1930s, therefore, psychologists developed tests of intellectual abilities that were supposedly independent from language (called nonverbal or **performance tests**), explicitly designed for the purpose of better evaluating the mental abilities of deaf children. Such changes notwithstanding, deaf children still generally scored lower than their hearing age-mates, even if the differences were small.

Looking back, it is now clear that many of those early nonverbal tests were not correctly constructed or used, and they may have been biased against anyone who lacked the "normal" sociocultural experiences of hearing, white, middle-class children. That is, they were not culture-fair for deaf children or many others who came from atypical early environments. Since that time, additional tests have been developed that are truly language-independent, meaning that they can be conducted without the necessity of understanding spoken or signed instructions, and culture-independent, at least within clearly stated limits.[1] Even now, when samples of deaf and hearing children are shown to have equivalent IQs according to some particular, usually nonverbal, test, the deaf children often lag behind hearing peers in school-related academic performance. Findings of this sort suggest that there are important factors other than intelligence that influence academic achievement in deaf children, seemingly a logical conclusion. Nonverbal tests may ensure that intelligence measures are not biased by a child's fluency in a particular language, but they do not address the fact that some skills and knowledge that are typically learned *through* language, even if they are separate from it.

Several investigators, myself included, also have suggested that because of differences in deaf children's early experience, there will be real differences between deaf and hearing children in the way that their minds and brains work.[2] These differences may result in different styles of processing information, some of which may be beneficial and some of which may not. Regrettably, such suggestions are frequently interpreted incorrectly to mean that deaf children are doomed to some kind of intellectual deficiency, and the conclusions are thus dismissed out of hand. The issue is actually much more subtle, and the possibility that deaf children might have a different configuration of intellectual abilities than hearing children requires serious consideration. If true, these abilities might well demand particular kinds of educational experiences to optimize deaf children's academic and intellectual growth. The lack of such experiences might explain some shortcomings in the academic achievement of deaf children even when they obtain normal scores on intelligence tests. In addition to being of central importance for promoting the education of deaf children, research on this question would help us to understand the interrelations among language, cognitive development, and social development.

Confounding Factors in Intelligence

THE LANGUAGE ISSUE

Most commonly, when deaf and hearing children are compared on intelligence tests, the focus is on the manipulation or completion of test materials in ways intended to reflect abstract as well as concrete reasoning abilities. On one hand, a reliance on nonverbal tests seems eminently fair, because most deaf children with severe to profound hearing losses are not fluent in English. But if nonverbal tests provide fair and accurate assessments of intelligence, why do we persist in using verbal tests for hearing individuals?

The answer, I believe, is that the "verbal" part of intelligence tests tell us a lot about children's ability to deal flexibly with information, because of the abstract, symbolic nature of language.[3] Sign language-based intelligence tests for deaf children should work just as well as spoken language-based tests for hearing children, if they are appropriately developed and administered. Eliminating verbal abilities (different from vocal abilities) from assessments of deaf children requires acceptance of the fact that we are tapping only one part of intelligence as it is typically understood. Most of what is learned in school settings "comes in" through language, and thus deaf children can achieve high scores on nonverbal tests while still struggling in school. In this case, the IQ tests and the demands placed on children in school settings are different, and one may not be a predictor of the other.

If the presence or absence of language demands in a particular classroom or testing situation was all that mattered, deaf and hearing children would appear comparable in areas that do not require language. Deaf children, however, frequently have difficulty in nonverbal academic tasks, lending support to the earlier suggestion that their learning and behavioral styles may be different from those of hearing peers. Just as important as what is explicitly taught to children is the wealth of knowledge they obtain incidentally, either by overhearing the conversations of others or via informal interactions with adults and other children. Such implicit learning usually will be more frequent in hearing than deaf children because there usually will be more "teachers" around who share a common language. Even when parents and others in a deaf child's environment do know some sign language, they typically use it only when they are directly addressing the child. This situation is very different from the natural language-learning environment of children who share a first language with those around them, and far less effective.

PHYSIOLOGICAL AND PSYCHOLOGICAL CONTRIBUTIONS

Another potentially confusing factor in analyzing of deaf children's intellectual skills is the possibility that any particular deaf child might have some mentally handicapping condition in addition to a hearing loss. For the 50 percent of the deaf population for whom hearing loss is hereditary, such a linkage is unlikely. As outlined in chapter 2, however, some early onset hearing losses are caused by medical conditions that also can have effects on the brain, and these effects may not become apparent until much later. The fact that approximately 30 percent of deaf children have experienced such severe illnesses means that we must be extremely sensitive to learning difficulties that cannot be attributed solely to early environments or language abilities. Early identification and attention to special needs are essential in these cases.

Meanwhile, it occasionally has been suggested that hearing loss, and especially hereditary hearing loss, might confer some intellectual advantages for deaf children. Deaf children with deaf parents tend to score higher on various tests of intellectual ability than deaf children of hearing parents, presumably because they share an early language and a fully rich environment with family members and members of the Deaf community. Interestingly, deaf children with hereditary hearing losses also score higher than deaf children with nonhereditary losses when the effects of early environment are equated. One research team has suggested the possibility that naturally occurring cultural or historical selection factors could have resulted in some kinds of hereditary hearing losses being linked to superior nonverbal intelligence. Another possible explanation of superior functioning by deaf children of deaf parents lies in the ways that their brains develop. Findings from variety of studies suggest that deaf and hearing children raised in signing environments have more balanced right and left sides of their brains (less **hemispheric specialization**) in both language and visual abilities. The result is slightly different organizations in the brains of deaf and hearing children, which may make the best use of potential information available to each (see Note 2).

Unfortunately, such findings raise more questions than they answer, because our understanding of cognition in deaf children, like our understanding of the relations between brain and mind, is still in its infancy. For example, we know that deaf children tend to rely on concrete experience and examples more than hearing age-mates. Is this a product of their educational experiences or does it have some more basic, cognitive or **neuropsychological** origin? An anecdote might make this issue clearer: Recently, a colleague and I were investigating the different problem solving strategies used by deaf and hearing children from age seven to fourteen. We assumed that the older children would perform the task much like adults, but we tested a few deaf college students just to be sure. Although we were right in our assumption, we hit one roadblock: Our experiment focused on how students spontaneously solve problems without any instructions or examples. Several of our student participants nonetheless asked for examples, and they became somewhat agitated when we explained that we could not offer any without defeating the purpose of the experiment. One student even signed, "You have to give examples. Deaf students always get examples!" and he refused to participate. While the strength of his preference for concrete examples may not be typical, the orientation is not unusual among deaf students. The problem is that most people—and parents in particular—would attribute this attitude to the student's being deaf. I don't think that's the reason. Much more likely is that the way that this student was educated, both at home and at school, led to this orientation. In essence, the student has been trained to deal with new information in this relatively specific or concrete manner, at least in part because of the poor communication between him and his parents and teachers. Alternatively, he might have been able to perform the task just fine without any help, but he did not know that and would not try.

This one case aside, it should be obvious that an example-bound approach to the world would affect a child's performance in a variety of social and academic areas. At a specific level, this orientation may explain some of deaf children's apparently concrete orientations as revealed in intelligence tests and other cognitive tasks. At a more general level, it may partially explain why deaf and hearing children frequently appear to differ in the ways they go about solving problems, even if they are equally successful in the end: It may be that the two groups have developed different cognitive styles. The question then becomes how we can teach in a way directed to those skills rather than trying to make deaf children perform more like hearing children. Today most educators believe that political and philosophical aspects of this issue should take a back seat to the question of what leads to better academic success for deaf children. It does not seem to be of any service to the deaf population to ignore the possible role of language skills, signed or spoken, in the ability to deal effectively with problem solving either inside or outside of the classroom. Whether or not deaf children obtain intelligence scores equal to their hearing peers is not the issue. The issue is the need to determine the relative strengths and weaknesses in deaf children's abilities and to develop means of using the former to offset the latter.

Striving for Success

When most educators and researchers talk or write about cognitive development or the intellectual skills of deaf children, they tend to focus on topics like those discussed above: IQ, problem solving, language, and nonverbal performance. Noticeably lacking is any mention of a potent factor recognized by parents and teachers but not often investigated in this regard: motivation to achieve. If deaf children are to succeed academically, occupationally, and in life in general, both they and their parents have to be sufficiently motivated to overcome obstacles related directly or indirectly to hearing loss during childhood. Studies involving hearing children have shown that parents' spending time with their children, facilitating their academic and extracurricular interests, and answering their questions in supportive environments all foster academic excellence as well as emotional maturity. Similarly, families' constant support of deaf children's endeavors have been shown to lead to higher levels of achievement in academic domains. Such encouragement may not be as frequent for deaf children in hearing families because of communication barriers, and some parents are simply unable to sustain the will and energy that may be necessary for meeting their deaf child's special needs. This is not to imply that they are bad parents. It is simply an acknowledgement that having a special child can be difficult and require a special kind of parent.

Deaf children's successful experiences, whether in school, in making a cardboard box into a fort, or in a social encounter, build on each other. Discovering that they can accomplish a particular task motivates children to try similar and sometimes more difficult tasks. Success really does breed success, because the emotional and physical benefits of success motivate us to strive for more. Those individuals who are more motivated therefore achieve more, and those who achieve more are more motivated. As noted earlier, an essential component of this process is that children have to notice that the outcomes of achievement-related behaviors are self-produced. This relation is apparent in the fact that intellectually achieving hearing children are more likely to believe that they have control over their academic success, and they are more independent than hearing peers who are less successful. Achievement and independence, meanwhile, are two dimensions on which deaf children tend to vary more widely and frequently lag behind hearing age-mates.

The relative lack of achievement by deaf children in academics has often been linked to their apparent tendency to behave in a less reflective, forward-thinking manner than hearing children and frequent failures to generalize information learned in one context to other situations in which it is applicable. True, reading, writing, and math involve some abstract kinds of knowledge, but the benefits of having such skills also may be viewed very differently by deaf children than by hearing children. We know, for example, that deaf children generally spend less time studying than hearing peers, but we don't know whether this is because they tend to have fewer demands placed on them or because they are less invested in achieving success in these areas. We also know that deaf children with more positive attitudes toward communication tend to be higher achievers. That could be because they are more positively disposed to learning in general, because they also tend to have higher self-esteem, or because they are more likely to have positive experiences in particular areas such as interpersonal interactions or reading than children who have poorer communication skills. Deaf children who are more **reflective** rather than **impulsive** in their approaches to learning and problem solving also tend to do better in school (see Chapter 9). This link is not surprising, insofar as most school learning requires problem solving of one sort or another. Impulsive behavior is unlikely to lead to long-term solutions to problems either in the classroom or on the playground. Most interesting, perhaps, is the way in which high self-esteem, an internal **locus of control**, and academic success come together when families are accepting and supportive of deaf children.

Several studies have suggested that one of the most potent predictors of educational success for deaf children is the amount of personalized attention a child receives.[4] This relation was perhaps first seen in Spain during the 1600s and 1700s, when children had to be literate in order to inherit the wealth of their parents. Parents of deaf children engaged private tutors to teach their heirs how to read and write, and pursuits in other areas followed. Similarly, studies in the United States over the last twenty years have shown the benefits of intensive, one-on-one education for deaf students as well as hearing students. Such environments, with qualified and high-quality teachers, allow the optimal match between students' skills and needs and their exposure to new material. Few families, however, can afford such education. The fact that there are over 135,000 deaf and hard-of-hearing children in the United States makes the cost of private tutors prohibitive for public school. Providing private teachers just for the 68,000 students currently enrolled in special programs for deaf students would cost between $2 billion and $4 billion per year. That is more than ten times the amount of money spent each year on public education in the entire state of New York!

Creativity and Flexibility

Earlier in this chapter, I suggested that one of the most important aspects of intelligence is the ability to adapt to new situations. Whether we are thinking about learning physics, understanding a poem, getting along in a new school, or learning to fix an automobile engine, intelligent people are those who can apply their knowledge in new ways in new situations and go beyond what they already know. Sometimes, the range of possible new situations will be smaller or better defined, for example, the number of things that can be wrong with a carburetor. In others, it may be larger and less well defined, for example, ways to bring peace to the world. In either case, we have to be able to reason from what is known to what is unknown or desired. That is, we have to be creative and flexible.

If creativity and flexibility are hallmarks of intelligence, they are also areas in which deaf children have traditionally been seen as lacking, at least if one reads the literature aimed at their teachers. Meanwhile, in the book *Deaf Persons in the Arts and Sciences: A Biographical Dictionary* Harry Lang and Bonnie Meath-Lang provide accounts of numerous deaf artists, musicians, writers, and scientists who achieved eminence in fields that demand creativity. Clearly, we need to examine the issue further if we want to understand this apparent contradiction.

WHAT IS CREATIVITY?

Historically, characterizations of deaf children as literal and concrete in language and cognitive functioning derived from observations indicating that deaf children tend to lag behind hearing peers in their abilities to grasp complex or abstract concepts. Most frequently, however, assessments of deaf children's cognitive flexibility were made using English-based materials such as written compositions or standardized tests. It therefore is unclear to what extent reported lags in such abilities reflect language-specific difficulties rather than more general limitations on cognitive development. Deaf children have as *much* experience as hearing children, but we have already seen that they may have different *kinds* of experience than hearing children. These differences, in turn, may affect the ways in which they function in educational, experimental, or day-to-day settings that require flexibility and creativity. Note that *affect* does not necessarily mean *impair* here, and we have already seen the great resilience of children faced with less-than-ideal early environments. Nevertheless, within some educational settings, deaf children are not expected to exhibit much diversity or creativity in thinking. They thus may have language and cognitive abilities just as creative and flexible as hearing peers, but these qualities may not be easily tapped by the usual assessments involving the reading or writing of English. Luckily, there are a variety of nonverbal tests of creativity available, and for various reasons (some of them based on the misguided equating of speech and language) they have been used extensively with deaf children.

Among researchers who study creativity, there is some debate over exactly what it is, whether it can be learned, and whether it is an ability, an achievement, a disposition, or a strategy. For the present purposes, these issues are largely irrelevant, and I will simply accept two definitions of creativity. First is the psychological definition, one that fits nicely with the definition of intelligence adopted above: Creativity is the process of becoming aware of a need for objects or information, searching for solutions, and producing a result. Second is the artistic kind of creativity: Creativity is the expression of emotion, beauty, or new ideas through the invention of new things or the novel rearrangement of old things.

NONVERBAL CREATIVITY OF DEAF CHILDREN

As we found earlier in the discussion of intelligence, nonverbal measures of creativity generally indicate that deaf children are more competent than is suggested by language-based measures. Recent evidence, for example, indicates that young deaf children show considerable creativity and imagination in their play, an area that is popular in studies of hearing children's creativity and intellectual flexibility. Communication abilities of deaf children and their parents seem to be an important predictor of success here, even when nonverbal behavior is observed. That is, investigations have suggested that hearing children, as a group, show somewhat more creative and imaginative play than deaf children do as a group. However, when only those deaf children with good mother-child communication are considered, the difference disappears. This result could have several causes, but they all relate to the fact that better-communicating mother-child pairs will have engaged in more complex and creative play than mothers and children who do not communicate well. Those children thus become more "skilled" in play and are likely to transfer their learning to situations in which they play with others. At the same time, play teaches children a lot about rules, about causes and effects, about objects that are played with, and about other peoples' perceptions and beliefs. Play clearly can be creative, and creative play leads to increased creativity.

Mothers also affect their deaf children's creativity by taking or giving up control during play. Recall that hearing mothers of deaf children were earlier described as more directive and less permissive than deaf mothers of deaf children or hearing mothers of hearing children. These characteristics can be seen when they are playing with their deaf children, as hearing mothers may try to direct activities and games where they would not do so with hearing children. In those situations, the mothers also tend to be less flexible, less encouraging, and less imaginative than they are when playing with hearing children. Better-educated mothers, however, are more likely to treat deaf and hearing children equally during play.

In addition to studies of play, deaf children's nonverbal creativity also has been studied using standardized creativity tests, similar to the tests used to measure intelligence. When we glean those studies that appear to have been correctly conducted and interpreted from the many that have not, deaf children do quite well, even though the tests were originally designed with hearing children in mind. Some studies even suggest that deaf children, at least in the eleven- to twelve-year-old range, are more flexible in their non-verbal thinking (for example, in construction tasks) than hearing age-mates. Others have indicated that deaf children can learn to be more creative within particular test contexts. The extent to which such learning occurs in natural situations and the characteristics of the situation that make such learning more or less likely remain to be determined.

VERBAL CREATIVITY OF DEAF CHILDREN

Because of the importance given to the link between language and cognition, much more research has been conducted concerning verbal than non-verbal creativity. Nonetheless, it is still surprising how little attention has been given to deaf schoolchildren's verbal creativity, especially in books intended for their teachers. This is likely due to the common assumption that deaf children have little verbal creativity to evaluate. That assumption is clearly wrong. Conclusions about deaf children's lack of creativity in language have largely been based on observations of their flexibility within English. Although the need for literacy in English is a laudable goal for an educational system that seeks quality education for deaf children, drawing conclusions about their cognitive and language abilities on the basis of their performance in English is likely to underestimate those abilities. Assessment of deaf children's verbal creativity thus should be seen as a somewhat different enterprise from assessment of their capabilities within any particular language. In particular, we need to consider their comprehension and production capabilities in sign language as well as English.

Studies of deaf children's verbal creativity based on their skills in English have found that those children with better English skills, spoken or written, appear more creative. On average, however, deaf children will not perform as well as hearing children on English-based tests of creativity, if only because hearing children have much more experience in the language than deaf peers. Certainly, there are exceptions to this assertion, but the generalization is as valid as it is obvious. Similarly, I know that I am not seen as very creative when I write in Italian, and would never dream of writing anything in that language other than scientific papers, which tend to be rather dry and stuffy anyway.

One alternative means of evaluating deaf children's verbal creativity involves examination of their use or their comprehension and production of figurative language—expressions like *dry and stuffy*. Do deaf children, or even hearing children, understand such phrases? Figurative language is assumed by educators and psychologists to reflect both verbal and nonverbal flexibility, as well as a general ability to consider the world from alternative perspectives—again, an essential component of intelligence. More specifically, figurative-language abilities depend on the ability to see abstract relations across different domains. If deaf children were as cognitively rigid as some investigators have reported, they would not be expected to either comprehend or produce figurative language. Consistent with that view, several studies during the 1970s found that deaf children did not understand English expressions like *knowing it by heart* or *looking a gift horse in the mouth*. Notice, however, that most children learn these kinds of figurative expressions from their families, teachers, or peers; they normally would not have to figure them out for themselves. The spontaneous use of such expressions is a sign of fluency in English, or whatever language the expression is drawn from, and does not really tell us very much about deaf children's verbal creativity per se. More recent studies, therefore, have looked at deaf children's use of figurative language within sign language.

Usually, such studies have examined the stories that deaf children tell on fantasy themes like what it would be like if animals and people changed places, but similar results are obtained when they describe less interesting day-to-day events. At the outset, such studies are interesting because they have shown deaf children to be very skilled in telling stories within sign language, even if some of them have trouble with writing stories in English. In fact, both their signed stories and their written stories are generally very well structured, consisting of all of the elements that make up good stories: settings, goals, actions to achieve goals, occasional barriers to success and ways to get around them, and conclusions (see Chapter 7). At least from eight years of age onward, deaf and hearing children's written stories are fully comparable in this sense, even if they differ in the quality of their English vocabulary and structure.

Deaf children's signed stories are interesting not only because they have good story structure, but also because they contain a wealth of figurative language. We have now recorded stories told by dozens of deaf and hearing children, and time after time we find that the deaf children are at least as creative as their hearing peers, and sometimes more so. Part of this creativity comes from the fact that deaf children are more skilled with the creative tools of sign language than they are with the creative tools of English. They use gestures, pantomime, and creative modifications of existing signs much more frequently than hearing children use gestures, pantomime, and creative modifications of words. Just as importantly, deaf children use and create the same kinds of figures of speech as hearing children, but they do it in sign language. For example, we have seen deaf children refer to people as being like birds, insects, machines, and monsters, and they do so just as often as hearing children. In short, as in other areas, deaf and hearing children show different kinds of verbal creativity, but the two groups are more similar than they are different. Deaf children do not appear any less creative than their hearing peers when they are evaluated in ways that are unbiased with respect to their language and experience.

Summary

Early investigations of deaf children's thinking skills routinely found them to lag behind hearing peers by several years. The tests used in those studies often required comprehension of English, and many confused language and intelligence. More recently, a variety of intelligence tests and other tests of cognitive ability have been developed that depend only on nonverbal performance measures. Although there are still differences observed between deaf and hearing children, these often are more qualitative than quantitative.

The question of whether language is independent of intelligence or IQ scores is made more confusing rather than clearer by evaluation of deaf children. The problem is that those deaf children who are most lacking in language abilities are also likely to be different from other deaf children and hearing children in other ways, including the diversity of their early experiences and the quality of their relationships with parents and peers. Carefully constructed performance tests sometimes have eliminated differences between deaf and hearing children, but in other cases, differences have remained. Such findings indicate that there are factors beyond communication that contribute to children's intellectual development. They also rule out any simple link between language and cognitive abilities in deaf children.

This chapter reviewed a variety of evidence concerning verbal and nonverbal creativity of deaf children. In general, in both nonverbal and verbal areas, deaf children often appear just as creative as their hearing peers. Factors that hinder deaf children's creativity include excessive control by adults, lack of communication and interaction with teachers and parents, and less diversity in early experiences than hearing age-mates enjoy. Deaf children appear less creative than hearing children when they are evaluated using printed materials. When evaluated in terms of their sign language production, however, deaf children are found to be just as creative as their hearing peers. These findings support the hypothesis that deaf children have great intellectual and creative potential that may not be easily tapped by testing in English or other spoken-written languages.

Because individual differences among deaf children are so large, more evidence is necessary before we can make any generalizations about their intellectual development or creative processes. What evidence is available nonetheless strongly indicates that they are far more capable than earlier books and reports suggest. Although the charge that they are more "concrete" than hearing peers may be warranted for some deaf children in some domains, the reasons for that characteristic may be due more to the way in which they have been educated than to anything directly related to their being deaf.

Notes

1. To clarify what is meant by culture-fair tests, consider the following example. One might expect that tests that involve the rearrangement of geometric shapes or construction of objects using blocks would be universally appropriate for testing the intelligence of young children. However, there are cultures in the world where there are very few right angles, in which geometric shapes have little relevance, and in which children do not have experience with things like Tinker Toys, Lego, or bricks. Tests involving such materials therefore would not be measuring the same things that they measure in children living in New York City and may not be culture-fair for individuals without such experience.

2. The suggestion that deaf and hearing people's brains may be different is not meant metaphorically. We know, for example, that rats raised in rich environments, with objects and places to explore, have many more interconnections in their brains than rats that are raised in relatively sterile environments. Similar differences would be expected in human brains. In addition, different parts of the brain will be used more or less in particular situations depending on the kinds and amounts of information they have encountered in the past, and enhanced brain activity in some areas has been identified in both deaf children and hearing children raised in homes where ASL is the dominant language.

3. *Verbal* should not be confused with *vocal* here. The use of *verbal* in *verbal intelligence* refers to language. Most intelligence tests consist of verbal and non-verbal (performance) parts and some yield separate scores for verbal intelligence and nonverbal intelligence.

4. The important ingredient here most likely is not the one-on-one situation per se, but its promotion of greater time-on-task activity. Traditionally, in-depth, continued attention to communication and educational topics was maximized for deaf students through personal tutors. Computers in education now may provide a far a less expensive alternative.

9

Deaf Children to Deaf Adults

*I never met a deaf adult when I was a kid, so I always assumed that I
would be able to hear when I grew up. I was shocked when I started at
a school for the deaf and saw teachers and houseparents with hearing
aids! Wow! They were just like me! It really changed the way I
thought of myself and about being deaf.*

Marvin, a Deaf accountant

Chapters 1 and 4 explored the beginnings of social development in deaf
children during the first months of life. The focus there was primarily on
the early interactions between infants and their parents, which were also
shown to have a role as the foundation for later social development. The
present chapter moves beyond infancy and the influences of particular
individuals to consider the ways that deaf children develop socially and
emotionally as they pass through the school years and into adulthood.[1] In
this context, we can look at the influences of early social interactions on later
social behavior, but we also have to consider the skills and preferences that
children acquire during the early years—characteristics that help to make
up their personalities. Throughout the chapter it will be useful to keep in
mind that we are discussing general observations and broad but imprecise
statements about social and emotional functioning. Not all deaf children
will fit these stereotypes, and they are not meant to be prescriptive for any
particular child or family. Similarly, because children and families vary
widely, the rules, customs, and behaviors that any child learns in the home
will not always apply to social situations outside of the home, and those
learned in the immediate neighborhood may not apply in school. These differences may be even more pronounced for deaf children, and particularly
deaf children of hearing parents.

Differences in the generality or relevance of social rules for deaf and
hearing children can result from the fact that deaf children tend to have

fewer playmates during the early years, from their parents having more restrictive rules for behavior, or from parents not being as able to communicate expectations about social interactions. For example, it is common to see a teacher or parent react to one hearing child hitting another by saying something like "Janie, don't hit Jonathan. How does it feel when someone hits you? It hurts, doesn't it? You wouldn't like it if Jonathan hit you, would you?" This kind of response is more likely to lead to positive changes in behavior than spanking or yelling "Stop that!" at the child, and it begins the process of internalizing the rules and expectations of the society.

Parents who do not share a common, fluent language with their children cannot engage in such moral teaching as effectively as parents who do. Their children are not as likely to learn the reasons for social rules at home. This is not to say that deaf children will be any less polite or well behaved than hearing children or that parents need to have any special tools for bringing up their deaf children. Quite the contrary: Deaf children will learn about social interactions and will develop personality characteristics in precisely the same way as hearing children. The important issues are who their teachers and role models will be, and how the children see themselves as part of the social world. Growing up is hard enough when it comes to friends, social pressure, falling in love, and "doing the right thing." Growing up deaf adds some extra dimensions.

Personality and Emotional Growth during the School Years

Deaf children from deaf families often are more comfortable socially than deaf children from hearing families. Children from deaf families are likely to have had a wider range of social interactions within the Deaf community, and they will have experienced greater understanding and acceptance from others inside and outside the family. Deaf children of deaf parents also are more likely than those with hearing parents to have experienced consistent parenting behaviors and effective communication from an early age. Social interactions with deaf individuals outside of the immediate family thus are more likely to be similar to those within the family. Partly as a result of this consistency, deaf children of deaf families tend to have relatively greater social confidence, self-esteem, and a greater sense of being in control of their own lives. This latter characteristic, known as locus of control, is an important predictor of academic as well as social and career success and has surfaced at various points in other chapters. Deaf children of hearing parents can be just as confident and secure as those of deaf parents, but it may require more conscious planning by hearing parents to ensure that their children have the right kind of personality-building experiences.

As young children become more social, the variety of their relationships with family, peers, and other adults (including teachers) increases far beyond that established with their parents and other family members. Most children will naturally be attracted to other people who will serve both emotional and practical roles in their lives. That is, all children have a need to be liked and emotionally close to others, and so they seek approval and affection from adults and, later, from peers. At the same time, they often depend on others to help them or show them how to achieve their goals. Both of these kinds of attention-seeking are referred to as dependence, and they are normal and healthy parts of children's (and adults') personalities. Even children who are said to be independent still display appropriate dependence, but they blend dependent behavior in some situations with self-reliance and assertiveness. Children who are overly dependent on others may not feel in control of their own lives and are said to have an external locus of control. Children who blend independent and dependent behavior and feel "in control" are said to have an internal locus of control.

Children who are physically or psychologically challenged are likely to encounter difficulties in establishing their independence. In part, their need for more assistance from others is a real one, with the kind and extent of such help varying with the nature of the child's handicap. Nonetheless, the frequent overprotection of handicapped children by well-meaning adults creates further barriers to social independence and physical competence, as the children are often able to perform a variety of tasks that others typically do for them. The resulting social immaturity could have been avoided. As Kathryn Meadow-Orlans, a prominent researcher in the field, once noted:

> Parents generalize from the narrow range of tasks that the handicapped child actually cannot do, and assume that there is a much larger spectrum of tasks of which he is incapable. Eventually, the assumed inability becomes a real inability because the child does not have the opportunity to practice tasks and develop new levels of expertise. In addition, it takes more patience and time for handicapped children to perform the trial-and-error process of skill acquisition—time and patience that parents may not have or be willing to give. For deaf children with deficient communication skills, it takes additional time and patience merely to communicate what is expected, required, and necessary for the performance of even a simple task.

Meadow-Orlans's suggestion concerning the importance of effective communication between deaf children and their parents and peers is supported by observations of researchers and teachers in a variety of settings. Because they typically receive fewer explanations for the causes of other people's social and emotional behaviors, deaf children may have more difficulty controlling their own behavior and learning from social experience. Communication barriers also may cause deaf children and adolescents to have less knowledge about social rules, and their lack of social skills may impede the development of independence and self-esteem. Yet another hurdle for social development is the fact that deaf children often lack social role models with whom they can identify and communicate. All of these factors help us to explain the observation that deaf children of deaf parents have greater social maturity than those of hearing parents. Nonetheless, we have to remember that descriptions of whole groups as socially mature or socially immature are broad generalizations, and that many deaf children are just as socially and behaviorally adjusted as hearing children of the same ages.

As in other areas, some children are faster or slower social learners. Some will have families that are more or less instructive with regard to social interactions outside of the home. Deaf children are often seen to be more involved with their families than are hearing children in hearing families. In some sense, family interactions are more important for deaf children than for hearing children, because a greater percentage of their social experience happens with family members than with others outside the home. This makes family members very important as role models. Role modeling plays a central role in development, helping children to learn about different roles, about their cultural heritage, about the values and morals of their family and community, and about more specific things like religion, politics, preferences for particular sports teams, and favorite foods. The ability to identify with others and to model their behavior first depends on children believing that they are similar to the model. Boys, for example, learn how to act like boys by watching their fathers and other boys, not by watching their mothers and older sisters. As children discover ways they are like others, they try to act like them and think like them, eventually developing similar likes and dislikes. Finding that their parents have the same last name as they do or that they look like one of their parents can contribute to this development in the same way that sharing cultural or ethnic characteristics often makes children act more like others with similar backgrounds.[2]

Perhaps an example will help to make the general point: When I was growing up, my family did not have a strong distinction between "girl" things and "boy" things. We were all involved in cooking, cleaning, painting, fixing, and so on. It was primarily my father who taught me to sew and to cook, and with him as my role model, both activities became very natural for me (I now do both more often, if not better, than my wife). A colleague of mine was eager to have his two daughters grow up the same way, and so he made a point of having them help him paint the house and taking them out into the garage to build things with him or work on the family car. It did *not* work. Why? Probably because it was their father who always did the "boy" things with his daughters. If their mother had built the bird houses with them and their father had taught them to cook (as my father did with me), perhaps the gender roles would have seemed more flexible. As it is, they are both wonderful teenagers, but they are not very interested in the kinds of activities that we think of as being done by males.

Modeling plays an important role in giving children a sense of identity, both as individuals and as part of a larger community. By sharing characteristics with others in their family or their community, they come to see themselves as part of a group, as *belonging* (see the quote at the top of this chapter and Note 2). Deaf children in hearing families will have a sense of family identity, but their sense of being part of the larger community often will be colored by whether or not they know other deaf people. Deaf children normally will learn about Deaf culture only by being around Deaf children and Deaf adults, and that is why the Deaf community sees residential schools as so important.

Living with Parents and Peers

Early language experience for deaf children has been shown to have a significant impact on their personalities and emotional development, just as it does with hearing children. Most research in this area has focused on the benefits of early exposure to sign language, but the important thing is to have consistent two-way communication, regardless of whether it is spoken or signed. For example, studies have shown that children enrolled in preschool intervention programs utilizing Total Communication are more likely to respond appropriately to their mothers' requests and use far more communication with them during play (see Chapter 6). These interactions tend to be longer, more relaxed, and more gratifying on both sides. Deaf children who have established good communicative and social relationships within the family thus will be better equipped to venture out into the social world.

Thinking back to the school years and our social lives during that time, many adults agree that they were the best of times and the worst of times. There are many fond memories of friends and events, but there were also many conflicting pressures (and most people say they would not want to go through them again). We were supposed to act like individuals, but we also wanted to fit in with the crowd. We were supposed to be successful in academics, but also liked by others. As school and our school friends became major social influences, we started to accept the values of our peers and our role models, sometimes even when those values were in conflict with values of our families. During the school years, we had to face problems of self-esteem, gender identity, and of trying to figure out who we were and what we wanted. Sometimes, it seemed that our parents were not much help.

Deaf children encounter all of the same social problems and find the same social solutions as other children. Depending on their environments, they also might face other challenges. In a public school setting, for example, being deaf makes them different, and parents who think being different in school does not matter are forgetting a lot about their own youth. In residential school or day school programs, deaf children find others who are like them, but the hearing world is still all around them. Chapter 6 described the impact of residential and mainstream settings on deaf children's social adjustment. In general, the evidence indicates that students in mainstream programs tend to feel more isolated and lonely than students in residential schools.

When children share common characteristics and attitudes with others, when they are part of a group, their self-esteem grows. A variety of studies have examined the self-esteem of deaf children and identified factors that promote or hinder its development. Most generally, it is now well documented that deaf and hearing children do not differ, overall, in their self-esteem, a finding that holds from age three all the way through college. Deaf children with multiple handicaps do have lower self-esteem than those who do not, but they are no different from hearing children with multiple handicaps. Deaf children whose parents are better signers have been shown to have higher self-esteem than children whose parents do not sign as well, and for this and other reasons cited above, deaf children of deaf parents have higher self-esteem than deaf children of hearing parents. Deaf children enrolled in Total Communication programs also tend to have higher self-esteem than children in programs that focus on spoken language, but the extent to which this is a consequence of communication skill per se rather than improved social relations or other factors is unclear. Similarly, deaf children in residential schools have higher self-esteem than children in mainstream programs (a finding that may surprise advocates of inclusion), although the reasons for that relation are undoubtedly complex.

For this and other reasons, most Deaf adults believe that residential schools are a vital source of social growth for deaf children, and available findings linking social development to school placement make it difficult to make a case for any other school setting. Hearing proponents of mainstreaming and inclusion sometimes argue that the "artificial" nature of such schools might result in a narrow view of social responsibility and social interaction, but there is no support for such a position from existing research. Moreover, the fact that many hearing parents do not have fluent communication with their deaf children means that the socialization they receive at home can also be rather narrow, and it is difficult to know which situation would be better or worse for any particular child. The apparent advantages of residential or day school programs for deaf children's social development do not supersede their need for a secure family life. Nevertheless, special programs represent a fertile ground for social interactions with peers and deaf adults that go beyond what is available in most homes and preschool programs. In that setting, deaf children will have more playmates and more communication during play than they will in public schools. They also will be less overprotected and intruded upon by well-meaning adults. Some of the benefits of the larger social circle gained in residential or day school settings may seem trivial: things like going to the mall with a group of friends, telling jokes in the hallway, and flirting on the playground. But I think that the importance of those behaviors for normal social and personality development during the school years cannot be ignored. This kind of experience leads directly to children's acquisition of an accurate assessment of their personal strengths and weaknesses (**self-image**), leadership skills, and self-esteem. These characteristics, in turn, play an important role in children's desire for achievement and eventual success in academic and social settings.

Clearly, the most important part of raising a deaf child is trying to give them as normal a childhood as possible. Social, language, and educational experiences all enter into the normal mix, but *normal* does not mean *business as usual*. As I cautioned earlier, having a deaf child affects the whole family, and a deaf child in a mainstream setting affects the entire class. This means that some day-to-day activities may have to change if deaf children are to have access to the experiences and opportunities available to hearing children.

Influences of Brothers and Sisters

Most people who have brothers or sisters recognize that siblings have an effect on each other's personalities and development. In general, siblings are less emotionally tied to each other than they are to their parents, and they thus can serve as confidants and behavior-modifying critics for one another.

Siblings observe and evaluate each other in ways that can contribute to social growth and maturity. They also learn from each other and share resources in a variety of contexts. They can protect each other from emotional or physical harm and serve as a buffer between each other and the parents or outside world. They can make life simpler or more complex, more comfortable or more difficult.

We actually know very little about how sibling relationships might be affected when one child is deaf. Some changes will be subtle, others not so subtle, and all will vary depending on the parents' ability to adjust to having a deaf child. When the parents accept their deaf child, they are more likely to help their other children come to an acceptance of their deaf sibling. Hearing siblings of deaf children, nonetheless, sometimes become angry and resentful toward their deaf siblings. In addition to normal sibling rivalry during childhood, hearing siblings may be frustrated at the lack of communication in the family and at first may not understand what it means to be deaf. Hearing siblings may be jealous of the increased attention that a deaf child receives from their parents and upset at sometimes having to act like caretakers, explaining to people outside of the family that their brother or sister is deaf. At other times, the relationships may be seamless, and deaf and hearing siblings may have especially warm feelings for each other. Positive relationships among deaf and hearing siblings provide deaf children with social and emotional support as well as encouragement in dealing with the implications of their hearing losses outside of the home. Hearing siblings, for example, can serve as helpful resources in social as well as academic contexts. Deaf children with hearing siblings thus often show better social skills than deaf children with no hearing siblings.

With regard to the effects of siblings on deaf children's communication abilities, it is important to note that the quality and quantity of communication in a family with only one deaf child will be considerably different from that of a family with more deaf children. Consider first the situation where there is only one deaf child in an otherwise hearing family, the most common situation.[3] On average, deaf children appear to have more active communication with their hearing siblings than with their hearing parents. Hearing siblings are often more likely to use signed and nonsign gestural communication than their hearing parents, who often try to focus on spoken communication. Hearing siblings thus may serve as intermediaries between deaf children and their parents as well as with people outside of the family. Their possible interpreter role aside, older siblings will provide models of language use, allowing deaf children to "practice" communicating. Deaf children accordingly tend to achieve higher communicative functioning when they have older siblings, either deaf or hearing.

If sharing some mode of communication (either spoken, signed, or a combination) with deaf and hearing siblings has positive consequences for both deaf children and their families, the absence of a common language between siblings can lead either to negative consequences or to the failure to benefit from a potentially positive family setting. For example, it may be too difficult for hearing children to explain to their deaf siblings what is going on in a particular context, how to play a game, or why there is an argument between them. Hearing siblings thus may cut short or avoid more complex social interactions, even if they are on good terms with their deaf siblings. This reduced interaction will not only have a direct effect on social interaction, is will affect the learning of social skills and the ability to resolve conflicts.

Consider now the situation where there are several deaf children in the same family. Such families are likely to have histories of deaf members, indicating hereditary causes of hearing loss (see Chapter 2). Such families not only will tend to be more accepting of people who are deaf, but they are more likely to accept gestural and signed communication, and may have considerable sign skills. In the promotion of social growth, there is likely to be a considerable difference between a hearing family with only one deaf child, who will tend to be the center of family attention, and a family with several deaf children, which will function more naturally. Growing up with deaf siblings provides a rich environment for modeling and all of the typical characteristics of sibling relationships. Although more research needs to be done, what we know so far indicates that these relationships have only positive effects on deaf children, both socially and cognitively.

Understanding the Feelings and Values of Others

The ability to consider the feelings of other people is intertwined with both social and cognitive development. Over time, children learn to balance social roles, the feelings and goals of others, and the values that their families and culture place on different kinds of behavior. To behave in a socially appropriate way, children have to consider alternative perspectives in social situations, and role taking therefore is an essential component of mature social functioning.

Traditionally, deaf individuals, and deaf children in particular, have been described as having difficulty taking the perspective of others, thus being emotionally egocentric, lacking in empathy, and insensitive to the needs of those around them.[4] Such reports are common in the literature, but they often overlook the fact that role-taking ability is strongly related to children's language skills. That is, children who have the benefits of early communication are better able to consider the perspectives of others in social situations, probably because they have gotten more explanations of the causes and effects of behavior. Among such children, any delays observed in their role-taking ability during the preschool years tend to disappear by the middle school years.

Children's understanding the perspectives of others and of their culture is an important part of deciding what is right and what is wrong. Moral development requires that children understand the reasons for avoiding bad behaviors and performing good behaviors. Punishment and rewards can also accomplish this at some superficial level, but unless children internalize the values of the family and society, the effects are often short-lived and limited in generality. When children truly understand how others view their behavior, they are more likely and more able to try to follow social rules. Moral development thus is related to role taking and, more generally, to children's cognitive development. Research studies over the past twenty years have shown that deaf children lag behind hearing children in their abilities to judge other people's behavior in terms of their intentions rather than the outcome. For example, they might see a child who accidentally breaks a dish while trying to help in the kitchen as being just as bad as the child who intentionally breaks a dish in a fit of anger. Deaf children are also more likely to behave out of fear of punishment rather than because they understand the principles underlying appropriate behavior. As a result, they may be more likely than hearing age-mates to be disruptive in school or to get into trouble if they think they can get away with it. Unfortunately, for reasons cited above, deaf children may also be more likely than hearing children to misjudge their chances of getting caught.

Any explanation of the above behaviors needs to take into account the social and cultural context in which they occur. For example, hearing parents may have fewer opportunities to teach their deaf children the family's rules or the culture's morals directly. They also tend to give in to their deaf children's demands when they lack sufficient communication skill to explain the reasons for delays or for denying children something they want. These children will experience inconsistency in responses to their actions when behavior permitted at home is not allowed in school or neighborhood play settings. Such inconsistency often leads to resistance to parental values by the time children reach the middle school years, thus accelerating the movement to identification with peers (regardless of whether peers model acceptable or unacceptable conduct). The resulting behavior will further affect socialization and may be interpreted as indicating underlying psychological problems if it is consistently negative. While there are certainly many more factors that affect the mental health of either deaf or hearing children, the ways they behave in interpersonal interactions are often a primary indicator of psychological well-being or psychological difficulties from the perspectives of concerned parents and teachers. We thus now consider mental health issues in more detail.

Mental Health in Deaf Children and Deaf Adults

In the previous section, we saw that deaf children may lag behind hearing children in recognizing the reasons for other people's behavior, in part because deaf children are less likely than hearing peers to receive explanations for other people's social behaviors. As a result, deaf children might not always understand why people respond to them the way they do. One investigation involving seven- to eight-year-olds, for example, showed that the deaf children were less successful than hearing peers in matching faces showing different emotions with emotionally-related scenes. The deaf children understood and could name the emotions on the faces, but they had trouble connecting the emotions with the right contexts. Findings of this sort suggest that deaf children might sometimes behave inappropriately or misunderstand others' behavior in ways that can lead to perceptions of emotional difficulty. For example, some people believe that deaf children (and adults) tend to act more immaturely or aggressively than hearing peers. In particular, deaf children are often said to be more disruptive and more impulsive in school, whereas deaf adults are sometimes described generally as oversensitive, depressed, or even paranoid. Is there any truth to these descriptions? As in most areas, the research findings on this issue are mixed and the conclusions we draw may depend on the assumptions we have when we start. Perhaps most importantly, there is a long history of misdiagnosing hearing loss in children as mental retardation, autism, or other psychological disturbances. Mistakes like these are disgraceful and potentially devastating for deaf children and their families, but they do occur. Clearly, they reflect a lack of information about hearing loss on the part of parents, pediatricians, and teachers. Beyond such confusions, however, there is a variety of factors that may put deaf children at risk for psychological stress.

ARE DEAF CHILDREN IMPULSIVE?

Perhaps the most common psychological problem attributed to deaf children is impulsivity. The term *impulsivity* has two closely related meanings. Normally, we apply the word *impulsive* to people who seem to act without thinking, usually behaving in a way that seems to satisfy their immediate desires without concern for others or for long-term implications. Considering this everyday kind of impulsivity, educators and researchers have claimed that deaf children's behavior often shows a desire for immediate gratification. This need is reflected either in an inability to wait for what they want or a willingness to settle for less if they get it sooner rather than getting what they really want later. In deaf children, such behavior is often attributed to the lack of early language interaction with hearing parents and teachers, who may not understand what a deaf child is asking for or may not be able to explain why children cannot have what they want when they want it. Although other possible explanations for impulsive behavior are considered below, hearing parents of deaf children frequently do yield to demands for attention, assistance, or objects in order to avoid the possibility of temper tantrums. Part of the problem is that once such an episode starts, parents might not have sufficient communication skill to be able to stop it.[5] That is, without enough language proficiency to relate the present to the past and to the future, hearing parents unintentionally might be teaching their children that dependence and demands will be immediately rewarded. This attitude may then be carried over into the classroom, where deaf children are more likely than hearing children to "act up" and get in trouble.

So much for the common use of *impulsive*. When psychologists use that term to describe a child, they normally are not referring to how children behave on the playground, but to the way they solve problems. From the psychological perspective, impulsivity is one end of an impulsivity-reflectivity dimension, one of several dimensions that comprise a child's cognitive style. Although the standard tests of impulsivity-reflectivity examine cognitive or academic problem solving, the underlying dimension also relates to social problem solving. Impulsivity and reflectivity are most easily seen in the trade-off between speed and accuracy in doing a task or in making a decision. Tests for younger children generally involve choosing which of several pictures is the same as or different from a target picture. For preschoolers, this might involve a target picture of a bear and a child's having to choose from among pictures of another bear, a horse, a cat, and a mouse. Children in the second grade might be asked to choose from among several clown pictures and pick the one that has exactly the same pattern of striped clothing as the target. Children who make their choices quickly and with frequent errors will fall into an impulsive range, whereas those who take more time to consider the alternatives before making (more often correct) decisions will fall into a reflective range. Similarly, when older children are asked to trace through mazes printed on paper, those who take longer but stay in the lines are rated as more reflective than those who go more quickly, but bump into lines and have to backtrack out of dead ends.

Despite all of the stories about impulsivity in deaf children, relatively few research studies have been conducted to determine whether or not they are really more impulsive than hearing peers in any formal sense. This question is important in part because we know that for both hearing and deaf children, those who are more reflective tend to have better academic achievement scores in school than those children who are more impulsive. The few studies that have been done in this area have suggested that deaf children of deaf parents may be more reflective than deaf children with hearing parents, that deaf children enrolled in early intervention programs will show better impulse control than those without such intervention (see Chapter 6), and that deaf children who learn sign language earlier in life may be less likely to be impulsive than those who learned to sign later.[6] There is no evidence that I am aware of, however, linking reflectivity or impulsivity to the presence or absence of hearing. In fact, the only study I know of which actually compared deaf and hearing children is a recent one that I conducted with Victoria Everhart. In that investigation, we compared hearing and deaf children, all of whom had hearing parents, in three different age groups: seven to eight years, ten to eleven years, and thirteen to fourteen years. Our test of impulsivity-reflectivity for all three groups was a standard one, involving tracing paths through mazes. The results were clear: There were no significant differences in impulsivity-reflectivity between the deaf and hearing students in any of the three age groups.

It is difficult to say whether impulsive behavior on school tasks results in poor performance, or poor performance and frustration in school lead to impulsive behavior. In any case, given the evidence showing positive relations between (1) early language experience and reflective problem solving, (2) parental involvement with children and academic success, and (3) reflectivity and academic success, it seems safe to conclude that effective communication and involvement of parents in their deaf children's schooling are important for avoiding impulsivity. Impulsivity is not a consequence of hearing loss, but there are avoidable hurdles in growing up deaf that can lead to impulsive behavior in some children and may have implications for later psychological functioning. The first goal should be to prevent such problems in childhood.

PSYCHOLOGICAL FUNCTIONING IN ADOLESCENCE AND ADULTHOOD

It has sometimes been said that if deaf people did have greater emotional difficulties than hearing people, it would be understandable. After all, some deaf children grow up in homes where there is little acceptance of their hearing losses and less understanding of their special needs. Surely they would be expected to have some anger or to show other effects of such an upbringing. Even in more accepting families, there may be emotional consequences to a lack of effective communication between parents and children. In stressful situations, deaf children may not fully understand what is happening, what is wrong, who was bad, or what their role is in the episode. Similarly, the constant frustrations of not being able to communicate with the hearing-oriented worlds of education and business surely must have some impact on deaf adults, especially when someone is the only deaf person in a company or a small community.

There are also misconceptions by hearing professionals concerning deaf people that may lead to erroneous conclusions about psychological functioning. Difficulties of diagnosis because of communication barriers are well documented. Relatively few qualified therapists are fluent signers, and most deaf people who want counseling or therapy need a sign language interpreter to assist either them or the therapist, depending on your point of view. Some years ago, a deaf acquaintance pointed out to me that it is difficult enough to discuss serious personal problems with a psychotherapist, but sharing them at the same time with an interpreter who may be a neighbor and who works with all of your friends can be very intimidating. Certified interpreters have a very strict code of ethics about such matters, but the situation still can be an awkward one.

Research has shown that the quality of a therapist's sign language skills can directly influence the range of psychological symptoms identified in children and adolescents. In addition to the simple language barrier, most psychotherapists are unfamiliar with deaf people and Deaf culture, and may not understand social and emotional differences between them and hearing clients. This situation can result in the failure of a deaf person to benefit from the therapeutic situation, but it occasionally will lead to misdiagnoses as well. For example, a doctoral student in clinical psychology once came to me concerning a deaf adolescent girl with whom he was working. He was beginning to think that the girl was paranoid, because she reported that her parents were talking about her "behind her back," using spoken language. She also apparently refused to make eye contact with him during their sessions. This was the student's first deaf client, and he was seeking some books or articles on mental health in deaf people, but I sent him back to the girl rather than to the library. He eventually discovered that, as I suggested, the girl's parents actually *were* talking about her when she was present. It seems that neither parent could sign very well, and they had never really discussed their daughter's future with her. Often, however, she would do something that would start the parents talking about their plans and hopes for her future. They would look at her during those conversations, but when she would ask what they were talking about, they would say, "Nothing." Apparently, they were trying to avoid having to explain their parental concerns, and they never realized how much anxiety they were causing their daughter. As for eye contact, moving the interpreter to a seat beside the therapist rather than beside the client solved the problem.

As in other areas, access to mental health services for deaf people is improving in this country, as are the opportunities for deaf people to enter the mental health field. At the University of Rochester School of Medicine, for example, there is a program that provides doctoral-level training for clinical psychology students who are deaf. Most of those students will later become therapists themselves, with both deaf and hearing clients. Along with other deaf and hearing psychologists, some of them will also conduct research to better understand mental health and mental illness in people who are deaf.

Much of what we currently know about mental health among deaf people comes from relatively old studies, including a famous statewide study in New York in the early 1960s, about which many articles and books have been written. In general, the New York Project suggested that the more severe forms of mental illness, such as psychoses, bipolar (manic-depressive) disorder, and schizophrenia, are equally frequent among hearing and deaf populations. That finding has been confirmed several times since then in both the U.S. and England. Other studies have suggested that deaf people may be less likely than hearing people to be mentally retarded or to suffer from severe depression. One study conducted with college students, in contrast, indicated that deaf students were considerably more likely than hearing students to report *mild* depression. What makes this most interesting is that both deaf and hearing students who reported that their mothers were overprotective during their childhoods were more likely to report being depressed as young adults. Insofar as we know that hearing mothers of deaf children tend to be relatively overprotective, the greater incidence of mild depression among the deaf students perhaps follows quite naturally. At the same time, this result can serve as another reminder to parents of the need for normal and natural parenting of deaf children.

The finding that deaf college students might experience mild depression more frequently than hearing college students is consistent with findings suggesting that deaf students in mainstream settings may feel isolated and lonely compared to students in special programs (most of the students in the above study came from mainstream schools; see Chapter 6). Similarly, there is some evidence that deaf adults and adolescents may be prone to more posttraumatic stress disorders. For deaf people who are not involved with the larger Deaf community, there may be considerable social isolation that leads to difficulty when parents or other people who are close die or move away. These feelings may be reflected in either depression or post-traumatic stress reactions. Generally speaking, however, even though deaf children might have more frequent behavior problems than hearing children, there do not appear to be any serious, long-term psychological effects of such behavior. Some studies have even suggested that growing up deaf might make individuals more resistant to psychological problems. Parents might take some consolation in such findings, but there is still a variety of practical issues to make raising a deaf child a challenge for most people.

Summary

Childhood and adolescence are a time of growth, as personality and social skills emerge from interactions of children with others in their environments. Regardless of whether children are hearing or deaf, they seek the same kinds of emotional and practical support, learn the same kinds of behaviors, and are influenced by the same kinds of factors. Communication plays an important role during these years, as children learn their roles as members of a family, a gender, a community, and a culture. Deaf children who have access to other people's interactions and explanations for behaviors better understand social dynamics. Those who have access to social rules and can consider the perspectives of others develop the moral codes of others who they try to emulate.

In early childhood, parents are the primary source of implicit and explicit teaching about social expectations. As children get older, siblings, playmates, and adults outside of the home take on greater roles in this regard. During the school years, deaf and hearing students seek to be accepted by their peer groups and adopt the values, preferences, and behaviors of children and adults who are their role models. Modeling teaches children about appropriate (and inappropriate) ways of behaving. They are more likely to model people who are perceived as similar to them, and over time they become more like those models. Having higher self-esteem and a sense of control better enables children to think for themselves and make good decisions about how to act and who to emulate.

Families play a relatively larger role in deaf children's socialization than in hearing children's socialization, if for no other reason than that deaf children are likely to have a relatively greater proportion of their social interactions with family members than are hearing children. Siblings generally have an important role in childhood, providing a safe opportunity to try out new roles and get feedback on behavior. Deaf children, in particular, benefit from siblings both emotionally and in terms of communication skills.

Other deaf children in residential schools can play similar roles, and that environment provides deaf children with lifelong friends and social-emotional support. Residential schools do not lead deaf children away from their families, but provide them with an important kind of social support that they cannot get at home. There they find children of various ages who are like them and who accept them as brothers and sisters. Meanwhile, deaf adults who work in residential schools can serve as important role models, much like aunts and uncles, promoting accurate self-images and higher self-esteem.

Deaf students often show more behavior problems in school than hearing students. These can result from inconsistent social experiences, misunderstandings about social rules, and frustration with lack of communication. Behavior that might be referred to as *impulsive*, however, should not be confused with the psychological sense of *impulsivity*, referring to problem-solving strategies. Contrary to many unsubstantiated claims, there is no evidence to suggest that deaf children or adults are any more likely than hearing peers to have impulsive cognitive styles. At the same time, better communication skills and consistent parenting seem to lead to more reflective, successful problem solving.

Deaf children and adults also do not appear much different from hearing peers in terms of the incidence of mental health problems. More serious illnesses are equally frequent in deaf and hearing populations. Deaf people may be slightly more prone to some mild disorders, but they appear to be less prone to others. Full access to competent mental health services is difficult for deaf people, usually requiring the services of a sign language interpreter in addition to the barriers faced by hearing people. Further, mental health professionals need to become better informed about social and cultural differences between deaf and hearing people if they are to provide effective services and avoid misdiagnoses and lost opportunities.

Notes

1. Portions of this chapter were written with Cristina Vaccari, from the University of Bologna.

2. Identification and modeling are the sources of behaviors that underlie stereotypes: The more a child feels like an *X*, the more she will try to act like an *X* and seek out other *X*s to socialize with and have as friends.

3. Nationally, almost 80 percent of deaf children have hearing siblings only, while almost 10 percent have both deaf and hearing siblings.

4. *Egocentric* here is meant in the psychological sense of being self-ori-

ented. When used in its everyday sense, it implies arrogance or vanity. In its developmental sense, it refers to young children's frequent inability to understand that the world may look different to other people. Thus children often cannot consider the feelings of others or even understand that a visual scene looks different from different vantage points. The simplest way to demonstrate this is to show a two-year-old both sides of a card (or a page in a book) that has, for example, a dog on one side and a cat on the other. If you hold it up so that the dog is facing him, he can tell you that he sees the dog, but when you ask what *you* see, he often will say "dog" as well.

5. As difficult and embarrassing as temper tantrums might be in public places, most psychologists suggest simply removing the child from the situation for a "time out." Punishing children who are already upset usually makes the situation worse. Ignoring them might work, but parents' embarrassment often pushes them to the point where they resort to physical punishment anyway.

6. As described earlier, there are a variety of differences between deaf children who are involved in early intervention programs and those who are not. We therefore should not draw any simplistic conclusions from these findings.

10

Where Do We Go from Here?

Fate takes by the hand those who will follow.

Italian proverb

In the preceding chapters, we have explored what it means to be deaf, technically, practically, and culturally. We have examined a variety of issues confronting children who grow up deaf, as well as their parents and teachers. In discussions of everything from language to laws and from education to caption decoders, the emphasis has been on providing deaf children with access to all that they need for normal and successful lives. Beyond this, there is much more.

Deaf children deserve more than just TTYs, captioned films, and classes they can understand. They deserve the commitment of people around them to give them every opportunity to achieve excellence in their own ways, in their own chosen careers. They have the right to a free and appropriate public education, but they also have just as much right as hearing children to be involved in decisions that affect them. For that, they need access. I recently heard an interview with the world-famous violinist Itzhak Perlman, who had polio as a child and now walks with leg braces and crutches. He was discussing the issue of access and lamented that even now he sometimes has to take freight elevators or struggle up flights of steps to reach the stage of concert halls in which he is performing. Perlman said that for him, true access would be the freedom to walk into a public place with his family and friends when they do and through the same entrance. Understandably, he resents having to call ahead to arrange for a security guard to unlock a back door for him. Perlman asked simply for "access with dignity." Is this a society that will deny him that? How can we continue to deny such access for the millions of adults and children who are deaf?

In several chapters, I have discussed past and current opportunities for people who are deaf and the hurdles they encounter. Although generalizations are dangerous and deaf children vary widely, we have seen that most deaf children enter school already at a disadvantage relative to hearing children in language proficiency and in the knowledge that contributes to social and cognitive development. In part, these hurdles have their origins in early childhood, when late discovery of hearing losses and lack of information available to parents can result in barriers to effective communication and to many kinds of early childhood experiences. If deaf children's needs are met, the differences between them and hearing children disappear as they get older. If those needs are not met, deaf children will face a long, uphill struggle.

Overall, deaf children are similar to hearing children in many more ways than they are different. To the extent that there are differences, most of them relate more to issues of communication than to being deaf. Deaf children who have early exposure to language turn out to be those who are most successful in school and in their quality of life. Throughout this book, I have placed considerable emphasis on sign language for two reasons. First, spoken language is simply inaccessible for the vast majority of deaf children. Second, but not unrelated, the overwhelming preponderance of research evidence indicates that deaf children exposed to sign language from an early age are more likely to be academically and socially successful than those exposed only to spoken language.

At the same time, I have tried to impress on readers the importance of natural language. From my own reading of the available literature, I have concluded that a combination of American Sign Language (ASL) and English are necessary to optimize the opportunities for deaf children. It does not appear that artificial systems, such as Signed English or SEE1 and SEE2, are sufficient to provide deaf children with access to all of the information they need to achieve their full potentials. ASL *and* Signed English or ASL *and* Cued Speech seem much more likely to succeed, but the key is consistency. Unfortunately, we cannot produce both ASL and either Signed English or Cued Speech at the same time. Therefore, I have suggested an emphasis on ASL first, later supplemented by other systems to facilitate reading and speech skills when children are ready for them. Contrary to some honest misconceptions and some ill-informed claims, there is no evidence at all to suggest that learning sign language interferes with deaf children's learning of English or their potential for using spoken language. Children who learn sign language early generally are more, not less competent in English reading and writing skills and more socially and emotionally secure. Most importantly, parents and children need to be able to communicate effectively with each other.

Being a Parent of a Deaf Child

Throughout this book, I have described the social, language, and cognitive growth of deaf children. At every age level, we have seen that the context for learning and growth plays an essential role in making children who they are. That context will determine whether a deaf child will be satisfied with short-term success or will strive for a lifetime of excellence. Who decides what the context will be? We do. It is parents, teachers, politicians, and educational administrators who will either provide deaf children with access to excellence or deny it.

Generally speaking, we have seen that children whose parents are more actively involved with them will have better success in language learning, social interactions, and academic performance. This is not just true for deaf children, it is true for all children. Similarly, virtually all children will benefit from preschool programs that provide enriched language and social experiences. I have argued for the importance of early intervention (preschool) programs for deaf children, in particular, and provided considerable evidence in support of them. The goal of such programs is to start as early as possible to give deaf children the kinds of experiences they need and to ensure that parents are able to be full participants in their children's growth and education. This kind of opportunity may be especially important for deaf children of hearing parents, who are less likely than other children to have such experiences at home. Language is not the only issue here, although I believe that it is perhaps the most important one. Self-esteem, learning strategies, and social skills are also promoted in good preschool programs, and their importance should not be underestimated.

Perhaps above all else, I have argued that we need to make the educational and other experiences of deaf children as normal as possible. This conclusion is not a call for mainstreaming deaf children into regular classrooms. Concerns about the appropriateness of a separate, special environment for deaf education have been with us for over a hundred years, and they are likely to be with us for some time to come. Public Law 94-142 (IDEA, see Chapter 6) mandated that deaf and other handicapped children should be educated with nonhandicapped children to the greatest appropriate degree. But it also recognizes that regular classrooms may be inappropriate for some deaf students. Being in a regular classroom does not necessarily provide deaf children with the same education as hearing peers. Quite the contrary, in the absence of comparable early environments and appropriate accommodations, many deaf children will be unable to gain from either the content or the context of a regular public school classroom. Such a setting would be neither "normal" or helpful.

Public school thus needs to be one option within a range of educational opportunities for deaf children. As affirmed by the U.S. Department of Education, the decision of which kind of school program is best for any particular child has to include a variety of considerations, some directly related to school curricula and some related to social development. Parents need to be informed and supported through that decision process, not preached to or bullied. If laws like IDEA and the Americans with Disabilities Act are to be fruitful for deaf children and deaf adults, I believe that the focus of attention must be placed prior to the classroom, on early detection of hearing loss (see Chapter 2) and support for parents (Chapter 1), including in most cases some instruction in sign language. The problems facing deaf children go beyond their inability to hear, or speak, or read. Most of those problems did not develop during the school years, and it is unlikely that they can be easily resolved there.

In the back of this book, I have provided a list of organizations and programs that might be of help or interest to parents or others involved with deaf children and to people who are deaf themselves. One would expect that organizations such as the American Society for Deaf Children and the National Association of the Deaf would be obvious resources for parents of deaf children. Unfortunately, they often are discovered only after a long period in which parents do not know their child is deaf and then a longer time still in which they search for good advice from people who seem to know what they are talking about. Along the way, they will be pulled by those favoring one language orientation or another and one educational philosophy or another. Occasionally, they will be misled by those who, as the biochemist Sam Pennington once said, "may be wrong but are never uncertain."

Being a parent of a deaf child may not be easy. Particularly for first-time or younger parents, changes in family life when a child is born take considerable adjustment. Finding out that your child is different from others or will have special needs can be daunting, but having a deaf child will be no less rewarding, less enjoyable, or less exciting than having a hearing child. There are some emotional and practical issues that parents will need to resolve, but the issues do get resolved, and we move on. Dealing with these matters requires both professional information and the sharing of experiences with others who are in similar situations. For parents, such support can come from parent-infant programs and preschools within the community as well as from national organizations. For teachers and other professionals, such support can come from workshops and other professional development opportunities that focus on the needs of deaf students. Meanwhile, it is essential that both basic and applied research relating to deaf children continue to ask the hard questions and help to establish an agenda for change.

Recognizing that deaf children are in some ways different from and in some ways the same as hearing children is an important step for educators and parents. As much as we might want them to be like hearing children, forcing deaf children into that mold does them no service and may do them harm. If deaf children are to receive help in those areas in which they need it, they must be appreciated in their own right, and we should recognize that they might need more or different educational experiences to derive the same benefits. Similarly, if they are to be allowed to develop on their own in areas in which they do not need help, we must try to allow deaf children all of the freedoms and experiences of hearing children without being overly controlling of their behavior either at home or at school. It therefore is important to keep in mind that methods for understanding the competences of hearing children might not always be appropriate for deaf children—differences should not be equated with deficiencies.

Looking back, the two themes I have tried to emphasize most are the need for early and consistent exposure to language and the importance of flexible learning strategies. Together, these tools will promote deaf children's abilities to interact with and gain from interactions with the world. This was found to be true in social as well as cognitive domains, both of which are enhanced by natural and normal experiences with other deaf children and deaf adults as well as family members. Both explicitly and implicitly, I have placed much of the responsibility for these needs on parents and teachers. Throughout the book, I have urged them to take an active and proactive role in deaf children's educations. Flexibility, patience, and communication skill are essential for the parents and teachers of any child. Deaf children may require a greater quantity of each of these, but the quality of the stuff is essentially the same.

Glossary

[Words in **bold** have separate entries.]

acoustic: Relating to the physical properties of sound. Often contrasted with **auditory**, relating to sound as it is heard.

ADA: See **Americans with Disabilities Act.**

adventitious: Accidental. Here referring to relatively sudden loss of hearing.

American Sign Language (ASL): The sign language used in the United States and English-speaking parts of Canada.

Americans with Disabilities Act (ADA): Enacted by the United States Congress in 1990, the ADA prohibits discrimination against individuals with disabilities and requires public and private agencies to provide reasonable access to services.

ASL: See **American Sign Language.**

attachment: The emotional link between young children and mothers or other caregivers. Most extensively studied in children eight to eighteen months old.

attention deficit disorder: A psychological/behavioral condition characterized by short attention spans and often accompanied by hyperactivity.

audiology: The science of hearing. Audiologists study and test hearing and are involved in the design and application of hearing aids.

auditory: Relating to how sound is heard. Often contrasted with **acoustic,** relating to the physical properties of sound.

bilingual-bicultural programs: Often called "bi-bi" programs, these academic programs emphasize both ASL and English while encouraging children to learn about both Deaf and hearing cultures.

caption decoder: An electronic device used to decode television signals that carry closed captions. Decoder boxes are now being replaced by decoder chips built into televisions.

classifier: A handshape in ASL used to represent a class of referents (people, animals, vehicles, round things, etc.). Some spoken languages also have classifier structures.

CODA: Child of deaf adults.

cognitive development: The development of children's skills in thinking, memory, problem solving, etc.

cognitive style: A multidimensional description of a child's thinking styles. Includes **impulsive** versus **reflective** problem solving and strategic versus nonstrategic approaches to novel situations.

congenital: From birth. Congenital or early-onset hearing losses occur prior to language learning and typically result from hereditary factors or from maternal or infant illness.

Cued Speech: Supplementing of spoken language through several handshapes placed in different locations around the face, used to distinguish sounds that look similar on the lips.

cumulative trauma disorder (CTD): Musculoskeletal problems resulting from high-acceleration, repetitive movements like sign language interpreting. Characterized by numbness and soreness in hands, it can cause long-term disability. (It differs from carpel-tunnel syndrome, which affects nerves in the wrist.)

day school programs: Special school programs that serve deaf children. May be housed at a public or residential school, but do not involve living on campus.

decoder: See **caption decoder.**

demographics: Characteristics of populations (e.g., income, ethnic origins, occupation, hearing status).

directional signs: Signs which can be made in various directions to communicate *from* and *to* (e.g., I LOOK-AT YOU, YOU LOOK-AT ME).

early onset: See **congenital.**

etiology: Medical origin or cause.

FAPE: Fair and appropriate public education, required by **IDEA.**

fingerspelling: Use of the manual alphabet within a sign language to spell words.

Gestuno: An informal combination of gestures and signs used by deaf people from different countries to communicate with each other.

grammar: The set of internalized rules that allow the fluent user of a language to produce essentially an infinite number of correct ("grammatical") utterances. Also called *syntax.*

hemispheric specialization: The **neuropsychological** specialization of the two halves of the brain for some differing functions. In most right-handers, language is predominantly in the left hemisphére and visual-spatial functioning in the right hemisphere.

home signs: Special signs that develop within deaf families and may not be understood by others. May result from children's early sign mistakes, dialects, or idiosyncratic uses.

iconic: Visual. Refers to signs that look like their referents (e.g., CAMERA, GOLF)

IDEA: Individuals with Disabilities Education Act. Originally enacted in 1975 as the Education for All Handicapped Children Act and subsequently amended by other laws, IDEA is aimed at ensuring fair and appropriate public education for children who might otherwise be excluded from equal access due to various handicaps.

IEP: See **Individualized Education Plan.**

impulsivity: Cognitive style characterized by fast but often wrong responses. See also **reflectivity.**

inclusion: Educational philosophy advocating the mandatory education of all children in the same public-school classrooms.

Individualized Education Plan (IEP): Required by **IDEA** to ensure appropriate educational programming for children with disabilities, IEPs allow teachers and parents to develop an education plan especially suited to the needs of a particular child.

inflection: Often refers to tone of voice, but here the term relates to the modification of words or signs to indicate number, tense, manner, or other **grammatical** information.

intelligence: The set of abilities that allows an individual to understand and respond appropriately to novel situations, to learn. Measured by tests that yield intelligence quotients (IQs) as estimates of intelligence.

IQ: See **intelligence.**

least restrictive environment (LRE): Mandated by **IDEA** to ensure that handicapped children are not forced into inappropriate academic programs. LRE is sometimes incorrectly equated with **inclusion.**

lipreading: See **speechreading.**

locus of control: Personality characteristic relating to whether individuals see their lives as under their own control (internal locus of control) or under the control of others (external locus of control). Internal loci are related to academic success, social success, recovery from health difficulties, etc.

LRE: See **least restrictive environment.**

mainstream: Attendance by deaf children at a public school for part or all of the school day, with support of interpreters and other services.

manually coded English: Artificial systems using **ASL** signs and special **grammatical** markers to communicate English through the hands (e.g., Signed English, SEE1, and SEE2).

name sign: A sign used to refer to a particular individual (i.e., not the fingerspelling of his or her name).

neuropsychological: Relating to brain or nervous system processes. Can influence emotional, physical, or cognitive functioning.

otitis media: Infections of the middle ear that cause inflammation and can damage the ossicles (hammer, anvil, and stirrup) or the eardrum; a leading cause of childhood hearing loss.

performance tests: Portions of intelligence tests that do not require language for administration or responding.

Pidgin Sign English (PSE): A hybrid of ASL and Signed English often used in communication between Deaf and hearing signers.

prelingual hearing loss: Hearing loss prior to learning language (see **congenital**).

prevalence: Extent of practice, existence, or acceptance. Prevalence of hearing loss refers to the total number of people with losses, in contrast to the number who might be born deaf or become deaf in a given year.

progressive hearing loss: Hearing that declines over time (versus acute hearing loss), often due to hereditary factors or aging.

pure tone average (PTA): The average hearing loss, in decibels, across all frequencies in an individual's better ear.

reciprocity: The alternating interactions and mutual cuing of infants and caregivers that develops with time and experience.

reflectivity: Cognitive style characterized by slower but more often correct responses. See also **impulsivity.**

residential school: Schools at which children can live on campus. Residential schools are a central feature of the Deaf community.

residual hearing: Hearing that remains following significant hearing loss. Hearing aids and other amplification devices depend on residual hearing for effectiveness.

self-esteem: Self-pride or self-respect. The extent to which individuals like who they are; can be positive or negative.

self-image: One's view of their own strengths and weaknesses; can be accurate or inaccurate. Often confused with **self-esteem.**

Signed English: A form of **manually coded English** originally intended to facilitate deaf children's reading and writing skills (sometimes "Sign English").

signing space: Roughly square area in front of a signer within which most signs are made, from waist to top of head and equal width.

Simultaneous Communication (SC): Simultaneous production of both sign and speech (see also **Total Communication**).

speechreading: Formerly called lipreading. Understanding spoken language through visual analysis of mouth and face movement. Usually effective only with significant **residual hearing,** it is extremely difficult and tiring, especially for those spoken languages (like English) that have many similar mouth shapes.

synchrony: The meshing of behavioral patterns between infants and caregivers (especially mothers) that develops with time and experience.

syntax: See **grammar.**

TDD: Telecommunications Device for the Deaf (see **TTY**).

telegraphic speech: The stage of language development in which two or more words or signs are strung together without "function" words, often resembling a telegram (e.g., "want milk").

tinnitus: A perceived ringing or humming due to inner ear or sensorineural disfunction. Can occur in deaf or hearing individuals, vary from soft to very loud, and persist indefinitely.

Total Communication (TC): Communication method which makes use of all potentially available sources of linguistic communication, including sign, speech, and amplification.

TTY: "Visual telephone" for people who are deaf, using keyboard and written visual display.

Information Sources and Organizations Serving Deaf Children

ABLEDATA
8455 Colesville Rd., Suite 935
Silver Springs, MD 20910
Voice/TTY: (301) 588-9284
Voice/TTY: (800) 227-0216
FAX: (301) 587-1967
An information and referral project that maintains a database of more than 20,000 assistive technology products. The project also produces fact sheets on types of devices and other aspects of assistive technology.

ADARA: Professionals Networking for Excellence in Service Delivery with Individuals who are Deaf or Hard of Hearing
(formerly AMERICAN DEAFNESS AND REHABILITATION ASSOCIATION)
P.O. Box 251 554
Little Rock, AR 72225

Voice/TTY: (501) 868-8850
FAX: (501) 868-8812
Promotes and participates in quality human-service delivery to deaf and hard-of-hearing people through agencies and individuals. ADARA is a partnership of national organizations, local affiliates, professional sections, and individual members working together to support social services and rehabilitation delivery for deaf and hard-of-hearing people.

ALEXANDER GRAHAM BELL ASSOCIATION FOR THE DEAF, INC.
3417 Volta Place NW
Washington, DC 20007
Voice/TTY: (202) 337-5220
Gathers and disseminates information on hearing loss, promotes better public understanding of hearing loss

Courtesy National Information Center on Deafness, Gallaudet University. Reprinted by permission.

in children and adults, provides scholarships and other financial and parent-infant awards, and promotes early detection of hearing loss in infants.

AMERICAN ACADEMY OF AUDIOLOGY
1735 N. Lynn St., Suite 950
Arlington, VA 22209
Voice/TTY: (703) 524-1923
Voice/TTY: (800) 222-2336
FAX: (703) 524-2303
A professional organization of individuals dedicated to providing high-quality hearing care to the public. Provides professional development, education, and research, and promotes increased public awareness of hearing disorders and audiologic services.

AMERICAN ASSOCIATION OF THE DEAF-BLIND
814 Thayer Ave., Room 302
Silver Spring, MD 20910-4500
TTY: (301) 588-6545
FAX: (301) 588-8705
Promotes better opportunities and services for deaf–blind people. Its mission is to assure that a comprehensive, coordinated system of services is accessible to all deaf-blind people, enabling them to achieve their maximum potential through increased independence, productivity, and integration into the community. Annual conventions provide a week of workshops, meetings, tours, and recreational activities.

AMERICAN ATHLETIC ASSOCIATION OF THE DEAF
3607 Washington Blvd., #4
Ogden, UT 84403-1737

Voice: (801) 393-8710
TTY: (801) 393-7916
FAX: (801) 393-2263
Governing body for all deaf sports and recreation in the United States. Twenty different sports organizations and two hundred member clubs are affiliates of the AAAD, which. sponsors a U.S. team for the World Games for the Deaf and other regional, national, and international competitions.

AMERICAN HEARING RESEARCH FOUNDATION
55 E. Washington St., Suite 2022
Chicago, IL 60602
Voice: (312) 726-9670
FAX: (312) 726-9695
Supports medical research and education into the causes, prevention, and cures of deafness, hearing losses, and balance disorders. Also keeps physicians and the public informed of the latest developments in hearing research and education.

AMERICAN SOCIETY FOR DEAF CHILDREN
2848 Arden Way, Suite 210
Sacramento, CA 93825-1373
Voice/TTY: (800) 942-ASDC
The ASDC is a nonprofit parent-helping-parent organization promoting a positive attitude toward signing and deaf culture. Also provides support, encouragement and current information about deafness to families with deaf and hard-of-hearing children.

AMERICAN SPEECH-LANGUAGE HEARING ASSOCIATION
10801 Rockville Pike

Rockville, MD 20852
Voice/TTY: (301) 897-5700
Helpline: (800) 638-8255
A professional and scientific organization for speech/language pathologists and audiologists concerned with communication disorders. Provides informational materials and a toll-free Helpline number for consumers to inquire about speech, language, or hearing problems. Also provides referrals to audiologists and speech/language pathologists in the United States.

AMERICAN TINNITUS
ASSOCIATION
P.O. Box 5
Portland, OR 97207
Voice: (503) 248-9985
FAX: (503) 248-0024
Provides information about tinnitus and referrals to local contacts and support groups nationwide. Also provides a bibliography service, funds scientific research related to tinnitus, and offers workshops for professionals. Works to promote public education about tinnitus.

ARKANSAS REHABILITATION
RESEARCH AND TRAINING
CENTER FOR PERSONS WHO
ARE DEAF AND HARD OF
HEARING
University of Arkansas
4601 W. Markham St.
Little Rock, AR 72205
Voice/TTY: (501) 686-9691
FAX: (501) 686-9698
Focuses on issues affecting the employability of deaf and hard-of-hearing rehabilitation clients: career assessment, career preparation, placement, career mobility, and

advancement. Provides information and data bases related to the rehabilitation of deaf and hard-of-hearing people served by the federal/state Vocational Rehabilitation Program.

ASSOCIATION OF LATE-
DEAFENED ADULTS
10310 Main St., Box 274
Fairfax, VA 22030
TTY: (815) 899-3040
FAX: (815) 899-4517
TTY Hotline: (815) 899-3040
Serves as a resource and information center for late-deafened adults and works to increase public awareness of their special needs.

AUDITORY-VERBAL
INTERNATIONAL, INC.
2121 Eisenhower Ave., Suite 402
Alexandria, VA 22314
Voice: (703) 739-1049
TTY: (703) 739-0874
FAX: (703) 739-0395
AVI is dedicated to helping children with hearing losses learn to listen and speak. Promotes the Auditory-Verbal Therapy approach, which is based on the belief that theoverwhelming majority of these children can hear and talk by using their residual hearing and hearing aids.

BETTER HEARING
INSTITUTE
5021-B Backlick Road
Annandale, VA 22003
Voice/TTY: (703) 642-0580
Voice/TTY: 800-EAR-WELL
(Hearing Helpline)
FAX: (703) 750-9302
A nonprofit educational organization that implements national public information programs on hearing

loss and available medical, surgical, hearing aid, and rehabilitation assistance for millions of Americans with uncorrected hearing problems. BHI maintains a toll-free Hearing Helpline, a telephone service that provides information on hearing loss, sources of assistance, lists of local hearing professionals, and other available hearing help to callers from anywhere in the United States and Canada.

BOYS TOWN NATIONAL RESEARCH HOSPITAL
555 N. 30th St.
Omaha, NE 68131
Voice: (402) 498-6511
TTY: (402) 498-6543
FAX: (402) 498-6638
The BTNRH is an internationally recognized center for state-of the-art research, diagnosis, and treatment of patients with ear diseases, hearing and balance disorders, cleft lip and palate, and speech/language problems. Also includes programs such as Parent/Child Workshops, Center for Childhood Deafness, Register for Heredity Hearing Loss, Center for Hearing Research, Center for Abused Handicapped, and summer programs for gifted deaf teens and college students.

THE CAPTION CENTER
125 Western Ave.
Boston, MA 02134
Voice/TTY: (617) 492-9225
FAX: (617) 562-0590
A nonprofit service of the WGBH Educational Foundation with offices in Boston, New York, and Los Angeles. Produces captions for every segment of the entertainment and advertising industries and offers clients an array of services including off-line captions, real-time captions, and open captions. Sells open-captioning software and QuickCaption to enable schools and agencies to caption their own programs and events.

CAPTIONED FILMS/VIDEOS
National Association of the Deaf
814 Thayer Ave.
Silver Spring, MD 20910
Voice: (301) 587-1788
TTY: (301) 587-1789
FAX: (301) 587-1791
Free loans of educational and entertainment captioned films and videos for deaf and hard of hearing people.

CENTER FOR BICULTURAL STUDIES, INC.
5506 Kenilworth Ave., Suite 105
Riverdale, MD 20737-3106
Voice: (301) 277-3945
TTY: (301) 277-3944
FAX: (301) 699-5226
Promotes public education on interaction of deaf and hearing cultures and fosters public acceptance, understanding, and use of American Sign Language and other natural signed languages. Disseminates information, sponsors forums, public discussions, and video projects. Sister organization of the Bicultural Center.

COCHLEAR IMPLANT CLUB INTERNATIONAL
P.O. Box 464
Buffalo, NY 14223
Voice/TTY: (716) 838-4662
Provides information and support to cochlear implant users and their

families, professionals, and the general public.

CONFERENCE OF EDUCATIONAL ADMINISTRATORS SERVING THE DEAF
Lexington School for the Deaf
75th St. and 30th Ave.
Jackson Heights, NY 11370
Voice: (718) 899-8800
TTY: (718) 899-3030
FAX: (718) 899-9846
Focuses on improvements in the education of deaf and hard-of-hearing people through research, personnel development, advocacy, and training.

CONVENTION OF AMERICAN INSTRUCTORS OF THE DEAF
CAID Membership Office
P.O. Box 377
Bedford, TX 76095-0377
Voice: (817) 354-8414
TTY: (510) 794-3795
FAX: (510) 794-2409
Promotes professional development, communication, and information among educators of deaf individuals and other interested people.

DEAF AND HARD OF HEARING ENTREPRENEURS COUNCIL
817 Silver Spring Ave., #305-F
Silver Spring, MD 20910
TTY: (301) 587-8596
FAX: (301) 587-5997
Encourages, recognizes, and promotes entrepreneurship by people who are deaf or hard of hearing.

DEAF ARTISTS OF AMERICA, INC.

302 N. Goodman St., Suite 205
Rochester, NY 14607
TTY: (716) 244-3460
FAX: (716) 244-3690
Organized to bring support and recognition to deaf and hard of hearing artists. Goals are to publish information about deaf artists, provide cultural and educational opportunities, exhibit and market deaf artists' work, and collect and disseminate information about deaf artists. Also organizes one traveling art exhibit per year.

DEAFNESS AND COMMUNICATIVE DISORDERS BRANCH
Rehabilitation Services Administration
Office of Special Education and Rehabilitative Services
Department of Education
330 C St. SW, Room 3228
Washington, DC 20202-2736
Voice: (202) 205-9152
TTY: (202) 205-8352
FAX: (202) 205-9772
Promotes improved and expanded rehabilitation services for deaf and hard-of-hearing people and individuals with speech or language impairments. Provides technical assistance to RSA staff, state rehabilitation agencies, other public and private agencies, and individuals. Also provides funding for interpreter training and demonstration rehabilitation programs such as programs for low-functioning adults who are deaf.

DEAFNESS RESEARCH FOUNDATION
9 E. 38th St.
New York, NY 10016-0003

Voice/TTY: (212) 684-6556
Voice/TTY: (800) 535-3323
FAX: (212) 779-2125
The nation's largest voluntary health organization, providing grants for fellowships, symposia, and research into the causes, treatment, and prevention of all ear disorders. The DRF also provides information and referral services.

DEAFPRIDE, INC.
1350 Potomac Ave. SE
Washington, DC 20003
Voice/TTY: (202) 675-6700
FAX: (202) 547-0547
Works for the human and civil rights of deaf people and their families. The organization's empowerment and advocacy program brings together a diversity of people to work against internalized and systemic oppression for individual and institutional change.

THE EAR FOUNDATION
2000 Church St.
Box 111
Nashville, TN 37236
Voice/TTY: (615) 329-7809
Voice/TTY: (800) 545-HEAR
FAX: (615) 329-7935
A national, not-for-profit organization committed to integrating the hearing- and balance-impaired person into the mainstream of society through public awareness and medical education. Also administers the Meniere's Network, a national network of patient support groups that provides people with the opportunity to share experiences and coping strategies.

GALLAUDET UNIVERSITY
800 Florida Ave. NE
Washington, DC 20002-3695
Voice/TTY: (202) 651-5000
The world's only four-year liberal arts university for students who are deaf or hard of hearing. Established in 1864 by an act of Congress, Gallaudet offers more than fifty undergraduate and graduate degree programs and numerous education and summer courses. Disseminates information through such units as the Gallaudet Bookstore, Gallaudet University Press, Gallaudet Research Institute, Pre-College Outreach, College for Continuing Education, and the National Information Center on Deafness.

GALLAUDET UNIVERSITY ALUMNI ASSOCIATION
Alumni House
Gallaudet University
800 Florida Ave. NE
Washington, DC 20002-3695
Voice: (202) 651-5060
TTY: (202) 651-5061
FAX: (202) 651-5062
Represents more than 12,000 alumni of Gallaudet University across the United States and around the world. The GUAA, which is governed by a nationally elected board of directors, provides a variety of services that support and benefit the university, the alumni, and the general deaf community.

HEARING EDUCATION AND AWARENESS FOR ROCKERS
P.O. Box 460847
San Francisco, CA 94146
Voice: (415) 773-9590 (hotline)

Voice: (415) 441-9081
TTY: (415) 476-7600
FAX: (415) 476-7613
Educates the public about the dangers of hearing loss resulting from repeated exposure to excessive noise levels. Offers information about hearing protection, testing. and other information about hearing loss and tinnitus. Operates a twenty-four-hour hotline information, referral, and support network service and conducts a free hearing screening program in the San Francisco Bay area. Also launches public hearing awareness campaigns, programs for schools, and seminars, and distributes earplugs to club and concert goers. Initiated H.E.A.R. affiliates in other cites worldwide.

HEARING INDUSTRIES ASSOCIATION
515 King St., Suite 420
Alexandria, VA 22314
Voice: (703) 684-5744
FAX: (703) 684-6048
The association for hearing aid manufacturers and suppliers of component parts.

HEAR NOW
9745 E. Hampden Ave., #300
Denver, CO 80231
Voice/TTY: (303) 695-4327
Voice/TTY: (800) 648-HEAR
FAX: (303) 695-7789
Committed to making technology accessible to deaf and hard-of-hearing individuals throughout the United States. Raises funds to provide hearing aids, cochlear implants, and related services to children and adults who have hearing losses but

do not have the financial resources to purchase their own devices.

HEATH RESOURCE CENTER
1 Dupont Circle
Washington, DC 20036
Voice/TTY: (202) 939-9320
Voice/TTY: (800) 544-3284
FAX: (202) 833-4760 (American Council on Education)
The national clearinghouse on postsecondary education for individuals with disabilities, a program of the American Council on Education. Disseminates information nationally about disability issues in postsecondary education. It offers free publications and a toll-free telephone service of use to administrators, service providers, teachers, instructors, rehabilitation counselors, health professionals, individuals with disabilities, and their families.

HELEN KELLER NATIONAL CENTER FOR DEAF-BLIND YOUTHS AND ADULTS
111 Middle Neck Road
Sands Point, NY 11050
Voice: (516) 944-8900
TTY: (516) 944-8637
FAX: (516) 944-7302
The national center and its ten regional offices provide diagnostic evaluations. comprehensive vocational and personal adjustment training, and job preparation and placement for people who are deaf-blind from every state and territory. Field services include information, referral, advocacy, and technical assistance to professionals, consumers, and families.

HOUSE EAR INSTITUTE
2100 W. Third St., 5th Floor
Los Angeles, CA 90057
Voice: (213) 483-4431
TTY: (213) 484-2642
FAX: (213) 483-8789
National nonprofit otologic research and educational institute that provides information on hearing and balance disorders. The Children's Auditory Research and Evaluation (C.A.R.E.) Center does evaluation and therapy. Also offers professional and general public educational programs that include Safety Patrol, Bridging the Gap, Family Camp, and the Young Adult Work Program for deaf children and families.

INTERNATIONAL HEARING SOCIETY
20361 Middlebelt Road
Livonia, MI 48152
Voice: (810) 478-2610
Voice: (800) 521-5247 (Hearing Aid Helpline)
FAX: (810) 478-4520
Professional association of specialists who test hearing and select, fit, and dispense hearing instruments. The society conducts programs of competence qualifications, education, and training, and promotes specialty-level accreditation. The Hearing Aid Helpline provides consumer information and referral.

JOHN TRACY CLINIC
806 W. Adams Blvd.
Los Angeles, CA 90007
Voice: (213) 748-5481
TTY: (213) 747-2924
Voice/TTY: (800) 522-4582
FAX: (213) 749-1651

An educational facility for preschool children who have hearing losses and for their families. In addition to on-site services, worldwide correspondence courses in English and Spanish are offered to parents whose children are of preschool age and are hard of hearing, deaf, or deaf-blind. All services of the JTC are free of charge to the families.

JUNIOR NATIONAL ASSOCIATION OF THE DEAF AND YOUTH LEADERSHIP CAMP
814 Thayer Ave.
Silver Spring, MD 20910-4500
Call NAD (see next entry)
Also TTY: (301) 587-4875
Develops and promotes citizenship, scholarship, and leadership skills in deaf and hard-of-hearing high school students through chapter projects, national conventions, contests, and other activities The NAD also sponsors a month-long Youth Leadership Camp program each summer in Oregon.

NATIONAL ASSOCIATION OF THE DEAF
814 Thayer Ave.
Silver Spring, MD 20910
Voice: (301) 587-1788
TTY: (301) 587-1789
FAX: (301) 587-1791
The oldest and one of the largest consumer organizations advocating for equal access by people who are deaf or hard of hearing in the areas of employment, education, telecommunications, and rehabilitation. Also maintains the NAD publications department at (301) 587-6282

(voice) and (301) 587-6283 (TTY), deaf awareness information, legal defense fund, public information center, youth programs, and certification programs for interpreters and for sign language instructors.

NATIONAL BLACK DEAF ADVOCATES
246 Sycamore St., Suite 100
Decatur, GA 30030
TTY: (404) 687-9155
Voice: (404) 687-8290
FAX: (404) 687-8298
Promotes leadership, deaf awareness, and active participation in the political, educational, and economic processes that affect the lives of black deaf citizens. Currently has seventeen chapters in the United States and the Virgin Islands.

NATIONAL CAPTIONING INSTITUTE
1900 Gallows Road
Vienna, VA 22182
Voice/TTY: (703) 917-7600
Voice: (800) 533-9673
TTY: (800) 321-8337
FAX: (703) 917-9878
Provides closed-captioning service for television networks, program producers, cablecasters, producers of home entertainment videocassettes, advertisers, and other organizations in the federal and private sectors.

NATIONAL CENTER FOR ACCESSIBLE MEDIA (CPB/WGBH)
WGBH Educational Foundation
125 Western Ave.
Boston, MA 02134

Voice/TTY: (617) 492-9258
FAX: (617) 782-2155
A project of the Corporation for PublicBroadcasting and WGBH, NCAM aims to increase access to public mass media (television, radio, print, movies, multimedia) for underserved consumers, such as disabled people or speakers of other languages. NCAM researches and develops media access technologies that make them more inclusive or expand their use, and acts as a resource to broadcasters, producers educators, and consumers through consulting, training, journal articles, and conferences.

NATIONAL CUED SPEECH ASSOCIATION
1615-B Oberlin Road
P.O. Box 31345
Raleigh, NC 27622
Voice/TTY: (919) 828-1218
Membership organization that provides advocacy and support regarding use of Cued Speech. Information and services are provided for deaf and hard-of-hearing people of all ages, their families and friends, and professionals who work with them.

NATIONAL FRATERNAL SOCIETY OF THE DEAF
1300 W. Northwest Highway
Mt. Prospect, IL 60056
Voice: (708) 392-9282
TTY: (708) 392-1409
FAX: (708) 392-9298
Works in the area of life insurance and advocacy for deaf people. Has eighty divisions across the country.

NATIONAL INFORMATION CENTER FOR CHILDREN AND YOUTH WITH DISABILITIES

P.O. Box 1492
Washington, DC 20013
Voice/TTY: (800) 695-0285
Voice/TTY: (202) 884-8200
FAX: (202) 884-8441

NICHCY provides free fact sheets, state resource sheets, and general information to assist parents, educators, caregivers, advocates, and others in helping children and youth with disabilities become participating members of the community.

NATIONAL INFORMATION CENTER ON DEAFNESS

Gallaudet University
800 Florida Ave. NE
Washington, DC 20002-3695
Voice: (202) 651-5051
TTY: (202) 651-5052
FAX: (202) 651-5054

Serves as a centralized source of up-to-date, objective information on topics dealing with deafness and hearing loss. NICD collects, develops, and disseminates information about all aspects of hearing loss and services offered to deaf and hard of hearing people across the nation. Also provides information about Gallaudet University.

NATIONAL INFORMATION CLEARINGHOUSE ON CHILDREN WHO ARE DEAF-BLIND (DB-LINK)

Teaching Research
345 N. Monmouth Avenue
Monmouth, OR 97361
Voice: (800) 438-9376
TTY: (800) 854-7013

Collects, organizes, and disseminates information related to children and youth (up to twenty-one years) who are deaf-blind and connects consumers of deaf-blind information to sources of information about deaf-blindness, assistive technology and deaf-blind people. DB-LINK is a collaborative effort involving the American Association of the Deaf-Blind, American Foundation for the Blind, Helen Keller National Center, Perkins School for the Blind, St. Luke's Roosevelt Hospital, and Teaching Research.

NATIONAL INSTITUTE ON DEAFNESS AND OTHER COMMUNICATION DISORDERS INFORMATION CLEARINGHOUSE

1 Communication Ave.
Bethesda, MD 20892-3456
Voice: (800) 241-1044
TTY: (800) 241-1055
FAX: (301) 907-8830

A national resource center for information about hearing, balance, smell, taste, voice, speech, and language. The NIDCD clearinghouse serves health professionals, patients, industry, and the public.

THE NATIONAL REHABILITATION INFORMATION CENTER

8455 Colesville Road, Suite 935
Silver Spring, MD 20910
Voice/TTY: (301) 588-9284
Voice/TTY: (800) 346-2742
FAX: (301) 587-1967

Provides information and referral

services on disability and rehabilitation, including quick information and referral, data base searches of the bibliographic data base REHABDATA, and document delivery.

NATIONAL TECHNICAL INSTITUTE FOR THE DEAF
Rochester Institute of Technology
Marketing Communications
52 Lomb Memorial Drive,
LBJ Building
Rochester, NY 14623-5604
Voice: (716) 475-6400
TTY: (716) 475-2181
FAX: (716) 475-6500
Provides technological postsecondary education to deaf and hard-of-hearing students. Dissemi-nates informational materials and instructional videotapes on issues related to deaf people and Deaf culture.

THE NATIONAL THEATRE OF THE DEAF
5 West Main St.
P.O. Box 659
Chester, CT 06412
Voice: (203) 526-4971
TTY: (203) 526-4974
FAX: (203) 526-0066
Outreach: (203) 526-4971
Concentrates on artistic and theatrical professional development of deaf actors. Tours the United States and abroad. Also presents Little Theatre of the Deaf productions in schools, theaters, museums, and libraries. Sponsors a professional school and Deaf Theatre Conference for deaf individuals interested in the art of theater.

NORTHERN ILLINOIS UNIVERSITY RESEARCH AND TRAINING CENTER ON TRADITIONALLY UNDERSERVED PERSONS WHO ARE DEAF
1425 W. Lincoln Highway
DeKalb, IL 60115-9984
Voice: (815) 753-8687
TTY: (815) 753-6520
Voice/TTY: (800) 607-8464
FAX: (815) 753-1545
Conducts research, resource development, and training/technical assistance projects geared toward enhancing the employment, independent living, and quality-of-life outcomes for traditionally underserved people who are deaf. The NIU-RTC Clearinghouse provides information and referral on independent living and educational, vocational, mental health, and medical information related to deafness and this particular population. Current projects focus on three core areas: systems and program issues, individual interventions, and service provider interventions.

QUOTA INTERNATIONAL, INC.
1420 21st St. NW
Washington, DC 20036
Voice/TTY: (202) 331-9694
FAX: (202) 331-4395
Shatter Silence, Shatter Noise, and the annual Deaf Woman of the Year Contest are programs that Quota Clubs conduct through the Quota International Foundation to inform their communities about the needs and abilities of individuals who are

deaf, hard of hearing, or speech impaired.

RAINBOW ALLIANCE OF THE DEAF
P.O. Box 66136
Houston, TX 77266-6136
TTY: (713) 621-1103 evenings/weekends
FAX: (713) 520-2079 weekdays
RAD is a national organization serving the deaf gay and lesbian community. Represents approximately twenty-four chapters throughout the United States, Canada, and Europe.

REGISTRY OF INTERPRETERS FOR THE DEAF, INC.
8630 Fenton Street, Suite 324
Silver Spring, MD 20910
Voice/TTY: (301) 608-0050
FAX: (301) 608-0508
A professional organization that certifies interpreters, provides information on interpreting to the general public, publishes a national directory of certified interpreters, and makes referrals to interpreter agencies.

REHABILITATION ENGINEERING RESEARCH CENTER ON HEARING ENHANCEMENT AND ASSISTIVE DEVICES
Lexington Center, Inc.
30th Ave. and 75th St.
Jackson Heights, NY 11370
Voice/TTY: (718) 899-8000, ext. 363
FAX: (718) 899-3433
The RERC promotes and develops technological solutions to problems confronting individuals with hearing loss. Current projects include assistive devises for hearing impaired individuals with low vision, detection of hearing loss in infants using otoacoustic emissions, developing ASCII standards for TTY modems, and evaluating the use of assistive technologies in the community and workplace. Provides information and referral for consumer questions on assistive technology and research.

THE SEE CENTER FOR THE ADVANCEMENT OF DEAF CHILDREN
Main Office: P.O. Box 1181
Los Alamitos, CA 90720
Voice/TTY: (310) 430-1467
Branch Office: San Jose State University
Division of Special Education
Washington Square
San Jose, CA 95192
Voice: (408) 924-3784
TTY: (408) 924-3782
FAX: (408) 924-3713
Offers information and referral for parents and educators on deafness-related topics and Signing Exact English (SEE). Provides evaluation of sign skills, workshops, and consulting services related to communication in general and SEE in particular.

SELF HELP FOR HARD OF HEARING PEOPLE, INC.
7910 Woodmont Ave., Suite 1200
Bethesda, MD 20814
Voice: (301) 657-2248
TTY: (301) 657-2249
FAX: (301) 913-9413
Promotes awareness and informa-

tion about hearing loss, communication, assistive devices, and alternative communication skills through publications, exhibits, and presentations.

TELECOMMUNICATIONS FOR THE DEAF, INC.
8719 Colesville Road, Suite 300
Silver Spring, MD 20910-3919
Voice: (301) 589-3786
TTY: (301) 589-3006
FAX: (301) 589-3797
A nonprofit consumer advocacy organization promoting full visual and other access to information and telecommunications for people who are deaf, hard of hearing, deaf–blind, and speech impaired. Supports consumer education and involvement, technical assistance and consulting, application of existing and emerging technologies, networking and collaborations, uniformity of TTY standards, and national policy development that aids these goals.

TELE-CONSUMER HOTLINE
1331 H St. NW, Suite 201
Washington, DC 20005
Voice/TTY: (202) 347-7208
Voice/TTY: (800) 332-1124
FAX: (202) 347-7126
Impartial consumer information service about residential telecommunications concerns. Information and referrals about equipment and phone services for consumers with disabilities. Free publications about tele-

phone equipment, TTY directories, selecting a long-distance company, and more.

TRIPOD
2901 N. Keystone St.
Burbank, CA 91504-1620
Voice/TTY: (818) 972-2080
Voice/TTY: (800) 352-8888
Voice/TTY: (800) 2-TRIPOD
(California only)
FAX: (818) 972-2090
Provides a national toll-free hotline for parents and other individuals wanting information about rearing and educating deaf and hard-of-hearing children. TRIPOD operates a model parent/infant/toddler program, Montessori preschool/kindergarten an elementary and middle school, and a ninth grade in high school. The coenrollment programs for hearing, deaf, and hard-of-hearing children are within the Burbank Unified School District.

WORLD RECREATION ASSOCIATION OF THE DEAF, INC./USA
P.O. Box 92074
Rochester, NY 14692-0074
TTY: (716) 586-4208
FAX: (716) 475-7101
Established to foster the development of innovation in recreational and cultural activities for the deaf and hard-of-hearing community.

Following are state commissions or state offices mandated to serve deaf and hard-of-hearing people. While the scope of services differs from state to state, these programs provide a variety of valuable services including advocacy, information gathering and dissemination, referral to appropriate agencies, interpreting services, and job placement.

Alabama
Department of Rehabilitation
Services
(205) 281-8780 (V/TTY)
(800) 441-7607 (V/TTY)
in Alabama

Alaska
Division of Vocational
Rehabilitation
(907) 561-4466 (V/TTY)

Arizona
Arizona Council for the Hearing
Impaired
(602) 542-3323 (V/TTY)
(800) 352-8161 (V/TTY)
in Arizona

Arkansas
Office of the Deaf and Hearing
Impaired
(501) 296-1635 (V/TTY)
(501) 296-6669 (TTY)

California
State Office of Deaf Access
(916) 387-4573 (V)
(916) 387-4577 (TTY)

Colorado
Vocational Rehabilitation Services
(303) 894-2650 (V/TTY)

Connecticut
Connecticut Commission on the
Deaf and Hearing Impaired
(203) 566-7414 (V/TTY)

Delaware
Delaware Office for the Deaf and
Hard of Hearing
(302) 577-2850 (V/TTY)

District of Columbia
Rehabilitation Services
Administration
(202) 727-0981 (V/TTY)

Florida
Florida Council for Persons who are
Deaf or Hard of Hearing
(904) 488-5087 (V/TTY)
(800) 451-4327 (V/TTY)
in Florida

Georgia
Division of Rehabilitation Services
(404) 657-3073 (V/TTY)

Hawaii
Hawaii State Coordinating Council
on Deafness
(808) 586-8131 (V/TTY)
(808) 586-8130 (TTY)

Idaho
Idaho Council for the Deaf
and Hard of Hearing
(208) 334-0879 (V)
(208) 334-0803 (TTY)
(800) 433-1323 (V) in Idaho
(800) 433-1361 (TTY) In Idaho

Illinois
Division of Services for Persons who
are Deaf or Hard of Hearing

(312) 814-2939 (V)
(312) 814-3040 (TTY)

Indiana
Deaf and Hard of Hearing Services
(317) 232-1143 (V/TTY)
(800) 962-8408 (V/TTY)
in Indiana

Iowa
Deaf Services Commission of Iowa
(515) 281-3164 (V/TTY)

Kansas
Kansas Commission for the Deaf
and Hard of Hearing
(913) 296-2874 (V/TTY)
(800) 432-0698 (V/TTY) in Kansas

Kentucky
Kentucky Commission on the Deaf
and Hard of Hearing
(502) 573-2604 (V/TTY)
(800) 372-2907 (V/TTY)
in Kentucky

Louisiana
Louisiana Commission for the Deaf
(504) 925-4178 (V/TTY)
(800) 256-1523 (V)
(800) 543-2099 (TTY)

Maine
Office of Rehabilitation Services
Division of Deafness
(207) 624-5318 (V)
(207) 624-5322 (TTY)
(800) 332-1003 (V/TTY)
in Maine

Maryland
Division of Rehabilitation Services
(410) 554-3278 (V)
(410) 554-3277 (TTY)

Massachusetts
Massachusetts Commission for the
Deaf and Hard of Hearing
(617) 727-5106 (V/TTY)
(800) 882-1155 (V/TTY)
in Massachusetts

Michigan
Division of Deafness
Michigan Department of Labor
(517) 373-0378 (V/TTY)
(800) 385-6811 (V/TTY)

Minnesota
Minnesota Commission Serving
Deaf and Hard of Hearing People
(612) 297-7305 (V/TTY)

Mississippi
Vocational Rehab. Services
(601) 853-5310 (V/TTY)
(800) 443-1000 (V/TTY)
in Mississippi

Missouri
Missouri Commission for
the Deaf
(314) 562-5205 (V/TTY)
(800) 796-6499 (V/TTY)

Montana
Rehabilitative/Visual Services
Division
(406) 727-7740 (V/TTY)

Nebraska
Nebraska Commission for the
Hearing Impaired
(402) 471-3593 (V/TTY)
(800) 545-6244 in Nebraska

Nevada
Rehabilitation Division
(702) 687-4452 (V)

(702) 687-3388 (TTY)
(800) 992-0900, ext. 4452 in Nevada

New Hampshire
Program for the Deaf and Hard
of Hearing
(603) 271-3471 (V/TTY)
(800) 299-1647 in New Hampshire

New Jersey
Division of the Deaf and
Hard of Hearing
Department of Human Services
(609) 984-7281 (V/TTY)
(800) 792-8839 (V/TTY) in
New Jersey

New Mexico
New Mexico Commission for the
Deaf and Hard of Hearing
(505) 827-7584 (V)
(505) 827-7588 (V/TTY)
(800) 489-8536 (V/TTY)
(800) 873-8892 (V/TTY) helpline
in New Mexico

New York
Office of Vocational and
Educational Services for Individuals
with Disabilities
(518) 486-3773 (V/TTY)
(800) 222-5627 (V/TTY)

North Carolina
Department of Human Resources
Division of Services for the
Deaf/Hard of Hearing
(919) 733-5199 (V)
(919) 733-5930 (V/TTY)

North Dakota
Office of Vocational Rehabilitation
(701) 328-3999 (V)

(701) 328-3975 (TTY)
(800) 755-2745 (V) in North Dakota

Ohio
Rehabilitation Services Commission
(614) 438-1325 (V/TTY)
(800) 282-4536 (V/TTY) in Ohio

Oklahoma
Services to the Deaf and
 Hard of Hearing
(405) 522-6377 Ext. 2920 (V)
(405) 424-2794 (TTY)
833-8973 (V/TTY) in Oklahoma

Oregon
Deaf and Hearing Impaired Access
Program
(503) 378-3142 (V/TTY)
(800) 521-9615 (V/TTY)
in Oregon

Pennsylvania
Office for the Deaf
and Hearing Impaired
(717) 783-4912 (V/TTY)
(800) 233-3008 (V/TTY)
in Pennsylvania

Puerto Rico
Vocational Rehabilitation
(809) 782-0011 (V/TTY)

Rhode Island
Commission on the Deaf and
 Hard of Hearing
(401) 277-1204 (V)
(401) 277-1205 (TTY)

South Carolina
Vocational Rehabilitation
Department
(803) 822-5313 (V/TTY)

South Dakota
Communication Services for
the Deaf
(605) 339-6718 (V/TTY)
(605) 361-5760 (V/TTY)
(800) 642-6410 (V/TTY) in South
Dakota

Tennessee
Tennessee Council for the Hearing
Impaired
(615) 741-5644 (V/TTY)
(800) 270-1349 (V/TTY)
in Tennessee
(615) 270-2655 (V/TTY) twenty-
four-hour answering machine

Texas
Texas Commission for the Deaf
and Hearing Impaired
(512) 451-8494 (V/TTY)

Utah
Division of Services for the Deaf
and Hard of Hearing
(801) 263-4860 (V/TTY)
(800) 860-4860 (V/TTY)
in Utah

Vermont
Division of Vocational
Rehabilitation
(802) 241-2186 (V/TTY)

Virginia
Virginia Department for the Deaf
and Hard of Hearing

(804) 225-2570 (V/TTY)
(800) 552-7917 (V/TTY)
in Virginia

Virgin Islands (U.S.)
Disabilities and Rehabilitation
Services
(809) 773-2323 (V/TTY)
(800) 774-0930 (V) in the
Virgin Islands

Washington
Office of Deaf and Hard of Hearing
Services
(360) 753-0703 (V/TTY)
(360) 753-0699 (TTY)
Message only lines:
(800) 422-7930 (V)
(800) 422-7941 (TTY)

West Virginia
West Virginia Commission for the
Hearing Impaired
(304) 558-2175 (V/TTY)
(304) 558-0026 (TTY)

Wisconsin
Office for the Hearing Impaired
Department of Health and Social
Services
(608) 266-8081 (V)
(608) 266-8082 (TTY)

Wyoming
Division of Vocational
Rehabilitation
(307) 856-2393 (V/TTY)

Suggested Readings

Chapter 1

Calderon, R., & Greenberg, M. T. (1993). Considerations in the adaptation of families with school-aged deaf children. In M. Marschark & M. D. Clark (Eds.), *Psychological perspectives on deafness* (pp. 27–48). Hillsdale, N.J.: Lawrence Erlbaum and Associates.

Higgins, P. C. & Nash, J. E. (1987). *Understanding deafness socially*. Springfield, Ill.: Charles C. Thomas.

Marschark, M. (1993). Origins and interactions in the social, cognitive, and language development of deaf children. In M. Marschark & M. D. Clark (Eds.), *Psychological perspectives on deafness* (pp. 7–26). Hillsdale, N.J.: Lawrence Erlbaum and Associates.

Moore, M. S., & Levitan, L. (1993). *For hearing people only* (2nd ed.). Rochester, N.Y.: MSM Productions.

Nash, A. & Nash, J. E. (1987). Deafness and family life in modern society. In P. C. Higgins and J. E. Nash (Eds.) *Understanding deafness socially* (pp. 101–121). Springfield, Ill.: Charles C. Thomas.

Padden, C. & Humphries, T. (1988). *Deaf in America*. Cambridge, Mass.: Harvard University Press.

Chapter 2

Cagle, S. J. & Cagle, K. M. (1991). *GA and SK etiquette: Guidelines for telecommunications in the Deaf community*. Bowling Green, Ky.: Bowling Green Press.

Carne, E. & Verlinde R. (1987). Caption decoders: Expanding options for hearing impaired children and adults. *American Annals of the Deaf, 132*, 73–77.

Cohen, L. (1994). *Train go sorry*. New York: Random House.

Erting, C., Johnson, R. C., Smith, D. L., & Snider, B. D. (1994). *The Deaf way: Perspectives from the International Conference on Deaf culture*. Washington, D.C.: Gallaudet University Press.

Higgins, P. C. (1980). *Outsiders in a hearing world*. Beverly Hills, Calif.: Sage Publications.

Higgins, P. C. & Nash, J. E. (1987). *Understanding deafness socially*. Springfield, Ill.: Charles C. Thomas.

Lang, H. (1994). *Silence of the spheres: The deaf experience in the history of science*. Westport, Conn: Greenwood Press.

Lang, H. (1996). *A phone of our own*. Unpublished manuscript.

Lang, H. & Meath-Lang, B. (1995). *Deaf persons in the arts and sciences: A biographical dictionary*. Westport, Conn.: Greenwood Press.

Luterman, D. (1987). *Deafness in the family*. Boston, Mass.: College-Hill Press.

Marschark, M. (1993). *Psychological development of deaf children*. New York: Oxford University Press.

Marschark, M. (1996). Consensus on cochlear implants? *Journal of Deaf Studies and Deaf Education, 1*, 213–214.

Schildroth, A. N. & Karchmer, M. A. (Eds.) (1986). *Deaf children in America*. San Diego, Calif.: College-Hill Press.

Tucker, B. P. (1995). *The feel of silence*. Philadelphia: Temple University Press.

Vernon, M. & Andrews, J. F. (1990). *The psychology of deafness: Understanding deaf and hard-of-hearing people*. New York: Longman.

Chapter 3

Bragg, B. (1995). Sign initialization/fingerspelling in ASL: Its impact on deaf people. *Deafness: Life and culture II* (pp. 7–9). Silver Spring, Md.: National Association of the Deaf.

Cornett, O. R. & Daisey, M. E. (1992). *The cued speech resource book*. Raleigh, N.C.: National Cued Speech Association.

Fischer, S. D. & Siple, P. (1990). *Theoretical issues in sign language research*. Chicago: University of Chicago Press.

Marschark, M. (1994). Gesture and sign. *Applied Psycholinguistics, 15*, 209–36.

Meier, R. P. & Newport, E. L. (1990). Out of the hands of babes: On a possible sign advantage in language acquisition. *Language, 66*, 1–23.

Shroyer, E. (1988). *Signing English*. Greensboro, N.C.: Sugar Sign Press.

Shroyer, E. & Shroyer, S. P. (1985). *Signs across America*. Washington, D.C.: Gallaudet University Press.

Chapter 4

DeCasper, A. J. & Fifer, W. P. (1980). Of human bonding: Newborns prefer their mothers' voices. *Science, 208,* 1174–76.

DeCasper, A. J. & Spence, M. J. (1986). Prenatal maternal speech influences newborns' perception of speech sounds. *Infant Behavior and Development, 9,* 133–50.

Greenberg, M. T. & Kusché, C. A. (1987). Cognitive, personal, and social development of deaf children and adolescents. In M. C. Wang, M. C. Reynolds, & H. J. Walberg (Eds.), *Handbook of special education: Research and practice: Vol. 3. Low incidence conditions* (pp. 95–129). New York: Pergamon Press.

Gregory, S. (1976). *The deaf child and his family*. New York: Halsted Press.

Koester, L. S. (1992). Intuitive parenting as a model for understanding parent-infant interactions when one partner is deaf. *American Annals of the Deaf, 137,* 362–9.

Lederberg, A. R. (1992). The impact of child deafness on social relationships. In M. Marschark and D. Clark (Eds.), *Psychological perspectives on deafness* (pp. 93–119). Hillsdale, N.J.: Lawrence Erlbaum.

Spencer, P. E. & Deyo, D. A. (1992). Cognitive and social aspects of deaf children's play. In M. Marschark and M. D. Clark (Eds.), *Psychological perspectives on deafness* (pp. 65–92). Hillsdale, N.J.: Lawrence Erlbaum.

Chapter 5

Bonvillian, J. D., Orlansky, M. D., Novack, L. L., & Folven, R. J. (1983). Early sign language acquisition and cognitive development. In D. Rogers and J. A. Sloboda (Eds.), *The acquisition of symbolic skills* (pp. 207–214). Chicago: Plenum.

Geers, A. E. & Schick, B. (1988). Acquisition of spoken and signed English by hearing-impaired children of hearing-impaired or hearing parents. *Journal of Speech and Hearing Disorders, 53,* 136–43.

Hadadian, A. & Rose, S. (1991). An investigation of parents' attitude and the communication skills of their deaf children. *American Annals of the Deaf, 136,* 273–77.

Mayberry, R. I. & Eichen, E. B. (1991). The long-lasting advantage of learning sign language in childhood: Another look at the critical period for language acquisition. *Journal of Memory and Language, 30,* 486–12.

Petitto, L. A. (1987). On the autonomy of language and gesture: Evidence from the acquisition of personal pronouns in American Sign Language. *Cognition, 27,* 1–52.

Petitto, L. A. & Marentette, P. F. (1991). Babbling in the manual mode: Evidence for the ontogeny of language. *Science, 251,* 1493–6.

Volterra, V. & Erting, C. J. (Eds.). (1990). *From gesture to language in hearing and deaf children.* Berlin: Springer-Verlag.

Chapter 6

Allen, T. E. (1986). Patterns of academic achievement among hearing impaired students: 1974–1983. In A. N. Schildroth and M. A. Karchmer (Eds.), *Deaf children in America* (pp. 161–206). San Diego, Calif.: College-Hill Press.

Cornelius, G. & Hornett, D. (1990). The play behavior of hearing-impaired kindergarten children. *American Annals of the Deaf, 135,* 316–21.

Kluwin, T. N. & Stinson, M. S. (1993). *Deaf students in local public high schools.* Springfield, Ill.: Charles C. Thomas.

Lederberg, A. R. (1993). The impact of deafness on mother–child and peer relationships. In M. Marschark & M. D. Clark (Eds.), *Psychological perspectives on deafness* (pp. 93–119). Hillsdale, N.J.: Lawrence Erlbaum.

Moores, D. & Meadow-Orlans, K. P. (1990). *Education and developmental aspects of deafness.* Washington, D.C.: Gallaudet University Press.

National Information Center on Deafness. (1991). *Mainstreaming deaf and hard of hearing students: Questions and answers.* Washington, D.C.: Gallaudet University Press.

Rawlings, B. W., Karchmer, M. A., DeCaro, J. J., & Allen, T. E. (1995). *College & careers: Programs for deaf students* (9th ed.). Washington, D.C.: Gallaudet University and Rochester, N.Y.: National Technical Institute for the Deaf.

Schildroth, A. N. (1986). Residential schools for deaf students: A decade in review. In A. N. Schildroth and M. A. Karchmer (Eds.), *Deaf children in America* (pp. 83–104). San Diego, Calif.: College-Hill Press.

Schirmer, B. S. (1989). Relationship between imaginative play and language development in hearing-impaired children. *American Annals of the Deaf, 134,* 219–22.

Spencer, P. E. & Deyo, D. A. (1992). Cognitive and social aspects of deaf children's play. In M. Marschark and M. D. Clark (Eds.), *Psychological perspectives on deafness* (pp. 65–92). Hillsdale, N.J.: Lawrence Erlbaum.

Chapter 7

Cornett, O. R. (1995). What price literacy? *Deafness: Life and culture II* (pp. 11–17). Silver Spring, Md.: National Association of the Deaf.

King, C. M. & Quigley, S. P. (1985). *Reading and deafness.* San Diego, Calif.: College-Hill Press.

Meath-Lang, B. (1993). The risk of writing outside of the margins: A reexamination of the notion of access. In R. Donmayer & R. Kos (Eds.), *At–risk students: Portraits, policies, programs, and practices* (pp. 381–394). Albany: SUNY Press.

Paul, P. V. (in press). *Literacy and deafness: The development of reading, writing, and literate thought.* Needham Heights, Mass.: Allyn & Bacon.

Waters, G. S. & Doehring, D. G. (1990). Reading acquisition in congenitally deaf children who communicate orally: Insights from an analysis of component reading, language, and memory skills. In T. H. Carr and B. A. Levy (Eds.), *Reading and its development* (pp. 323–373). San Diego, Calif.: Academic Press.

Chapter 8

Braden, J. P. (1985). The structure of nonverbal intelligence in deaf and hearing subjects. *American Annals of the Deaf, 130,* 496–501.

Braden, J. P. (1994). *Deafness, deprivation, and IQ.* New York: Plenum.

Kusché, C. A., Greenberg, M. T., & Garfield, T. S. (1983). Nonverbal intelligence and verbal achievement in deaf adolescents: An examination of heredity and environment. *American Annals of the Deaf, 128,* 458–66.

Marschark, M. & Clark, D. (1987). Linguistic and nonlinguistic creativity of deaf children. *Developmental Review, 7,* 22–38.

Neville, H., Kutas, M., & Schmidt, A. (1982). Event-related potential studies of cerebral specialization during reading. 2. Studies of congenitally deaf adults. *Brain and Language, 16,* 316–37.

Zweibel, A. (1987). More on the effects of early manual communication on the cognitive development of deaf children. *American Annals of the Deaf, 132,* 16–20.

Chapter 9

Bat-Chava, Y. (1993). Antecedents of self-esteem in deaf people: A meta-analytic review. *Rehabilitation Psychology, 38,* 221–34.

Desselle, D. D. (1994). Self–esteem, family climate, and communication patterns in relation to deafness. *American Annals of the Deaf, 139*, 322–28.

Kluwin, T. N. & Gaustad, M. G. (1994). The role of adaptability and communication is fostering cohesion in families with deaf adolescents. *American Annals of the Deaf, 139*, 329–35.

Meadow, K. P. (1984). Social adjustment of preschool children: Deaf and hearing, with and without other handicaps. *Topics in Early Childhood Special Education, 3*, 27–40.

Myers. R. R. (1995). *Standards of care for the delivery of mental health services to deaf and hard of hearing persons*. Silver Spring, Md.: National Association of the Deaf.

Rayson, B. (1987). Emotional illness and the deaf. In E. D. Mindel & M. Vernon (Eds.), *They grow in silence: Understanding deaf children and adults*. San Diego: College-Hill Press.

Stinson, M. (1994). Affective and social development. In R. C. Nowell & L. E. Marshak (Eds.), *Understanding deafness and the rehabilitation process*. Boston: Allyn and Bacon.

Stokoe, W. & Battison, R. M. (1981). Sign language, mental health and satisfactory interaction. In L. M. Stein, E. D. Mindel, & T. Jabaley (Eds.), *Deafness and mental health* (pp. 179–94). New York: Grune & Stratton.

Vernon, M. & Andrews, J. F. (1990). *The psychology of deafness: Understanding deaf and hard–of–hearing people*. New York: Longman.

Everyday Signs

animal

apple

bathroom

because

believe

book

bottle

breakfast

brother

church

class

come

complain

computer

day

dinner

dog English

fly friend

glass go

group   hearing aid

home   hotdog

how   hungry

important

jump

lunch

milk

month

paper

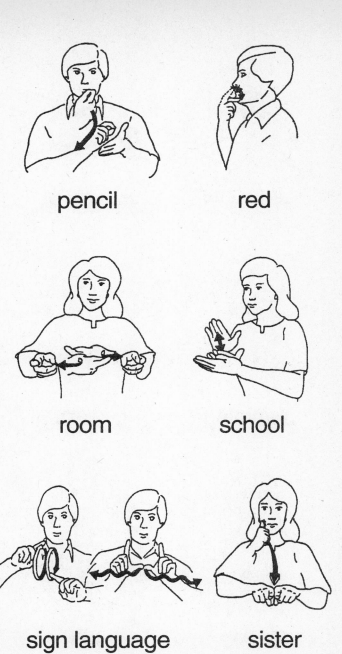

pencil

red

room

school

sign language

sister

spaghetti

together

vacation

want

week

what

where

why

work

year

Index